FLEXIBILE WORKING LIVES

The Changing Nature of Working Time Arrangements in Ireland

B. Fynes
T. Morrissey
W.K. Roche
B.J. Whelan
J. Williams

Oak Tree Press

Dublin

in association with

Graduate School of Business
University College Dublin

Oak Tree Press
Merrion Building
Lower Merrion Street
Dublin 2, Ireland

A catalogue record of this book is
available from the British Library.

ISBN 1-86076-002-3

Printed in Ireland by Colour Books Ltd.

CONTENTS

LIST OF TABLES

ACKNOWLEDGEMENTS

We wish to acknowledge the Department of Enterprise and Employment's funding of the original research, and in particular the support provided by John Travers, Greg Heylin and Bill Cox.

We are indebted to several colleagues in the ESRI who acted as internal readers on an earlier draft of the book and provided detailed readers' reports. In addition, the usual speed and efficiency of the ESRI's Survey Unit, General Office and Print Room at all stages of the project were very much appreciated.

The authors are solely responsible for the content and views expressed throughout the book as well as any errors or omissions.

CHAPTER 1

CONTESTED WORKING TIME

1.1 INTRODUCTION

One of the apparent contradictions highlighted by commentators on the current Irish economy is its strong performance, as measured by standard economic indicators, and the high levels of unemployment which co-exist with this strong performance. Much debate has centred on how high levels of unemployment can be accompanied by strong objective measures of growth. Employers, employees and their representatives, the unemployed, Government and political parties concentrate on different aspects of this issue. Each of these groupings focuses on its own concerns and as a result comes up with differing analyses and, by implication, differing solutions to the dilemma. In general, however, all would tend to agree that high levels of unemployment are 'bad' — either for the country, or for individuals.

Employers concentrate on measures that promote efficiency and effectiveness. Reports from the research literature on organisations outline recent trends in downsizing, business process re-engineering, the virtual corporation and the flexible worker.

World class manufacturing organisations are requiring greater flexibility, multi-skilling, teamworking and a rethinking of the way in which work is structured. Flatter hierarchies, empowered workers, outsourcing and crew training are some of the terms becoming more and more familiar in the literature on work and also more in common parlance as trade unionists, employers and politicians discuss the implications in the public domain. In the Irish context, recent discussions on the future of plants such as Packard in Tallaght, Dublin, have exposed people to terms such as 'flexible work practices', 'world class manufacturing' and 'team working'. The rapid rate of technological change is also impacting on the nature and structure of work, and in many instances is revolutionising the world of work.

While these changes may bring benefits to those who remain in work — for example, more responsibility and control, greater flexibility and increasing skill levels — they also can have wider effects in terms of the levels of employment and unemployment, and some argue that they may contribute to an increasing gap between those in work and those out of work.

Further, the nature of working arrangements is changing, with figures worldwide indicating a rise in part-time, contract and self-employed workers. In 1992, to compensate for the decline in their standard of living, workers in the US spent the equivalent of four more weeks a year at work than they had spent two decades earlier. The larger portion of this increase came from women entering the labour force in that time. While there may be increased flexibility for some, the downside could be increased unemployment or insecurity for others. And, in the attempts to become leaner, some organisations may be increasing the stress levels on remaining workers.

Employees also appear to be seeking greater flexibility to tailor both the amount of time they spend at work and the times at which they work to their wider life-styles and family, community and leisure activities.

Governments have also been looking at the potential of alternative ways of working as a means of reducing unemployment or of increasing employment levels. Does the global competitive environment offer much scope? Can public policy interventions impact on global trends, or can national governments at best have marginal effects, linked to their own spheres of influence — the public sector?

The key question is: how compatible are the driving forces for flexibility? This is the core issue addressed in this book. Employers, on the one hand, seek worker flexibility in terms of efficiencies and gains to the organisation through employee multi-skilling and hours worked in order to remain competitive; employees may be more concerned with flexibility as it affects their freedom of choice around balancing work and home life, and, at best, the potential employment spin-offs from flexible arrangements may be a secondary consideration; Governments may be seeking to achieve a greater balance so that more of the workforce can have access to paid employment and temporal flexibility can thus impact on rates of unemployment.

1.2 THE AGENDA OF EMPLOYERS

The past decade has been witness to a dramatic change in the competitive environments of nations, industries and individual firms. In the 1970s and 1980s, cost and quality began to dominate management's agenda. As we approach a new millennium, however, companies will have to compete on additional dimensions such as flexibility, innovation and time-based competition. World class organisations will thus need multiple capabilities to survive and prosper.

Although there is a considerable degree of speculation as to the future characteristics of competition, there is little or no doubt that it is the pace of change rather than change itself that needs to be managed in the future. The challenges that manufacturing and service organisations face today are probably greater than at any period since Henry Ford heralded the advent of mass production with the Model T. Having 'any colour as long as it is black' will not suffice in a world where Sony can launch four new products per day.

What then are the features of the product and service markets of the 1990s and how will such trends affect the nature of work? The emergence of Japan as the major industrial power in markets such as automobiles, electronics, telecommunications and information technology, has prompted companies in the Western world to search for reasons for such market dominance. A major research project carried out by a team at the Massachusetts Institute of Technology and documented in the best-selling book, *The Machine that Changed the World* (Womack et al., 1990) provides us with some useful insights. The study was carried out over a period of five years and examined the state of automobile manufacturing worldwide, but with a special emphasis on Japan. While it might seem somewhat incongruous to draw conclusions on the nature of global competition from a specific sector, trends in the car manufacturing industry (sometimes labelled 'the industry of industries') traditionally have determined the agenda in other manufacturing sectors. Furthermore, developments in manufacturing practices such as Total Quality Management also traditionally tend to be adopted at a later stage by a broader spectrum of service industries.

This research revealed that traditional mass-production strategies are being replaced by a new, post-bureaucratic paradigm which the authors labelled lean production. Although often used loosely in management jargon, the term 'lean' was defined in terms of a two-to-one performance gap. The lean organisation is twice as efficient and as effective as its more traditional competitor: it uses less of everything. It takes half the time and effort to design its products, half the human effort and tooling to make it with half the level of inventories and level of defects. As a result, the customer can be offered twice the number of products that can be built in half the normal volume.

The competitive advantage in terms of quality, cost, flexibility and speed-to-market accruing to such lean organisations is crystal clear. They can compete on not just one, but on a series of order-winning criteria in both global and local marketplaces. Approximately one-third of this two-to-one performance gap between best and worst practice organisations can be attributed to how production work is organised.

Production plants are now increasingly organised and focused on specific product-line and customer requirements rather than on traditional mass-production process principles. The emphasis within the workplace is on closeness to the customer, whether it be an 'internal' (co-worker) or 'external' (marketplace) customer. Empowerment, employee involvement and flexible working practices are additional features of the high-commitment workplace.

Similar trends are evident in the fast-growing service sectors. The delivery of services typically requires a relatively high degree of interaction between service provider and consumer: in such circumstances the role of the provider in providing service quality can be a critical success factor in customer retention. Furthermore, services frequently involve the consumer in the production of the service (co-production) — for example, booking a flight with an airline. In such instances, service availability may be of vital interest to the consumer, and it in turn may depend on the flexibility of the service provider.

Enterprises and agencies in the public sector are far from immune to similar competitive and commercial pressures. EU-instigated deregulation of public utilities is leading to major changes in the operation of public companies and to a more strident management emphasis on commercial criteria. Recent attempts to impose tighter controls on public spending are having a similar effect on the management of public services. In parallel with these developments, public-service consumers appear increasingly to be insisting on standards of service delivery, flexibility and convenience hitherto associated with services provided in the private sector.

Lean enterprises treat relationships with agents other than employees differently. The focus of their strategy is typically on what they regard as their core competence, with resources being directly allocated to such targets. Other ancillary activities are deemed to be 'non-core' and are typically subcontracted to suppliers. The range of 'non-core' activities, however, seems to be increasing exponentially. Only a few years ago subcontracting was limited to activities such as cleaning. Today, functions such as logistics, final packaging, invoicing and final assembly are being subcontracted. As a result, employees previously in a permanent and pensionable position now find themselves as a (sometimes highly dependent) supplier to their previous employer. A recent review of the emergence of post-bureaucratic/modern organisational structures suggests that 'the virtual organisation' will become the norm in the future. Virtual companies are typically a temporary yet dynamic alliance of companies formed in order to exploit volatile product-market niches opportunistically.

While such an organisational form remains more of an ideal than a reality, it is clear that information and communication technologies are already beginning to have a major impact on the nature of work. Unlike humans, information technology does not require recuperation time from long working hours, is not concerned about leisure/income trade-offs and is potentially highly flexible. This is particularly apparent in service industries where an alternative form of subcontracting occurs: customers do the work. Consumers now fill in their deposit and withdrawal slips at automatic telling machines, rather than asking a bank teller, and fill their cars with petrol rather than using an attendant.

Faced with these competitive pressures and new models of organising manufacturing and service operations, employers are increasingly likely to view working-time arrangements as but one aspect of the wider drive for flexibility and operating efficiency. Flexibility may be sought to use shift working to match productive capacity to peaks in demand. Alternatively, it is becoming increasingly common to phase out shift working in favour of annual working hours arrangements which permit weekly working hours to vary with demand within overall agreed annual working time limits. Other aspects of working time such as break periods and starting and finishing times are increasingly likely to be subsumed in the perceived commercial imperative of greater flexibility. Employer responses to issues such as job sharing, sabbaticals and early retirement are likely to be coloured by the commercial imperative and assessed coldly in the light of their contribution to the employer agenda.

1.3 THE AGENDA OF EMPLOYEES AND TRADE UNIONS

The motives for working-time flexibility are very different for those in employment. For employees, individual preferences regarding working time and leisure are at the core of any analysis of working-time flexibility. Personal choice dominates the agenda. Indeed, it could be argued that this individualism is quite contrary to the efficiency agenda of employers and the social concern agenda of Government.

In recent times, there appears to be little evidence of a substantial desire by workers to enjoy more leisure at the margin, even without real wage reductions. For example, a survey in Finland revealed that there was a 2:1 ratio of respondents who preferred current working hours and higher wages to shorter working hours and the same wages. Furthermore, only 2 per cent of respondents valued leisure time to such an extent that they would be willing to sacrifice existing income for substantially increased leisure time. This is hardly evidence of a 'willingness to share' attitude. Rather, those in employment appear to value the primacy of time worked and the control they have over trade-offs between work and leisure. The Irish data detailed in this book largely confirm this assertion.

For those not in full employment, the trade-off position may be quite different. Those attracted to work-sharing arrangements include women who wish to return to the workforce following child-rearing, retired and semi-retired individuals and those working part-time who want a more secure position. These categories are not typically classified as unemployed, so policy measures to alleviate chronic unemployment through work sharing may have the unintended consequences of increasing the supply of labour that wishes to avail of such arrangements. The impact on the primary target of policy measures, reducing unemployment levels, would thus be considerably diluted. This theme will be explored in some detail in this book.

1.4 WOMEN AND GENDER POLITICS

Work sharing can be a double-edged sword when it comes to gender equity. On the one hand, work sharing is seen as a means of giving greater flexibility to women who wish to combine career and family commitments. According to Handy (1994), the 'portfolio' approach to career, home-working and the organisation, whereby combinations of all three can be built up over one's lifetime, offers greater scope for women to deliver work in ways that meet these commitments.

The other edge of this sword, however, could mean that only women assume responsibility for family and career roles, thus reinforcing, rather than eliminating, the lack of equality of opportunity, and further marginalising women in terms of career development. There is evidence to suggest that the two-income family has yet to balance responsibilities for family and work, and that, more often than not, it is the woman who ends up managing the juggling act, either by working longer hours overall (by having a full-time job and also managing family and home), or by opting for some form of work sharing which may thereby limit career opportunities.

Another trend having an impact on women is the increase in service sector employment, which may be part-time, temporary or contractual. Many of the jobs created in this sector are considered attractive to women because they offer this flexibility to combine home and work. However, they may be further contributing to the marginalisation of women in work, as quite often these jobs are in the lower-paid categories.

While women carry the larger burden of house and family responsibilities, this dilemma will continue. Until a more equitable sharing of work and family responsibilities is seen as the norm, women will continue to run the risk of losing on the career front.

Work-sharing interventions targeted primarily at women, with the intention of allowing them greater flexibility, may in fact be counter-productive by reinforcing female stereotypes, allowing women to take on the larger portion of family care, and may result in limited career opportunities for women in the long run. Interventions, therefore, need to be promoted, which encourage greater distribution of these responsibilities between the sexes, and which do not, intentionally or unintentionally, reinforce gender inequity in the workplace.

The other issue hotly debated in the context of women's un-employment is how they are classified in the recording of un-employment figures. Women working in the home are technically 'unavailable for work' and therefore are excluded from the ranks of the measured unemployed. Some argue that if women working in the home (and technically 'unemployed' in the economic sense, in that they receive no remuneration of any kind including state benefit) were classified as 'out of work', then the true nature of unemployment would be far higher (closer to 50 per cent of the workforce). There are two basic responses to this. Firstly, that this is indeed the true nature of unemployment; secondly, that this could not be the true nature of unemployment as it creates too high a level of unemployment. The evidence to be presented in this book suggests, however, that women primarily avail of work sharing and, further, that if work sharing were more widely avail-able, more women would choose it. Therefore, the question to be posed is: if women are offered the choice of work sharing and avail of it, are they not technically available for work? Indeed, the ar-guments often put forward for the impact of work sharing on re-ducing unemployment are that there will be a displacement effect and scarcely any 'real' impact on unemployment. There is scope for further debate on this issue and the evidence to be presented in this book should focus and sharpen this debate.

1.5 THE AGENDA OF GOVERNMENT

The Government agenda around flexible working is driven by the need to generate jobs for the high numbers of unemployed in Ire-land. There is a perception in Government circles that freeing up working hours, through more flexible arrangements, will lead to employment creation and a more equitable distribution of paid work. Indeed, the study that forms the focus of this book is based on Government concerns about the role of working-time flexibility in the context of high levels of unemployment. The debate sur-rounding working time typically includes issues relating to indi-vidual preferences for trade-offs between work and leisure, changes in the composition of the workforce, technological pro-gression and social harmony. The present authors believe that all of these arguments are inextricably interwoven.

Unemployment, as Sinclair (1987) has wryly commented, is 'like an elephant: easier to recognise than to define'. Classifica-tions such as fully employed, under-employed, semi-employed, economically active and strictly unemployed have been suggested by labour force economists. But while measurement of unemployment continues to remain an issue for policy makers and economists, this is one 'elephant' that is not in danger of extinction. If anything, it has become an increasingly dominant species. The unemployment that accompanied the structural changes in many industrial sectors over the past 20 years is now intensifying in the white-collar ranks. The impact of changes in information and communications technologies has led to a new wave of restructuring in service sectors such as finance and retailing.

In the (then) 12 European Union Member States unemployment rose by 11 per cent to 18 million between the first quarters of 1993 and 1994. While much of this unemployment may be cyclical, there is reason to believe that a large proportion of the work population is chronically unemployed and a substantial number of workers (especially women) are in disguised employment — that is, workers involuntarily employed in part-time jobs.

The effects of unemployment are well known but often not fully understood, especially by those in full-time employment. While the financial consequences for the unemployed, those at work, and the exchequer are hotly debated, the social impacts in areas such as mental and physical health, suicide and crime tend to receive less considered attention. The unemployed are disproportionately represented amongst marginalised social groups. Typically they are more likely to be in their teens or early twenties or in the 'near retirement' (although not in the US) category than in other middle-age groupings. In addition, women, the less well-educated, ethnic minorities and the under-skilled tend to be over-represented among the ranks of the unemployed. Clearly an analysis of unemployment and work sharing inevitably must raise arguments regarding social equity and the composition of the labour force.

In the Irish context, Kennedy (1993) suggests that there is a distinct possibility of a conflict between the challenges of reducing unemployment and raising living standards. Arguing that the state now maintains a compensation system for the unemployed that was initially designed to counteract temporary rather than chronic unemployment, he contends that it would be more appropriate for the state to devise approaches, or finance the provision of work for the unemployed, beyond one year. While work sharing would appear to be one such measure, he does caution that the willingness of the employed to share is the real challenge. This will continue to be the case while work sharing is voluntary and not the result of direct Governmental intervention.

1.6 FLEXIBILITY: WHERE THE DIFFERING AGENDAS MEET

With such potential conflict between opportunity and overload (be it as an employee or as a subcontractor), some organisations are already beginning to have ethical reservations about the impact of recent attempts to respond to new patterns of competition. Whether or not such reservations become widespread is, however, open to conjecture.

Social, economic and technological developments will continue to intensify the demands for more flexible working patterns in both manufacturing and service sectors.

Technology continues to remain less sensitive than humans to working time. Management will continue to search for flexibility, functionally, numerically and temporally. For employees, the pattern of a working lifetime and time sovereignty may ultimately replace working time duration as a prominent issue. The question then is not *when* flexibility appears in the workplace but rather how it is brought about and by whom.

It has been suggested that organisations of the twenty-first century will be characterised by fair play and ethics, diversity, personal recognition, irreverence about hierarchy, continuous training, high competition and cosmopolitanism. In his second book on re-engineering, Champy (1995) recognises that the reason for the failure on many re-engineering projects has been the unbalanced focus of the projects, emphasising processes over human systems. There is now a need, he states, to recognise the social systems of the organisation if such efforts are to succeed. While this may augur well for those in organisations, it does not indicate how those outside organisations will fare, nor how these organisations may respond to demands from the outside for even more flexibility in terms of balancing home and work.

The flexibility agendas of Government, employers, employees and those currently outside the work environment (those officially registered as unemployed and those not, who may be wishing to participate in more flexible arrangements) appear incompatible in terms of what each is striving to achieve. The notion of 'full employment' appears irreconcilable with organisations' needs for competitiveness; the need for flexible arrangements for employers seems irreconcilable with the needs of those currently excluded from the official workforce; Government's concerns with social equity and balance appear at odds with global competitiveness. This book highlights the differing perspectives on, and requirements for, flexibility in work by the various players. The research presented here also suggests that the picture is not that clear-cut; that there is not a simple connection between flexible working arrangements and levels of unemployment; that the equation is not necessarily linear; that hours saved do not translate automatically into extra jobs; that significant gaps exist in the perception of flexibility; that individual self-interest can and does exert more influence around working time than does concern for the greater good; that global competitiveness is a far more pervasive argument for flexibility than the need to generate employment. The main players — employers, employees and their representatives, the unemployed, those officially not even in the workforce and Government — do in fact have quite distinct and incompatible agendas.

Is it a distribution issue? A definition issue? An equity issue? A competitiveness issue? Can interventions on the margins of current arrangements, without fundamentally rethinking those arrangements, offer the radical solutions hoped for in some quarters?

There is a need for more widespread debate, more understanding of the agendas of the various players, more creative thinking about the nature of work and work-flexibility implications. This book is intended as an empirically-based contribution to this major economic and social debate in the context of Ireland as it approaches the twenty-first century.

CHAPTER 2

TYPES OF WORK SHARING AND DATA COLLECTION

2.1 ARGUMENTS FOR CHANGES IN WORKING TIME

As long as we have one person seeking work who cannot find it, the hours of work are too long (Gompers, 1887, cited in Humphreys, 1986: xii).

The notion of sharing work out more evenly has a beguiling simplicity, yet one that fails to reflect the complexities of actual work time patterns and the relationship between working time and issues of cost and control. Moreover, much of the work-sharing discussion has assumed that all work contexts can be treated more or less equally for purposes of calculating the job-creation potential of different hours reductions, or the disposition of work groups (all ages, income levels etc.) towards work sharing (Blyton, 1985: 166).

Arguments for changes in working time stem from the changing nature of work itself, as the control of time is critical to the control of work. The main arguments have been summarised by Blyton (1985) and fall into the following categories:

1. *Discretion/Choice Argument*: The idea of worker participation in decision making has received attention in recent times. Management and unions have taken different approaches to this choice issue. Management has concentrated effort in promoting worker commitment and productivity, while unions have been more concerned with issues around power sharing. Decisions around working time have, however, been more restricted with real choice still quite limited.

2. *Labour Force Change Argument*: Changes in the composition of the labour force have been dramatic in recent years with in-

creases in the participation rates of women, the trend towards smaller families and the growth of employment in the service sector. The traditionally male structure of the working week is coming under pressure, with demands for part-time and job-sharing alternatives to the eight-hour five-day week.

3. *Equality/Harmonisation Argument*: Inequalities between different groupings are being highlighted and calls are being made to reduce inequalities between male and female and white- and blue-collar workers. These demands will continue to exert pressure for changes in conditions of employment.

4. *Technology and Organisational Efficiency Argument*: Major changes in technology and in the infrastructure of manufacturing industry, along with changes within the workplace, are contributing to the need for corresponding changes in work flexibility and in patterns of working time more suited to these changing circumstances.

5. *Broader Social Arguments*: Increased life expectancy, increasing congestion in the transportation system, the relation between work and non-work activities and other wider issues are contributing to the debate on the relevance of existing working time patterns.

6. *High Unemployment/Work-Sharing Argument*: The idea that by sharing out the available work, fewer individuals will experience full-time unemployment and that this will have beneficial economic and social effects.

The above arguments reflect the changing nature of economic, social and technological factors, life-cycle variables, the demand for greater choice and flexibility and the nature of time arrangements themselves. Such issues as the increasing participation of women in the workforce, smaller family sizes, growth in the service sector, rapidly changing technology, the balance between work and non-work, changes in preferences and high levels of unemployment, are all contributing to the debate. The notion is common that changes in working time are somehow desirable, albeit for different motives.

2.2 WORK SHARING AND EMPLOYMENT

The high unemployment/work-sharing argument is the focus of this book. As such, it should be viewed in the wider context of pressures for changes in working time, which have more to do with issues of choice and flexibility, than merely job-retention or job-creation issues. There is also some overlap in the different perspectives, in that wider social and technical variables impact on the work-sharing debate and vice versa.

While the work-sharing argument forms part of the working-time debate, it can also be placed within the context of employment policy. Work sharing is perceived as having a contribution to make in reducing unemployment or in job retention. More particularly, in periods of high unemployment, work sharing re-emerges for discussion (Drèze, 1985; Blyton, 1985; Geoghegan, 1985; Walsh, 1979). Work sharing has been defined as 'redistributing work over people so as to reduce the extent of involuntary employment' (Drèze, 1985: 1) and as 'those measures that concern the redistribution of working time by those in paid jobs, for the purpose of sustaining or increasing employment' (Humphreys, 1986: 2). A more elaborate definition is provided by the European Union:

> the aim of work sharing is to redistribute the total volume of work in the economy in order to increase employment opportunities for all those wishing to work. This does not mean that the volume of work [needs to] remain constant. Rather it is based on the observation that this volume is at present inadequate and that we must try to redistribute it (Commission of the European Communities, 1978: 2).

Work sharing therefore encompasses those measures which reorganise and restructure existing paid working time, which implies that existing incumbents must be prepared to adjust to this restructuring in order for those not in paid employment to benefit. There is another aspect of work sharing which receives less attention in the literature and that is the role of work sharing in terms of job retention. Work sharing can also be seen as a means of improving productivity or reducing costs, rather than as a means of dealing with high unemployment rates. Indeed, there is some evidence to suggest that some forms of work sharing may in fact contribute to unemployment levels through reductions in international competitiveness and increases in the supply of labour and displacement.

The renewed interest in work sharing is reflected in the recent adoption of a new Working Time Directive by the European Union (European Industrial Relations Review, 1993a). In essence, this Directive establishes:

- A maximum legal work week of 48 hours (including overtime)

- A minimum time-off of 11 hours in every day

- One full rest day in every week

- A minimum paid annual holiday entitlement of 4 weeks

- A basic limit of 8 hours on night shifts.

EU countries have three years to incorporate the Directive into domestic law, although a considerable number of sectors can avail of derogations. The European Trade Union Confederation (ETUC) has expressed disappointment with the measure, arguing that:

> its weakness and its failings give an inconsistent image of Community social policy . . . it is riddled with holes if one considers the number of sectors that have been left out of the Directive, and the list of sectors subject to derogation by simple national vote (Employment International, 1993a: 7).

The issue of working time is also considered in Commissioner Flynn's recent Green Paper on *The Future of European Social Policy*. The intention is that this document will generate a widespread public debate on issues such as employment, the situation of women in the labour market, education and training, the fight against social exclusion, social standards and social dialogue (Employment International, 1993b). More recently, the Delors White Paper on *Growth, Competitiveness and Employment* highlighted the issue of internal flexibility, and called for the development of Japanese-style work practices aimed at greater staff flexibility, the integrated organisation of work, flexible working hours and performance-related pay (Hourihan, 1993).

2.3 A TYPOLOGY OF WORK SHARING

Generally speaking, work sharing includes measures such as reductions in normal hours, job sharing and job splitting, sabbaticals and other forms of paid and unpaid extended leave, early and phased retirement, reductions in overtime, part-time working, increases in annual holidays and phased entry through extended education and training.

Drèze (1985) divides these measures into three types:

1. *Trading Hours for Jobs*: this involves *reducing standard working time* (weekly or annual) and/or *controlling overtime* to create new jobs.

2. *Sharing Jobs,* using either of two forms: the first is where a worker is replaced on a part-time basis as in progressive retirement schemes; the second is where part-time workers are hired in and do not replace existing workers.

3. *Trading Jobs*: replacing an existing worker under contract with a new entrant; *early voluntary retirement* accompanied by replacement is the most obvious form of job trading.

Of course, all of the above can be carried out in combination or as separate schemes. The implications for reductions in unemployment levels or in maintaining employment levels are not clear-cut. However, one point is apparent. Unless these measures are accompanied by, firstly, a mandatory policy of replacement, and secondly, an understanding that work conditions and practices for existing contracted workers must also change to accommodate these measures, their impact will be questionable in terms of employment.

We have adopted Drèze's description for the purposes of reviewing the international experiences and reporting on our survey findings. Chapters 3 and 4 consider trading hours for jobs, Chapter 5 considers sharing jobs and Chapters 6 and 7 address key issues, international experiences, survey findings for both the private and public sectors and conclusions. The remainder of this chapter addresses the methodological aspects of data collection.

2.4 APPROACH AND QUESTIONNAIRE DESIGN

The primary research underpinning this book involved four types of data collection:

- Interviews with managers in a random sample of companies

- Interviews with selected employees in each of these companies

- Interviews with a national random sample of persons outside the labour force

- Open-ended interviews with Trade Union Officials and other significant actors.

Questionnaires for the first three of these groups were designed by the authors in consultation with the Department of Enterprise and Employment. The management questionnaire was divided into five sections as follows:

1. Background and classificatory variables

2. Job-splitting arrangements

3. Overtime arrangements

4. Unpaid career breaks/sabbaticals

5. Early retirement.

The employee questionnaire was divided into six sections as follows:

1. Job-splitting

2. Overtime

3. Early retirement

4. Unpaid career breaks/sabbaticals

5. Unpaid maternity/paternity leave

6. Background and classificatory variables.

The questionnaire for those outside the labour force asked respondents about their main reason for giving up their last job, extent of job search, willingness to take a part-time job, desired hours and desired pay.

These questionnaires were pilot tested in late 1993. Copies of the questionnaire are available from the authors.

2.5 SAMPLE SELECTION FOR THE MAIN SURVEY

Two major types of employer were considered in the course of the project: namely, those in the private sector and those in the public sector. Based on the *a priori* assumption that at least some aspects of employment practice may differ between these two sectors, it was decided to select two independent and discrete sam-

ples. The first was of private sector enterprises (not establishments). This included the *commercial* semi-state sector. The second was selected from the public sector (including non-commercial
semi-state bodies). Sample selection procedures for each are considered below.

2.5.1   The Private Sector Sample

To select a statistical sample it is necessary to have a good quality
list of all members of the population under study. In the present
context, this implies that what is necessary is a reliable list of
employing entities in the country. Unfortunately, no such list is
readily available in the public domain. From the experience
gained in the pilot test, it was decided to concentrate on two main
sources for selecting the majority of firms in the sample used in
the main survey, namely, the Golden Pages list of companies and
the *Business and Finance* Top 1,000 list of companies.

The former is a listing of business enterprises. The entries on
this list can be selected according to a detailed 2,000-fold classification or aggregate thereof. A sample of companies was selected from this list according to a broadly-based classification
as follows:

1. Retail services

2. Wholesale services

3. Non-distributive services

4. Manufacturing

5. Building and Construction.

In selecting the sample, the population was pre-stratified according
to geographical region; by the aggregated five-fold classification; by
the disaggregated 2,000-fold classification; and alphabetically by
firm name. This should provide a sample of private sector and
commercial semi-state companies.

In addition to this sample, a sample from the *Business and Finance* Top 1,000 list of companies was independently selected. To
do this, the sample was pre-stratified according to the broad five-
fold classification above (retail services; wholesale services, etc.)
and numbers employed. Recorded employment among these firms
is in the order of 407,000 persons. This represents approximately

42 per cent of the non-agricultural workforce. Given the topic under consideration, it is important to be able to ensure coverage of as many employees as possible in the sample. It is for this reason that a disproportionate number of the larger firms in the total sample were included. Depending on which aspect of work-sharing practices is being considered at any particular point, it may be desirable to talk about the experience of the *firm* or, alternatively, the potential for splitting or replacing the number of *positions* in the workforce. Different weighting systems were used depending on which of these two conceptually distinct units (i.e. *firms* or *jobs*) was being considered. This issue is discussed more fully under "Weighting" below.

The total target sample of firms for the main survey was 1,000. This was split between the Golden Pages database and the "Top 1,000" list on a pro rata basis of sectoral employment accounted for by firms on the "Top 1,000" list. For the main survey the aim was to interview at least three employees from each firm.

2.5.2 The Public Sector Sample

As noted above, a prerequisite of sample selection is a population list containing all the elements of interest in any study. In this context this refers to a complete and exhaustive list of all employing entities in the public sector. As no such list is readily available, it was necessary to compile one from a number of different sources. Two main sources were used, namely, the annual estimates for the public sector and the IPA directory. This list purported to cover all public sector organisations and bodies, with a few important exceptions as follows: the Gardaí; Defence Forces; Central Civil Service and First and Second Level Education. The reader should note, therefore, that the figures presented in this book on levels or trends in public sector work-sharing practices refer to public sector organisations exclusive of these four areas of public employment.

2.6 OPERATIONAL DETAILS OF SURVEY

Fieldwork for the pilot phase of the study took place in early December 1993 and for the main survey between March 1994 and July 1994. The sample for the pilot was made up of 50 firms selected from private sector manufacturing and services. The target sample for the main survey comprised 1,000 firms selected as described above.

In each of the sample firms the aim was to administer a management questionnaire to the managing director (or the person nominated by the MD). In addition, an employee questionnaire was to be administered to at least three employees in the company.[1] The three employees were nominated for interview by the person who completed the management questionnaire. The interviewer instructed management that these three should be selected with regard to occupational and gender composition of the firm's total workforce. This sort of selection control should go some way towards preventing bias in the composition of the employee sample.

All interviewing (for both management and employee questionnaires) was carried out by the Economic and Social Research Institute's (ESRI) panel of interviewers. A letter was sent to the managing director of each firm in the target sample outlining the purpose and content of the survey and explaining that one of the interviewers would be phoning in the following week to arrange a convenient time for interview. Management was told in the introductory letter that it was hoped to interview three employees from their company as part of the survey.

When the management survey was completed, the interviewer outlined the broad selection guidelines which the employer should use in selecting employees for interview. A copy of a letter of introduction was left with management for each of the selected employees. This outlined the purpose of the study and stressed that participation in the study was on a voluntary basis and that the study had nothing to do with the firm or the firm's management. The employer facilitated the initial contact between the interviewer and the three selected respondents. Once this initial contact was established, it was up to the employees to decide whether or not they would participate in the survey. No replacements were sought from management to substitute for non-response among employees.

---

[1]   Copies of both the management and employee questionnaires used are provided in the pilot.

2.7 RESPONSE RATES

Table 2.1 provides details on the response rates among firms. From the first column it can be seen that 348 firms successfully completed the management questionnaire. A total of 319 of these firms agreed to proceed to the second stage of the study (selecting the employees for interview). In the case of 29 firms, however, management refused to select the employees. It can also be seen from the table that a further 40 firms were identified as being closed in the course of fieldwork and 235 were small self-employed businesses with no employees. As these no longer con-stitute valid elements in the population, they should be excluded from the calculation of response rates among valid firms. When this is done, it can be seen from the third column of the table that just over 43 per cent of firms completed the management ques-tionnaire and selected the employee names to allow the inter-viewer to proceed to the second stage of the survey. A further 4 per cent of firms completed the management questionnaire but refused to co-operate in the selection of the three employees. Some 30 per cent of companies refused to complete the questionnaire, while a further 11 per cent could not be contacted despite re-peated calls. The final 4 per cent of companies did not respond for a variety of reasons specific to the individual situation of the firm.

Table 2.1: Response Rates Among Firms

	No. of Firms	Per Cent of Firms	Per Cent of Valid Firms
Successfully completed*	319	31	43
Management only completed*	29	3	4
Refusal	224	22	30
Firm closed	40	4	—
Non-contact despite repeated calls	113	11	15
Firm has no employees	235	23	—
Other	64	6	9
Total *	1,024	100	100

* Includes 24 questionnaires from the pilot.

Table 2.2 provides details on response rates among employees. From the table it can be seen that the expected number of poten-tial employee respondents was 957 (three employees in each of the 319 companies which completed the management questionnaire and which allowed the employee stage of interviewing to proceed). Successful interviews were completed by 759 of these respondents, representing an employee response rate of almost 72 per cent among firms which successfully completed the management questionnaire.

Table 2.2: Response Rates Among Employees

	No. of Employees	Per Cent within Responding Firms
Successfully completed	759	79.3
Refusals	198	20.7
Total	957	100.0

2.8 WEIGHTING

Given the complex nature of the sample and the diverse sources from which it was drawn, it was necessary to devote considerable time to developing an appropriate set of weights for the data. The first step was to derive estimates of the total population of firms (workplaces) and the corresponding levels of total employment. These were based on the Labour Force Survey, the Census of Industrial Production and the Census of Distribution.

Two separate weighting schemes were developed for the management data:

1. A set of weights based on the size and sector of the firm so that valid generalisations could be made about the population of *firms*. This set of weights allows the development of unbiased estimates total, means or percentages. In other words, it allows the provision of estimates of the likely responses if all 40,000 firms had been interviewed.

2. A set of weights based on total employment in each firm. This is equivalent to giving each firm a "vote" proportional to its total employment level. Estimates derived on the basis of these weights gives an indication of the number or proportion of employees working in firms with certain characteristics.

In most of the tables presented in the following chapters, the figures in the body of the table are weighted using method 1 while estimates based on method 2 are given in the right-hand column.

The employee data were weighted by reference to the firms from which they came with a subsequent ratio-based adjustment for the gender mix of the employee labour force. The data relating to the persons outside the labour force are presented in unweighted form.

2.9 SAMPLING ERROR

The samples used in this survey were small. It is, therefore, very important to bear in mind that the results may be substantially influenced by sampling fluctuations, particularly if the estimate concerned is based on a subset of the data. The effect of such sampling errors is exacerbated by the large weights that were used. As a rough guide to sampling errors, the following shows the confidence intervals for simple random samples of the size used in the present survey. It is likely that these understate the true confidence intervals because of the operation of a "design effect" greater than 1. Therefore, confidence intervals derived on the basis of a design effect of 2 are also shown. (See Kish, 1965 for a further discussion of design effects and Moser and Kalton, 1971 for empirical justification of assumed magnitude of the design effect.)

Table 2.3: Sampling Errors and Confidence Intervals for Samples of Different Sizes, given an observed sample percentage of 50 per cent

Sample Size n	Standard Error	Confidence Interval (assuming simple random sampling)	Confidence Interval (assuming a design effect of 2)
50	7.1	13.9	27.7
100	5.0	9.8	19.6
348	2.6	5.3	10.6
500	2.2	4.4	8.8
759	1.8	3.6	7.1

As already noted, the following chapters are based on Drèze's classification of working time and report in detail on the key issues, findings from the international experience and survey findings for both the public and private sectors in Ireland.

CHAPTER 3

CHANGES IN STANDARD WORKING TIME

3.1 THE ISSUES

The length of the working period, together with wages, has been a central issue in the history of industrial relations. Labour has typically been purchased in temporal units (hours, days, weeks), thereby emphasising time rather than task as the primary concern in the wage-effort bargain (Blyton, 1989a). Throughout this century, working time has been altered through reductions in the length of the working week, increased holiday entitlement and reduction in the working lifetime (by way of late entry to and/or early exit from the labour market), while the incidence of part-time work increased significantly. The underlying rationale for such developments has been documented by Hinrichs (1991). From the employee's perspective, these developments include:

- In the initial stages of industrialisation, sufficient time for recuperation from work

- As economies developed in the 1950s and 1960s, the attainment of leisure

- As preferences for more individualised lifestyles emerged in the 1970s, flexibility of working time.

Developments underlying employers' attempts to move from the system of standardised working hours include:

- The requirement, necessitated by the intensive use of capital, that employees work time schedules that are outside the normal, socially established time structure

- The departure from an evenly regulated and stable distribution of working hours that result from changing and volatile patterns of demand, particularly in the growing service sector

- The attraction of employing workers whose working hours meet exactly with job requirements.

Thus, current preferences of employees for flexibility are based on the concept of *time sovereignty*, while management's desire for flexibility is founded on the increased uncertainty surrounding input prices, production possibilities, and product demand, largely as a result of the coincidence of the economic recession and the development of new, flexible manufacturing technology (Hill and Blyton, 1987). It is in this context that the international experience with reductions in standard working time are reviewed.

3.2 THE INTERNATIONAL EXPERIENCE WITH REDUCTIONS IN STANDARD WORKING HOURS

3.2.1 Country by Country Details

Belgium

Demands for a reduction in working hours in Belgium have been closely linked to the development of the labour movement, but, as elsewhere, over the course of time they have acquired a different meaning. Prior to the Second World War, union demands concentrated on the social and cultural aspects of a reduction in working hours. An emphasis on an improved lifestyle for workers dominated the debate. After the war, the system of industrial relations that evolved was founded on the basis of a tripartite social partnership agreement between unions, employers and government. Demands for reduction in working hours now lost their priority: the emphasis was placed on wages and social security. More recently, it has been suggested that Belgium, by the late 1970s, had come to the forefront of working time change and served as a 'social guinea-pig' for competing countries (de Rongé and Molitor, 1991). Evidence of such experimentation includes the following:

- The government-defined '5-3-3' policy formula of 1982: this implied a 5 per cent reduction in working hours, a recruitment rate of 3 per cent, and a 3 per cent decrease in wages with the overall objective of creating 75,000 jobs.

- The 1983 legislation (l'arrête 179) presenting firms with the opportunity of combining the reorganisation of work with modifications of working hours: employers now began to argue that working time flexibility was a prerequisite for reductions in working hours and creating/safeguarding jobs.

- The Hansenne experiments which were aimed at reorganising the working times of firms with a view to redistributing the work available. This set of provisions allowed companies to extend production time and react to demand within the existing legal framework. In 1987, 65 firms employing 26,000 workers participated in these experiments, leading to the creation of 900 additional jobs.

In terms of employment effects, de Rongé and Molitor have argued that the trade union campaign for reduced working hours and compensatory recruitment in Belgium has not achieved its goals. Developing the argument that there is a potential conflict between the reduction in working hours seen as a collective concern by the trade unions and the ever-increasing and varied preferences of their individual members (Hinrichs et al., 1985), they claim that the chances of a collective interest existing are greatly diminished if the probability that people might become unemployed varies significantly by sector, region or even gender. De Rongé and Molitor conclude that the union movement has progressively lost ground on working time reductions because of its adoption of a defensive position to social experiments such as the Hansenne provisions, variable timetables and part-time work. In fact, the unions have continued to put forward the same arguments for working time reductions as they did in the 1930s, despite the technical and organisational changes in manufacturing that have occurred since then.

In December 1993, the Government intervened to provide a framework for the redistribution of available labour (Blanpain and Engels, 1995). Joint committees could enter into collective bargaining agreements, determining what measures they feel are most appropriate. 'Company Plans' for the redistribution of available labour can be established using at least one of the following measures:

- Voluntary part-time working with split of available jobs

- Reducing working time

- Reducing overtime

- Introduction of a right to educational leave

- Introduction of a system of part-time pre-pension

- Introduction of shift work

- Introduction of flexible working time patterns

- Introduction of the four-day working week.

All of these measures must be accompanied by additional hiring. If the company plan is approved by the government and it results in a net increase in employment, the employer can avail of reduced social security contributions.

Britain

It has been suggested that employers' resistance to reductions in standard working time has been greater than their resistance to increases in wages in Britain this century (Bienefeld, 1972). The rationale of this argument is that cuts in working hours can increase labour costs and lead to further industrial disputes because of the more complex scheduling of production that occurs as a result of the reduction. Bienefeld also argues that economic buoyancy is a necessary condition for progress in reducing working hours because it improves employers' negotiating strength and provides the opportunity to pass on any increased costs to the consumer by way of price increases.

His central thesis, however, is the existence of a cyclically recurring and income-related shift in the demand for leisure, claiming that a sharp rise in money wages in the years preceding the rounds of hours reductions caused a shift in employees' preferences from pay rises to more leisure. Thus, as real income rises, the desire for more leisure is non-cumulative: each decision on whether unions should demand pay increases or hours reductions (increased leisure) is discrete or taken without reference to previous leisure opportunities foregone. Roche (1987) contests the validity of Bienefeld's thesis, arguing that the desire for leisure is intensified in hours campaigns through an 'inspection effect': hours campaigns focus employee attention on opportunities for leisure foregone in past negotiations, thereby increasing the marginal value of leisure. This explanation provides a direct motivating role to past choices and wage/leisure trade-offs.

In contrast to Bienefeld, Roche (1991) has emphasised the role of *structural* and *cyclical* factors, rather than (income/leisure trade-offs) as the primary forces impacting on innovations in working time in Britain. These factors include:

- Changes in patterns of consumption, and the application of new technologies, particularly with regard to shift working

- The emergence of on-call and stand-by arrangements

- An incomes policy that has facilitated 'unsocial hours premia'

- The development of internal labour and markets which have facilitated employee-oriented temporal flexibility arrangements

- An emphasis on the productivity contribution from increased capital utilisation.

In support of this argument, he contends that the 1959–66 round of hours reductions was the result of a relatively loosely organised campaign, which sought to trade income off against leisure in the light of fears of technological unemployment. This round ensured that the 40-hour week had become standard by the late 1960s. Simultaneously, productivity bargaining became increasingly popular during this period. These negotiations involved the bargaining of pay rises in return for changes in working practices and what employers perceived to be instances of 'leisure at work'. They also sought to extend work into what had traditionally been regarded as leisure time, by way of increased shift work and the introduction of 'on-call' arrangements.

The 1970s witnessed the demise of productivity bargaining, although shift work and other forms of flexible working arrangements continued to increase. This was particularly so in the service sector, which gradually came to dominate economic activity. It was in the wake of such structural changes in the economy, coupled with rising unemployment, that the unions were prompted once more to address the issue of working hours. The landmark of this campaign was the 1979 engineering dispute which was to be one of the most acrimonious in the history of British industrial relations. While initially demanding a 35-hour week, the eventual settlement was based on a 39-hour week, although this typically involved marginal reductions in finishing times rather than the reduction of a complete one-hour block (McKinlay and McNulty, 1992). In terms of employment effects, it appears as if the reductions have been offset by increased overtime and higher productivity resulting from changes in technology and work pace; increased employment was negligible (White and Ghobadian, 1984). From a flexibility perspective, it has been suggested that the reorganisation and rescheduling of working hours that occurred in Germany after the 1984 agreement had no parallel in Britain, although it is unlikely that this will be the case in the longer term (Roche, 1991; Blyton, 1992).

More recently, the 1989–90 engineers' dispute ended with a settlement which established the 37-hour week as the national standard *without* conceding the workforce and temporal flexibility

standards demanded by the employers. Ultimately, it appears that
the next frontier time in the British engineering sector will be a
renewed campaign for the 35-hour week in the second half of the
1990s (McKinlay and McNulty, 1992).

Denmark

Unlike its Scandinavian neighbours, Denmark has no statutory
maximum working week. Scheur (1992) has observed that all of
the reductions in weekly working hours (from 48 hours in 1945 to
37 hours in 1987) have been the result of collective bargaining.
This has occurred irrespective of whether the negotiations took
place at central level or were decentralised to sectoral or plant
level. The proportion of Danish employees covered by collective
bargaining is, at 74 per cent, somewhat lower than the union
density of 87 per cent; in the private sector it is even lower at 57
per cent.

The employment argument for reduction in weekly hours
dominated the debate in Denmark throughout the 1970s and
1980s. However, the 1987 bargaining round which featured a
phased cut from 39 to 37 hours was, for the first time, accompanied
by provisions for extra flexibility, allowing for variations in weekly
hours. For instance, in the meat industry, employers introduced a
four-day working week of 9.25 hours. Although employees took
strike action, they were eventually forced to concede to the employers' arguments in respect of improved equipment utilisation
and savings resulting from the elimination of a night shift.

The European Industrial Relations Review (1993b) has reported that reductions in working hours have meant that workers
have had to work somewhat more overtime. For a given reference
week, overtime had increased from 6.3 per cent in 1986 to 7.6 per
cent in 1990 in the private sector, while over the same period
salaried employees (who generally are not covered by collective
bargaining) had seen their normal working week increase above
that prevalent in the general labour market.

It appears that less standardised and more flexible working
time patterns appear to be spreading slowly (Schönemann-Paul et
al., 1992). There has been a marginal decline in the proportion of
full-time employees engaged in 'day-working' from 83.6 per cent
to 81.7 per cent between 1988 and 1991. Over the same period,
shift work increased from 6.7 per cent to 10 per cent of full-time
employment.

France

In France, the 1936 legislation introducing the 40-hour week with two weeks of paid holidays per year is considered to be the beginning of modern policies regarding working time. However, the gap between statutory and effective working time was not bridged for almost half a century. Developments during this period included:

- Before 1962, working time increased while employment remained stable and unemployment very low. This was mainly caused by a combination of increased demand for labour as a result of fast economic growth, and a demographic check on the supply side accounted for by a low pre-war birth-rate.

- Between 1962 and 1968, further economic growth resulted in job creation, while working time started to decrease slowly. This labour supply response can be attributed to the post-war 'baby boom' generations reaching adulthood.

- From 1968 to 1974, employment continued to increase at the same annual rate, while working time decreased faster than in the previous period, but neither of them fast enough to cater for the ever-increasing supply of labour. Unemployment reached half a million in 1974.

- Between 1974 and 1980, a slow-down in the rate of economic growth was coupled with increases in labour productivity. Despite further reductions in working time, the supply side demographic pressures and an increasing rate of female participation in the labour force saw unemployment reach 1.5 million by 1980.

- From 1980 to 1985, despite government intentions to reduce the duration of the working week, unemployment continued to grow.

The government initiatives of the early 1980s with regard to a reduction in standard working hours have been documented in some detail (Jallade, 1991). In 1981, the new socialist government put into effect an across-the-board policy of reducing the statutory working week on a step-by-step basis from 41 hours in 1981 to 35 hours in 1985. Initially, the statutory duration was reduced to 39 hours per week, coupled with the introduction of leave, with full wage compensation. It is important to put in context the task facing the government, industry and social partners at this time:

- The 35-hour week target in five years was treated with justifiable scepticism, given that it had taken almost half a century for the 40-hour week to become a reality.

- The initial transition to the 39-hour week was on the basis of a government decision to award total compensation (i.e. there was to be no drop in the monthly wage, implying a consequent increase in the hourly rate). Industry argued that reduction in working time ought to have been designed to enhance firms' competitiveness, thus giving them an incentive to employ additional workers.

Assessing the employment effects, the Institut National de la Statistique et des Études estimated that 110,000 jobs were created or maintained as a result of the measure, while, in response to a survey on the reactions of industrial firms, it was found that no more than 20 per cent had recruited individuals on a permanent basis (Boisard, 1982). Jallade argues that whatever small employment benefit was achieved was more than offset by the damage caused to competitiveness as a result of rise in wage costs and the emergence of a 'hiring-freeze' attitude amongst employers. He points to three critical lessons of the French experiment:

- Any uniform solution imposed from above is ineffective because it is ill adapted to the circumstances of many firms: some can tap productivity reserves while others are approaching the limit of their capabilities.

- There are very real risks attached to accelerating a trend that reflects economic constraints.

- There are practical difficulties in promoting work sharing by means of a reduction in the working week: if the reduction does not go far enough, the result is higher productivity with no additional jobs; if it goes too far, wages may go out of control.

Since the early 1980s, the emphasis in French policy has been on a more intensive use of plant and equipment, resulting in an increase in shift work coupled with the shortening of shifts. At plant level, the higher wage costs resulting from more shift work were compensated by significant gains in overall efficiency and a higher return on capital investment. From a government perspective, more shifts has meant more jobs.

Jallade concludes that governments, rather than focusing on the relationship between working time and employment, need to look at working time in the context of enhancing industrial competitiveness and, indirectly, job creation. They can have a role in this regard in two important ways: firstly, by setting international standards with respect to working time (possibly in the context of trade and tariff negotiations), and secondly, with regard to legislating for financing non-working (leisure) time out of working time, by way of higher taxes or social security contributions from those at work.

Currently, the government's five-year plan to combat unemployment again addresses the issue of reductions in working time (Industrial Relations Europe, 1993b). Initially, the draft legislation proposed a phased cut from 39 to 37, and eventually, 32 hours. However, Labour Minister M. Michel Giraud has indicated that the extension of present regulations to enable companies and unions to negotiate a whole panoply of flexible arrangements is a central policy objective. The legislation that finally passed through parliament was watered down considerably, with all references to a 32-hour week deleted from the text. The revised provisions included the following:

- Companies will qualify for lower social charges if they reduce individual hours by at least 15 per cent (just over 33 hours).

- The calculation of hours is to be on an *annual* basis.

- An initial increase of 10 per cent in the number of employees is mandatory.

- There is a guarantee that the total size of the workforce will not drop below the starting level for three years,

- There are to be corresponding pay reductions.

- The details of any arrangement must be set out in company-level agreements.

This final requirement is a major stumbling block for the French unions, as they do not want to sign any deals involving pay cuts. Likewise, a survey by UIMM, the engineering employers' federation, has revealed that a move to a 33-hour week with proportionate pay reductions would boost employment by no more than 2 per cent and probably jeopardise competitiveness.

Germany

The reductions in standard working time that occurred in Germany throughout the 1950s and 1960s culminated in the phased introduction of the 40-hour working week. By 1971, 77 per cent of blue-collar workers and 52 per cent of salaried employees had collectively agreed this standard. Initially, employees' preferences for 'bunched leisure' (the two-day weekend) stimulated this demand for a shorter working week (Hinrichs, 1991). More recently, employee concerns have developed to the stage where the *quality* rather than the quantity of leisure time has become a critical issue. This change in employee preferences was reflected in the negotiations for further reductions in working hours in 1984 and 1987.

When unemployment reached 2 million in 1982, reduction in working hours as an employment-creation policy attracted the attention of the powerful IG Metall union. Hinrichs has observed that the union recognised the difficulty in mobilising support for a reduction in working hours because:

- It was no longer realistic to rely on the support of a collective demand (i.e. forsaking individual preferences in the interests of class solidarity) for a reduced working week since work-leisure-income preferences had become much more individualised as the labour supply became increasingly heterogeneous in the 1970s.

- Future employment effects were uncertain.

- There were perceived fears of increased workloads and reduction in job security.

As an initial step in negotiations, IG Metall proposed a *single* reduction to a 35-hour week, arguing that this would lead to a 50 per cent employment effect. However, it was the intransigence of the employers' federation in preliminary negotiations that fuelled support for the union's demand. The union embarked on a strike that was to last for seven weeks. The essence of the union's strategy was the financing of indefinite strikes at a limited number of high-profile companies in order to win path-breaking precedents for the industry as a whole (McKinlay and McNulty, 1992). Following arbitration, the 40-hour norm was eventually breached, with both parties to the dispute agreeing to a 38.5 hour week (averaged over a two-month period) with full wage compensation. IG Metall's victory was essentially a Pyrrhic one: the 1984 agreement delegated the power to vary working hours to individual management and works councils, thereby furthering the decentralisation of collective bargaining from industry to plant level (Jacobi and Muller-Jentsch, 1990). Furthermore, the agreement contained a clause that the introduction of shorter hours must not lead to a reduction of the firm's processing time, which, by implication, facilitated further potential for flexible working time regimes on the part of the employers.

In 1987, a second series of negotiations, once more based on the 'working time for extended flexibility' principle, paved the way for a reduction in average weekly hours to 37.5 hours in 1988 and 37 hours in 1989. The period over which this average was calculated was extended from two to six months. In addition, IG Metall failed to obtain guarantees on the maximum of an 8-hour day or the preservation of Saturday as a free day. Hinrichs has suggested that the negotiations over working hours in the 1984–87 period are unique in that:

- It was the first time that the unions attained a working time reduction (with full wage compensation) solely by means of their own power during a period when the labour market was in crisis.

- It was also the first time the employers not only tried to defend the status quo, but also brought their own demands for the reorganisation of working time, which ultimately facilitated a compromise.

- As a result of the 'working hours for flexibility' exchange compromise, the unions may ultimately have sacrificed a central platform of collective bargaining, and inadvertently, or otherwise, facilitated the establishment of a new working time regime.

In terms of employment effects, IG Metall has estimated that approximately 100,000 jobs have been created or saved, although the employers suggest that no more than 24,000 jobs have been created. Hinrichs suggests that somewhere in between these two amounts is most realistic. Alternatively, it has been argued that employment trends are ultimately determined by economic growth prospects, while reduced working time increases the pressure on firms to rationalise, thus reducing the employment potential of economic growth (Neifer-Dichmann, 1991).

More recently, the German government considered the possibility of introducing three months' annual leave (with lower wages) in the interest of saving jobs (Gow, 1993). This 'achieving security through change' approach is mirrored in Volkswagen's decision in January 1994 to introduce a 4-day, 28.8-hour week as an alternative to axing 30,000 jobs, although other employers continue to doubt if this agreement has wider relevance (Industrial Relations Europe, 1993a). IG Metall's negotiating stance, however, continues to be one of full wage compensation for any proposed hours reductions.

The Netherlands

As in most industrialised countries, unemployment in the Netherlands increased sharply after the 1974 oil crisis. In addition, the Dutch labour supply continued to grow at a faster rate than most European economies throughout the 1980s, because of demographic and increased female participation effects. It was in this context that a centralised agreement on the reduction of working hours was reached between unions and employers in 1982. Employees were prepared to pay for the reduction in working time by waiving their price compensation (automatic indexation). The rationale for the agreement was two-fold: to raise profits and to reduce unemployment. By the end of 1984, the Central Bureau of Statistics estimated that 72 per cent of the nation's workers achieved some form of working time reduction. These reductions ranged from a few days per annum to a 36-hour working week, with the majority (50 per cent) of employees in the private sector settling for a 38-hour week. De Neuborg (1991) gives examples of how such reductions were achieved, including the following:

- Increase in the amount of unscheduled holidays

- Reduction of 15 minutes per day

- Straight cut in weekly hours

- Four days of nine hours (with five days production)

- Forty-five hours per week at peak periods and 27 hours per week at slack periods.

The Ministry of Social Affairs and Employment has examined the employment effects of the 1982 agreement. In a survey of 583 firms with more than 20 employees, 80 per cent of respondents had initiated or were planning working time reductions. Of these, 48 per cent maintained the same production time, while 45 per cent reduced it. New jobs were created in only 17 per cent of firms, although 26 per cent expected to be able to create new jobs. However, in 9 per cent of firms, jobs were lost or expected to be lost. The reasons for these low employment effects included productivity growth (35 per cent), overcapacity (22 per cent), reduction in production time (15 per cent) and reorganisational problems (9 per cent).

Further research by Elsendoorn and van Ginneken (1986) focused on working time reduction practices in companies that employed 21 employees or less (which accounts for about a quarter of Dutch employees). Of the survey respondents, only 37 per cent of firms had reduced working time, the remainder encountering problems such as planning and communication difficulties, negative impacts on customer service and the likelihood of a significant rise in production costs.

On the basis of these two surveys, de Neuborg has claimed that the most reasonable estimate of the employment rate is of the order of 20 per cent of the hours lost. This rate does not, however, address the issues of working time reductions leading to an *increase* in labour supply and the possibility of individuals taking on second jobs or moonlighting. Furthermore, working time reductions may activate part of the *non-registered* workforce. Using macroeconomic models, de Neuborg has contended that unemployment would diminish by approximately 1 per cent in the short term and, as such, cutting working time is a relatively ineffective policy instrument to combat unemployment. There are two other reasons which reinforce this conclusion. Firstly, inflation had been reduced to almost zero per cent per annum at the time of the reductions. As the reduction was to be paid for out of the price compensation (automatic wage indexation) mechanism, zero inflation rendered the financing of further working time reductions problematic. Secondly, workers' support was not strong and, in fact, diminished even further in the wake of the disappointing employment effects. This reasoning is a substantiation of van der Linden's (1987) conclusion that the employment effects of any hours reduction measures are critically dependent upon the attitudes of workers with regard to how a cut in working hours might impact on wages.

More recently, however, Social Affairs Minister Bert de Vries has indicated that he will introduce legislation in the near future to reduce the levels of bureaucracy imposed by the Labour Act, (Industrial Relations Europe, 1993d). This initiative coincides with growing public discussion about the four-day working week as a way of reviving employment. The union position continues to be one of wage compensation for reductions in hours.

Sweden

Post-war economic policy in Sweden has been based on an inte- grated equitable pay policy, structural rationalisation and an ac- tive labour market policy. A substantial raft of legislation exists in the areas of job security, holidays, parental leave and educational leave. The Swedish debate with regard to working time came to prominence with the Working Hours Act, 1970. This legislation included the following provisions:

- Normal working hours must not exceed 40 hours per week or an average of 40 hours over 4 weeks.

- Overtime must not exceed 50 hours per month and 200 hours per annum.

- Night work between midnight and 5 a.m. is prohibited (with some general exceptions).

The last two provisions may be overridden in the short term by local agreement, and the entire Act is discretionary in that collective agreements can replace it. Nevertheless, such agreements usually contain similar restrictions (Weigelt, 1991). As a result, since 1970, both manual and salaried workers have had a working week of 40 hours.

Throughout the 1970s and 1980s, the debate on working hours has concentrated on demands for a six-hour working day and a 30-hour working week. This debate has been stimulated by the in- creased level of female participation in employment, particularly in part-time work, and the fact that the number of such part-time employees working relatively longer hours per week has increased throughout the 1980s. As such, Weigelt observes a significant con- trast between the experience of other European countries and that of Sweden with regard to the debate on the reduction in working hours: it has been dominated by equality issues between men and women rather than employment or flexibility considerations. In fact, both employers and unions have adopted a rather conserva- tive approach to working time innovations, which can largely be attributed to the collectivist approach associated with the active labour management policy in Sweden.

Currently, as union leaders are considering a new campaign for working time reductions (Industrial Relations Europe, 1993c), Rehn's (1977) proposals for a flexible working *life* have begun to attract attention again. The rationale of his approach is to strengthen the position of the individual, and at the same time improve the efficiency of the labour market. This, Rehn claims, could be achieved by way of an insurance-funded entitlement to time off during one's working life. Whilst part of income credited to such a fund could be allocated to pension and retirement requirements, the remainder could be used on a discretionary basis for continuing education, sabbaticals or leisure. Rehn argues that this presents opportunities for employment stabilisation since such forms of leave could be synchronised to any downward cyclical fluctuations in demand. Developments of this nature, however, would require a comprehensive and dramatic overhaul of the social insurance system.

Australia

Like most industrialised countries, Australia experienced increasing unemployment throughout the 1970s and 1980s. The situation in Australia differed, however, from that in most of the other OECD countries. In particular, during this period, the Australian unemployment position has gone from below the average OECD unemployment rate in the 1970s to above the average rate in the 1980s. Since 1976, the Australian trade unions have undertaken a concerted campaign to reduce the length of the standard working week to 35 hours. Although this reduction has not been widely achieved, significant drops in the length of the standard working week have been achieved in most industries.

Mangan and Steinke (1987) have used multivariate analysis to examine the impact of reduced working hours, with particular reference to employment and labour cost. Using industry-level data, they found that consistent employment increases coincided with standard hours reduction in only a relatively small number of Australian industries. These were, in the main, tertiary public sector industries, relatively labour-intensive, and already had a significant part-time component to their workforce. They note that employment increases only followed standard hours reduction where the production function was essentially fixed in the short run and/or the industry was removed from direct competitive pressures (as in the case of the public sector). They highlight that no mainstream manufacturing industry which experienced reduced working hours experienced employment growth.

Turnridge (1981) has estimated the likely effects of an immediate move to a 35-hour standard working week in all Australian industries. Using econometric modelling techniques, the study made the following assumptions:

- A balance of trade constraint

- That employers initially attempted to maintain their levels of production

- That wage increases were by way of indexation.

The study considered three possible scenarios:

1. Employers initially maintain production through increasing employment while overtime is constant.

2. Overtime is initially increased while employment is constant.

3. Employment, overtime and productivity each initially increase sufficiently to offset a third of the production effect of the reduction in standard hours (i.e. there is a partial productivity offset).

Only under assumption 3, with the productivity offset provision in place, did employment show any significant and sustained increase, and under all assumptions standard hours reduction implied significant costs in terms of increased prices and production and consumption foregone.

The Bureau of Industry Economics (BIE) has used a survey approach to attempt to gain an understanding of the impact of reduced working hours (BIE, 1984). The sample of 54 firms known to have reduced working hours during the previous 5 years was drawn from 12 manufacturing industries and varied considerably in size. The findings are summarised in Table 3.1 below.

The findings lends further support to the argument that firms are more likely to increase overtime or productivity rather than employment in the event of a reduction in standard working hours.

Mangan and Steinke (1988) emphasise a conclusion common to all research programmes: the employment-generating potential of past or proposed working time reductions is not large, and is predominantly dependent upon offsetting productivity improvements or sales growth in the industry concerned. Indeed, some researchers (for example, Dixon, 1987) have warned of the cost implications of hours reductions, as the pattern of funding such reductions through increased overtime costs may indeed impact *negatively* upon employment in the future.

Table 3.1: Summary of Findings in Bureau of Industry Economics (BIE) on the Impact of a Reduction in Working Hours

Response to Working Hours Reductions	Proportion of Firms Making Response (%)		
	Increase	*No Change*	*Decrease*
Overtime	50	38	12
Employment	28	60	12
Output per hour	32	65	3
Unit cost	68	26	5
Prices	47	50	3

Source: Mangan and Steinke, 1988.

Japan

The emergence of Japan as a major industrial and economic power has frequently been attributed to the fact that employees there work *smarter* rather than *harder* (Wheelwright and Hayes, 1981). While it is clearly evident that the Japanese have emphasised the 'smarter' aspects of lean production, such as just-in-time manufacturing and total quality management (Womack et al., 1990), this is not to say that competitive advantage deriving from the more subjective term 'working harder' should be ignored. In Japan, working 'harder' means working longer.

In this context, Deutschmann (1991) has identified two significant aspects of Japanese working time practices:

1. By international standards, standard working hours and overtime are longer, while paid holidays are shorter.

2. There is no clear and formal distinction between working hours and leisure.

While the Japanese Wages and Welfare Department of the Ministry of Labour has been attempting to implement the 5-day working week for some time, only 28 per cent of industrial workers and 6.2 per cent of the country's 4.5 million companies were working thus by late 1986. The reasons for this include:

- Workers have become habituated to the notion that longer hours are a virtue.

- Nikkeiren, the employers federation, has historically viewed long hours as a way in which Japan can combat competition from newly industrialised Asian countries.

- The unions are reluctant to stress shorter working hours (Smith, 1988).

Tsujimura (1980) has commented that unions have consistently been more concerned with wage-rate negotiations than with shorter working hours. This, to a greater extent, mirrors the position in the US where employees have historically emphasised income rather than shorter hours. Similarly, lack of state intervention in social infrastructure effectively decreases the real value of household income in Japan, thereby providing the impetus for putting in longer hours. It has been claimed that the continued preference of Japanese workers for income over leisure is a quite rational response to the high cost of living (Cole, 1992).

Deutschmann has suggested that there are two other reasons why there is a gap between working hours in Japan and in Western industrialised countries. Firstly, the enterprise-centred structure of industrial relations and negotiation in Japan entails:

- An absence of the 'institutionally guaranteed spillover effect' that results from a centralised system of collective bargaining which is a feature of Western economies.

- Unions having historically to accept tough productivity-increasing measures which can outweigh the advantages of more leisure.

Secondly, the Japanese system of personnel management, with its emphasis on job rotation, quality circles and *group* responsibility imposes a very strong peer pressure on individuals not to be absent, to work longer, to perform (unpaid) overtime, not to take holidays and to socialise within a company-organised framework. In this regard, the practice of *rate-based manufacturing*, whereby a company produces at the daily sales rate (as typified by Sony's 'sell one, make one' approach), demands that employees continue to work until the daily production targets have been achieved.

In 1992, the Japanese government announced its five-year plan, entitled 'The Lifestyle Superpower Five-Year Plan — The Quest for Coexistence with Global Society', which specified economic goals such as improvements in social infrastructure and housing and reducing annual average working time by 2.2 per cent per annum from 2,008 hours to 1,800 hours. Fields (1992) has asserted that this would appear to be over ambitious, given that the greatest rate of reduction in working hours (1 per cent) was achieved between 1960 and 1973, when the country was starting from a much higher level. Such a view is supported by Deutschmann (1991) who concludes that declarations of plans to reduce working hours in Japan are to be considered in the context of principles rather than real intentions. Nonetheless, by 1994, the 39 hours average working week in Japan matched that of Germany (Japan Institute for Social and Economic Affairs, 1996).

United States

The *laissez-faire* character of business in the United States, with its emphasis on the freedom of the individual, is reflected in the traditional concerns of the American worker, with a particular emphasis on wage increases rather than on reductions in working hours. As evidence of this, 75 per cent of the increase in the standard of living in the United States between 1948 and 1975 was translated into increased wages rather than reduced working hours (Owen, 1976). Christopherson (1991) identifies three distinctive features of American industrial politics that contrast with the European experience and that have influenced the working time/wage debate:

1. Reductions in working time have largely been a regional rather than a national phenomenon, reflecting an ethnocultural dimension of working-class issues.

2. There has been an absence of national labour legislation and government intervention.

3. Workers have historically preferred to use hours restrictions as a way to increase earnings through overtime pay.

From an employer perspective, *employment stabilisation* practices (where every effort is made to provide continuous employment or income for its workforce and to put in place programmes to support this commitment) can be found in only two to three dozen enterprises in the United States (Kochan, 1985).

There has been considerable debate as to employment and working time patterns. Schor (1991: 1) maintains that 'in the last twenty years the amount of time Americans have spent at their jobs has risen steadily . . . working hours are already longer than they were forty years ago'. Likewise, Jones (1974), Kniesner (1976) and Owen (1979) report very little evidence of a declining trend in hours of work. Ehrenberg and Schumann (1982) have identified a rising trend in production workers' average weekly overtime hours, while Greis (1984) claims to have found a decline in average annual working hours since 1947.

However, there has been a significant change in the structure of the US economy since the early 1970s. The decline in traditional mass production, coupled with the emergence of the Japanese philosophy of *lean production* (Womack et al., 1990), has provided the backdrop to development of the service economy in the United States. Christopherson (1991) contends that the more responsive operating requirements of many service sectors has contributed to the proliferation of flexible working and employment patterns:

- Women have increased their hours of paid work by approximately 6 hours per week in the 1980s, mainly in part-time and temporary jobs.

- Per capita work hours were 14 per cent higher in 1986 than in 1985.

- The proportion of people holding second jobs has increased by 20 per cent between 1980 and 1987.

As a result, the concept of family-oriented working time flexibility with an emphasis on the role of women in the labour force *and* in the home has become a major issue in the debate on working time. Given that socially necessary work such as caring for children/the aged is still being carried out by women and has been historically viewed as a private rather than public responsibility, Christopherson forecasts that inequalities in the distribution of time and of wages will probably worsen for women in the future. Alternatively, it has been suggested that the duty to respect, protect and support family life in the context of work organisation is likely to become a major *ethical* issue in the future (Mele, 1989).

Ireland

Collective bargaining has played a major role in the regulation of working time in Ireland, particularly the normal weekly working hours and holidays of manual workers. The manner in which collective bargaining has addressed the issue of working hours, however, has been strikingly different from the manner in which it has addressed pay and conditions. Reductions in normal weekly working hours have tended to occur historically in infrequent general rounds. In the twentieth century these rounds have occurred at intervals varying from over 40 years to over 10 years. The economic and social circumstances shaping the occurrence of hours rounds have also been distinctive. The common thread running through the three hours rounds observed during the twentieth century has been widespread and intense concern on the part of employees and their unions over unemployment. This emerges from a brief review of the three hours rounds: the 1919–20 round; the 40-hour week round, spanning the 1960s and continuing for some groups into the 1970s; and the 39-hour week round of the years 1989–1990.

The post First World War round in Ireland, like the wider British round, was spurred by fears of mass unemployment associated with the ending of the wartime economic boom, a sharp rise in the level of unemployment, and military demobilisation. Many groups of workers secured the 48-hour week in this hours round, but the normal hours of manual workers, as laid down in collective agreements, still varied significantly by region, sector and occupation. Some groups of workers, especially in rural areas, still worked normal working weeks of 50 to 60 hours in the mid 1930s. Others, especially those in skilled trades in urban areas, had already progressed to a 44-hour week (Geoghegan, 1985). The Conditions of Employment Act, 1936 confirmed the 48-hour week as the standard working week.

After the Second World War, no general hours round occurred in Ireland. A six-day working week was to remain standard in most industries until the 1960s. The non-occurrence of an hours round in Ireland after the Second World War points to the contrasting features of the Irish and British labour markets. During the Second World War, real wages had fallen sharply in Ireland and the economy had stagnated. At the end of the War, there was no major demobilisation problem, although the return of migrants who had worked in Britain put added strain on the labour market. The priority of trade unions was to win wage rises to restore their members' pre-war living standards, as the threat of a sharp escalation in unemployment was a good deal more remote than in Britain.

A further round of reductions in normal working hours, ushering in the 40-hour week, commenced in Britain in 1959, and this was to be a factor encouraging further bargaining activity over working hours in Ireland. The subject of weekly working hours first became an objective of national trade union policy when, in September 1959, the newly united Irish Congress of Trade Unions (ICTU) held its first annual delegate conference and passed a resolution demanding a 40-hour week. A general movement aimed at securing a reduction in weekly working hours and the introduction of a five-day working week, without any loss in weekly earnings, was initiated by trade unions in 1960. As a result, a considerable number of workers obtained a shorter working week during that year, and in many instances the five-day working week was conceded. Thus, a five-day working week was conceded on a wider basis than hitherto, while reduced weekly working hours continued to be secured by an increasing number of workers. In the great majority of cases the five-day week and the reduction in the number of hours to be worked resulted from direct negotiations between unions and the employers concerned.

During the 1960s, a 40-hour week began more and more to become the norm, although there were some notable industrial disputes in the building industry and with maintenance craftsmen. In spite of the relative economic prosperity and labour-market buoyancy enjoyed by Ireland during much of the 1960s, the objective of work sharing was again apparent in the policies of trade unions in the 40-hour week round. As in the case of the 40-hours round occurring in Britain, fear of job losses arising from faltering economic growth and technological change was an important element in pressure for cuts in normal working hours. British unions with members in Ireland had already participated in policy debates in Britain on working time reductions as a response to such concerns.

At this stage, centrally bargained national pay agreements entered the picture. From 1970 to 1980, collective bargaining in Ireland was dominated by a series of nine consecutive national wage agreements. Their main effect was to confirm that the 40-hour week had now become standard for manual workers and that groups still working in excess of 40 hours might have 'sound and valid reasons' for seeking changes, provided that regard was had to the requirements of the industry or firm concerned and the date of any previous reductions in hours.

In the National Understanding of 1979 there was a provision that standard working hours would remain at current levels for the duration of the Agreement. The exceptions were cases where the Labour Court found that existing working hours in particular employments were out of line with those generally prevailing in the industry or region. There was also a commitment to introduce legislation. There was a supplementary provision in the National Understanding of 1980 that the employers agreed, in the event of negotiations for a further Agreement, to give consideration to a reduction in working hours in the context of the general social and economic situation and international developments.

Between 1982 and 1987, pay bargaining reverted to a decentralised round pattern. However, major changes in the conduct of pay bargaining emerged as decentralised rounds evolved during the next five years. Of particular importance was the emergence of company-level or company-by-company bargaining as the dominant level of collective bargaining. Throughout the 1980s, industrial and sectoral bargaining units gave way across a wide front to company-level bargaining. Little significant bargaining activity on working hours occurred in the private sector during the period of free collective bargaining up to 1987. A survey by the Federated Union of Employers, conducted in the mid-1980s, indicated that only about 7 per cent of companies had a normal working week for manual workers of less than 40 hours per week. The position was strikingly different in the case of clerical workers. Only 38 per cent of the companies surveyed operated a 40-hour week for clerical workers; 31 per cent operated a 37.5-hour working week. In the public service, a general agreement concluded in 1983 explicitly prohibited any changes in working hours during the currency of the agreement. Subsequent agreements contained no provisions for reductions in hours.

While little progress was apparent in collective bargaining, the issue of cuts in working time was coming earnestly back on the agendas of trade unions. This reflected both sharply rising unemployment and a resumption of emigration. It also reflected increased levels of trade union activity on working hours in Europe, particularly in Britain. In 1984, the ICTU campaigned for a reduction in working hours on the basis of what was happening in Europe. The Labour Court consistently declined to make any recommendation in that regard.

The re-emergence of national pay bargaining in 1987 saw the return of working time to the negotiating agenda. For the first time, a national tripartite agreement on wages, conditions and economic and social policy addressed the question of working time. The Programme for National Recovery 1987 (PNR) was a three-year agreement, and contained a clause that envisaged discussions between the social partners on reductions in standard working hours. This led to a 'Framework Agreement', in February 1989, between employers and the ICTU, which set the scene for negotiations at company level on reducing the normal working week. The Framework Agreement resulted in a round of reductions in working time and the advent of the 39-hour standard working week for most manual workers. The manner in which the cut of one hour was put into operation varied widely. In many instances, workers opted for a simple reduction of one hour per week, often on a Friday evening. In other instances, the parties opted to extend annual holidays by a number of days equivalent to the aggregate reduction in normal hours represented by a cut of one hour per week. A remarkable feature of the hours round introduced under the PNR was how little industrial conflict or friction arose in the process of adjusting working time through collective bargaining. The fact that the reductions occurred under the terms of a national tripartite agreement, and following an international trend towards reduced normal working hours, explains the ease with which negotiations were concluded.

The PNR was succeeded by a further three-year tripartite national pay agreement, the 'Programme for Economic and Social Progress' (PESP). The PESP contained no provisions for further reductions in working time, but did include a clause permitting the conduct of bargaining at local level, up to a ceiling of 3 per cent of basic pay cost. Reviews of the local round suggest that in instances where employers looked for concessions in return for the 3 per cent rise, revisions of working time arrangements were among the changes sought and agreed. It appears, however, that the changes to working time regimes involved were minor: for example, the abolition or tightening up of tea breaks. The local negotiations clause in the PESP may yet lead to a more significant change in the working time regime in the public service, where management is seeking to negotiate radical changes in the system of pay determination, grading structures and employment contracts.

O'Riordan's (1984) econometric analysis of the relationship between working hours and employment in 23 manufacturing industries between 1956 and 1971 leads him to the conclusion that the case for work sharing is weak in the context of employment generation. He argues that a reduction in hours would necessitate a more than proportional increase in employment for the level of output to be maintained: a 10 per cent cut in hours would involve a fall in output of 7 per cent, whereas a 10 per cent rise in employment would only raise output by 2 per cent. As such, even if reductions in hours were matched by proportional cuts in wages, extra labour and/or capital would be necessary to maintain output, which in turn would increase costs per unit. Roche (1988: 149), however, contests the statistical validity of this analysis and argues that, given the poor quality of working time data in Ireland:

> It is not possible to isolate the effects of variations in different facets of working time, such as, overtime working, short-time working, holiday entitlements and normal weekly hours

It bears emphasis that the 39-hour week round occurred in labour-market circumstances which had never before triggered an hours round in Ireland. Both in Ireland and internationally, hours rounds had tended to occur historically during periods of low unemployment and labour-market buoyancy. This was so in spite of the strong influence of fears about rising unemployment in changing the negotiating priority of unions from pay to hours. The hours rounds of the late 1970s and 1980s in a number of European countries and in Britain and Ireland occurred for the first time in circumstances of deep economic recession, high unemployment and often declining union membership and power. The chronic mass unemployment of the 1970s and 1980s, combined with a sharp decline in union confidence in the effectiveness of orthodox measures for combating the problem, helps to explain the historically unprecedented recent rounds of cuts. These same concerns have kept the issue of further cuts in working time on the industrial relations agenda.

3.2.2 Conclusion from the International Literature

Although calculating the employment effects of reductions in standard working time is a problematic exercise (Blyton, 1987), the international experience appears to have been disappointing, with some commentators suggesting the possibility of a negative effect. Of even more significance is the fact that these discouraging results have occurred irrespective of:

- The institutional variations in employer/union arrangements from country to country

- The differences in approach (legislative, collective bargaining or local agreement) that have been used to implement reductions

- The magnitude of the reduction.

There have, however, been some suggestions that a single, large-scale reduction would offer the greatest potential for employment (Cuvillier, 1984: 149), although in this context he cautions that:

> Large-scale reductions in working time would be required to split up the work to be done into a larger number of jobs and to bring about changes in the ways of living that would be sufficiently marked to give a spurt to industrial economies in difficulty. But it also appears that the larger the reductions and the faster they are carried out, the greater the danger of bottlenecks, and thus of arriving at results quite contrary to what was hoped for.

Given that most reductions in standard working time have been small and introduced on a phased basis, the experience has been that employers have largely absorbed such reductions through increased overtime and improved productivity. Nevertheless, there is some evidence from the 1984 reduction in hours in the German engineering industry to suggest that the work-sharing potential of hours cuts may indeed be significant where available opportunities to rationalise production and increase productivity *have already been taken* (Bosch, 1986). Similarly, Blyton (1985) has argued that, despite the absence of evidence of employment effects internationally, there are several points that may be made in support of the reduction in standard hours/work-sharing concept:

- Employer responses to a small cut in hours may not be an accurate guide to the responses generated by larger cuts.

- Little or no attention has been paid to the job *maintaining* effect of previous rounds of reductions.

- The timing of previous cuts (most recently in periods of uncertainty and unused capacity) may have acted against any work-sharing potential.

- Collective bargaining has generally not yet been extended to the point where agreements are made which restrict employers to increasing labour in order to maintain production.

Indeed, it increasingly appears as if employer preferences for improved flexibility will be the major *quid pro quo* for working time reductions. Mass production, based on the principles of product and part standardisation, vertical integration and specialisation of labour, thereby generating economies of scale, no longer forms the basis of the organisation of work. In an increasingly competitive marketplace, responsiveness to individualised demand is becoming more prominent, with forecasts that *mass customisation* will be the next form of production organisation (Westbrook and Williamson, 1993). Mass production and economies of scale will be replaced by advanced manufacturing technology (which is readily 'switchable' and 'extendible') that will be capable of generating economies of scope, with an emphasis on flexibility in relation to both products and volume (Goldhar and Jelinek, 1985).

Management will continue to search for flexibility both functionally (with greater multiskilling) and numerically (with regard to the size and structure of its workforce). For trade unions, the pattern of working time will replace work-time duration as the prominent issue, although they are constrained in this regard by individual requirements for greater flexibility and time sovereignty. It appears that 'the key issue will ultimately be one of matching numerical/functional flexibility with temporal flexibility' (Blyton, 1989a: 11).

3.3 STANDARD WORKING HOURS IN THE IRISH PRIVATE SECTOR

Four main aspects of standard working hours are addressed in our survey findings. First, we discuss average hours worked by various occupational grades as well as the extent of change in these hours over the five years preceding the survey. Secondly, we consider the effects in the operation of a number of aspects of private sector companies as a result of the reductions (if any) in standard working hours. Thirdly, we present information on managements' perceptions of the likely effects of any future reduction on the operation of their organisations. Fourthly, we look at employee preferences for implementing changes to working time arrangements. Each of these issues is considered initially for private sector companies before moving on to the public sector in Section 3.5.

3.3.1 Present Situation and Extent of Recent Changes

Table 3.2 presents details on the average number of hours worked in private sector companies for four occupational grades. Two sets of figures are presented for each grade. The first relates to the set of respondents when each firm is weighted in such a way as to provide unbiased estimates of the mean number of hours for the population of *firms* or *enterprises* — in other words, to provide estimates of the likely responses if all 40,000 firms had been interviewed in a census. The second set of figures provides estimates of average hours derived from a weighting system which was based on total employment in private sector companies. This second system is equivalent to giving each firm in the sample a 'vote' which is proportional to its level of total employment. Use of this second weighting system means that the experience of larger firms in the sample will be reflected to a greater degree in the reweighted sample statistics than will the experience of smaller firms. Consequently, the second weighting system will give an indication of the number or proportion of employees working in firms according to the selected characteristic.

Table 3.2: Estimated Mean Working Hours per Week for Various Grades of Employees

	Managerial / Professional and Higher Admin.	Clerical	Skilled Manual	Semi / Unskilled Manual
	(Mean Hours Per Week)			
Total All Enterprises	44.4	38.5	38.9	38.8
Total, Weighted by Employees	41.5	38.7	39.6	39.5

From the table it can be seen that the highest reported standard working hours (using both weighting systems) is for managerial/ professional workers who have an average figure of 44 hours per week. There was relatively little variation in the average between the other three categories, each of which fell within the range 38.5–38.8 hours per week. Table 3.3 presents these figures on a more disaggregated basis according to occupational grade and size/sector classification. It is clear from this table that there is a particularly low level of variability both within and between grades across the six size/sector groups for those outside the managerial/professional category. Not only is the overall average higher for the Managerial/Professional group relative to other workers, but the variation *within* that group between large and small firms in each of the three broad sectors is substantially stronger than for any of the other three grades included in the table.

Table 3.3: Estimated Means of Standard Working Hours for the Various Grades of Employees

Categories of Employers	Manuf. / Bld		Distributive Services		Non-Distributive Services		Total, All	Total weighted
	< 100 Emps.	100+ Emps.	< 20 Emps.	20+ Emps.	< 20 Emps.	20+ Emps.	Enter- prises	by em- ployment
	(Mean Hours Per Week)							
Managerial, Professional & Higher Admin.	44.5	40.4	44.3	39.9	45.4	39.4	44.4	41.5
Clerical	39.7	38.8	38.2	38.1	38.3	37.4	38.5	38.7
Skilled Manual	39.7	39.9	38.3	39.1	39.2	39.0	38.9	39.6
Semi-Unskilled Manual	39.8	39.7	37.8	38.2	39.1	39.6	38.8	39.5

Table 3.4 provides information on the extent to which there has been a change in the standard working hours over the five years preceding the study. Section A.1 presents details on manual workers, while A.2 presents information on non-manual workers. It can be seen that just under half (48 per cent) of private sector firms reported that standard working hours for manual workers had fallen over the five years preceding the survey. The percentage of firms reporting a fall in standard hours was substantially higher in larger than smaller firms across each of the three sectors. The fact that there were such substantial contrasts in the trends between large and small firms (with reductions in hours being more common in large firms) implies that there is a relatively large difference in the percentages of firms reported in the table, depending on which of the two weighting systems is used. The figure of 48.2 per cent of firms which experienced a reduction in standard hours worked relates to the enterprise-based weighting system which assigns a weight to each firm in a size/ sector category irrespective of the size of the individual firm in question. It can be seen that when the employee-based weight (which assigns a weight that is proportional to the number of employees) is used, the percentage jumps to 64.9 per cent. This means that 64.9 per cent of employees are accounted for by firms which experienced a reduction in standard hours among manual workers. The fact that the reduction in manual workers' standard hours is

more common among large firms results in a higher percentage emerging from the employee-based weight.

Table 3.4: (A) The Extent of Change in Standard Working Hours Over the Preceding Five Years and (B) Whether any Reductions in Hours were Negotiated under the Programme for National Recovery

A. Have standard hours changed in the five years preceding the study?	Manuf. / Bld		Distributive Services		Non-Distributive Services		Total, All Enter- prises	Total, weighted by employ- ment
	< 100 Emps.	100+ Emps.	< 20 Emps.	20+ Emps.	< 20 Emps.	20+ Emps.		
A1 Manual Workers' Hours	*(Per Cent of Enterprises)*							*(Per Cent of Employees)*
Have increased	—	—	—	2.6	2.4	—	2.7	0.3
Remained the same	58.6	17.7	81.8	30.8	78.6	48.4	51.6	34.8
Have decreased	41.4	82.3	18.2	66.7	19.0	51.6	48.2	64.9
A2 Non-manual Workers' Hours								
Have increased	—	—	—	2.6	4.8	—	1.3	0.5
Remained the same	74.6	38.7	90.2	48.7	87.1	70.3	68.8	55.8
Have decreased	25.4	61.3	9.8	48.7	8.1	29.7	29.9	43.7
B. For firms that had reductions, were these negotiated?	*(Per Cent of Enterprises)*							*(Per Cent of Employees)*
Under the PNR	75.0	88.2	50.0	68.0	50.0	81.3	76.5	88.9
Independently of the PNR	16.7	11.8	50.0	24.0	50.0	12.5	19.7	9.9
Never heard of (this provision of) PNR	8.3	—	—	8.0	—	6.3	3.8	1.2
Wgt'd	7000	500	17500	900	12400	1000	39300	
(Unwgt'd n)	(75)	(64)	(52)	(44)	(69)	(44)	(348)	(348)

In Section A.2 of Table 3.4 we can see that in 30 per cent of companies' non-manual workers experienced a fall in the standard number of hours worked, of which 69 per cent of companies indicated there had been no change for this grade of worker. The differences in the experience of large and small companies is generally in line with that of manual workers as outlined in Section A.1 of the table. When the employee weight is used it can be seen that just under 44 per cent of private sector employees are accounted for by firms which experienced a reduction in standard hours.

Section B of the table provides some insights into the framework of the reductions (if any) in standard working hours. The management in firms that experienced a reduction were asked whether or not that reduction was negotiated under the Programme for National Recovery (PNR). We can see from the table that, using the enterprise-based weight, a total of 76 per cent of firms that introduced a reduction did so under the PNR. In the remainder of firms the reduction was implemented independently of the programme.[1] In general, the reduction in standard hours was negotiated under the PNR in a higher percentage of large than small firms.

3.3.2 Effects of Reduced Working Hours

In the course of the management questionnaire respondents were presented with five options which could be used for reducing standard working hours. They were then asked to say which were used in their company to reduce standard hours for both manual and non-manual workers.

The options presented to respondents and the associated results are set out in Table 3.5. From this it can be seen that the overwhelming majority of firms effected the reduction by implementing a straight cut in normal weekly working time. This is the case for both manual and non-manual workers using both the enterprise-based and the employee-based weighting systems.

---

[1] On the assumption that the reduction could not have been negotiated under the PNR in the 4 per cent of firms that never heard of either the PNR in its totality or the specific provision relating to a reduction in standard hours.

Table 3.5: Ways in Which Standard Working Hours Were Reduced

	Enterprise Weight		Employee / Enterprise Weight	
	Manual Workers	Non-Manual Workers	Manual Workers	Non-Manual Workers
	(Per Cent)			
Straight out in normal weekly working hours	88.8	82.8	85.4	82.5
Increase in annual leave	12.9	20.9	13.5	15.3
Reorganisation of shift periods	1.3	0.8	4.3	1.2
Extension of flexitime	0.2	0.4	0.5	0.8
Other	2.0	3.2	17.7	25.5
Total*	105.4	108.0	121.4	125.3

*   This table is based on an open-ended question in which respondents were given
the opportunity to mention the relevant number of options applied in their firm.
Because multiple responses from individual firms were possible, the totals are in
excess of 100 per cent.

Table 3.6 gives details on managements' perceptions of the effects
of the reduction in standard working hours on a number of aspects of their operation. As in previous tables in this section results based on both weights are shown. The first weight in each
subsection is based on the enterprises only; the second is based on
the enterprises in proportion to their employment total. From the
table it can be seen that the strongest effect of a reduction in
standard hours was seen by management as being on labour
costs. Just under half of the firms (which accounted for 61 per
cent of the relevant private sector workforce) felt that the reduction had caused labour costs to increase. Other areas to have been
most affected by the reduction in standard hours were overtime
costs (increased in 23 per cent of firms, 36 per cent of the private
sector workforce) and overtime hours (increasing, as would be expected in the light of the previous statement, in 20 per cent of
firms which accounted for 33 per cent of the private sector workforce). The reduction in standard working time does not seem to
have substantially impacted on a number of employees — either
full-time or part-time. A total of 8 per cent of firms (accounting for
7 per cent of the private sector workforce) experienced an increase
in full-time employees. Comparable figures in respect of part-time
employees are 3 per cent of enterprises (accounting for 21 per cent
of the workforce). This divergence between the two figures reflects
the fact that the increase in part-time employment resulting from

Table 3.6: Effects of the Reduction in Standard Working Hours on a Number of Aspects of their Operation Among Those Firms which Experienced a Reduction in Standard Hours Over the Preceding Five Years

	Increase	*Same*	*Decrease*		*Increase*	*Same*	*Decrease*
Overtime Hours				**Productivity**			
Total All Ents.	20.2	76.2	3.6	Total All Ents.	4.7	82.9	12.4
Total, Wgt'd by				Total, Wgt'd			
Employees	33.3	66.4	0.3	by Employees	3.7	52.4	43.9
Overtime Costs				**Expenditure on Plant etc.**			
Total All Ents.	22.8	73.6	3.6	Total All Ents.	11.8	88.1	0.1
Total, Wgt'd by				Total, Wgt'd			
Employees	36.4	63.4	0.3	by Employees	6.8	92.7	0.6
Sub-Contracting				**No. Full-Time Employees**			
Total All Ents.	1.7	98.3	0.0	Total All Ents.	8.0	89.4	2.6
Total, Wgt'd by				Total, Wgt'd			
Employees	6.1	93.9	0.0	by Employees	6.7	91.6	1.7
Labour Costs				**No. Part-Time Employees**			
Total All Ents.	48.1	44.3	7.6	Total All Ents.	3.0	96.5	0.6
Total, Wgt'd by				Total, Wgt'd			
Employees	61.2	37.9	0.9	by Employees	21.3	78.0	0.7

the reduction in standard hours was exclusively concentrated in the larger firms. Using the enterprise-based weights, it was found that 14 per cent of the larger firms in the Manufacturing/Building sector which experienced a reduction in standard working hours experienced an increase in the number of part-time employees. Comparable figures for the larger distributive and non-distributive services sectors were 23 per cent and 6 per cent respectively. None of the smaller firms in any of the three sectors had experienced an increase in the number of part-time employees on foot of a reduction in standard working hours.

The final issue considered in this section is managements' views on the likely effects of a (further) reduction in standard working hours. From Table 3.7 it can be seen that respondents were asked to state their degree of agreement or otherwise with each of six statements on the likely outcome of a reduction (or further reduction if relevant) in the number of standard working hours. These statements were put to *all* respondents, not just to those who had already experienced a reduction in hours in the preceding five years.

From the table it can be seen that on most of the issues mentioned, firms' views seemed to be quite evenly divided. A majority thought that a (further) reduction in standard hours would have a negative impact on productivity and would lead to an increase in overtime. A total of 38 per cent felt that it would not facilitate negotiations on flexible working time, while 24 per cent felt that it would. Views on the employment impact of a (further) reduction seem to be particularly mixed. Approximately 30 per cent of firms felt that it would result in an increase in full-time and 35 per cent felt that it would lead to an increase in part-time jobs. As a counterbalance to this view, however, 54 per cent of firms did not agree that it would lead to any increase in full-time employees, while 47 per cent did not feel that it would lead to an increase in part-time employment.

Table 3.7: Firms' Views about the Effect of a Further Reduction in Standard Hours

Would a further reduction in standard working hours	Strongly Agree	Agree	Neither Agree nor Disagree	Disagree	Strongly Disagree	Total
	(Per Cent of Enterprises)					
Facilitate negotiations on flexible working time	5.0	19.5	37.8	16.6	21.1	100.0
Have a negative impact on productivity	30.1	23.6	24.5	18.9	2.9	100.0
Probably lead to an increase in the amount of overtime	33.0	24.6	19.9	15.5	7.0	100.0
Probably result in serious production re-scheduling problems	24.9	20.0	30.6	14.6	9.9	100.0
Probably result in an increase in the number of full-time employees	11.7	18.5	15.6	33.0	21.2	100.0
Probably result in an increase in the number of part-time employees	9.9	26.0	17.2	23.5	23.3	100.0
Wgt'd	7,000	500	17,500	900	12,400	39,300
(Unwgt'd n)	(75)	(64)	(52)	(44)	(69)	(348)

3.4 EMPLOYEE PREFERENCES FOR IMPLEMENTING CHANGES TO WORKING TIME ARRANGEMENTS

In the course of the employee questionnaire, respondents were asked to state their level of agreement or otherwise with two statements on different ways of implementing changes to working time arrangements. The first referred to a trade-off between standard working and pay, while the second focused on whether or not a pay rise would be preferred in the form of cash or time-off-in-lieu. In addition, respondents were asked to state which of these options they would choose to take extra time off from work: would they prefer a shorter working week; longer holidays; or extra days which could be taken during the year? By considering the replies to these three questions, some insights can be gained into the trade-off between cash and time-in-lieu. The results, disaggregated according to sex and age, are presented in Tables 3.8 and 3.9.

From Table 3.8 it can be seen that, in aggregate, 22 per cent of employees agreed that they would like to get more time off their current job, even if this meant a reduction in their current pay, while 73 per cent disagreed. In general, females were more positively disposed towards this proposition than males (26 per cent compared with 19 per cent respectively).

In terms of variations by age cohort, it can be seen that the highest level of agreement with this statement is among the 46–55-year age cohort. A total of 44 per cent of this group would seem to prefer more time off for less income. This is more than twice the aggregate average for all employees. Given that the 46–55-year cohort is the prime age cohort for take-up of early or phase retirement schemes, this trend may impact on the potential for such schemes. This will be discussed in Chapter 6.

The second statement in Table 3.8 considers employees' preferences for increased remuneration and, specifically, whether they would prefer to take some or all of a pay rise in the form of time-off-in-lieu rather than in the form of cash. Overall, 19 per cent said they would prefer to take a pay rise (at least in part) in the form of time-off-in-lieu, while just over 75 per cent disagreed.

As was the case with the first statement, a slightly higher percentage of females than males seem to be in favour of extra time-off-in-lieu (24 per cent compared with 17 per cent respectively). One can also see that the percentage of each age cohort which is in agreement with this statement increases progressively from 13 per cent for the youngest to peak at just over 23 per cent for the

46–55-year age group. As noted above, this may have implications for the introduction of early or phased retirement packages, which would be primarily aimed at this age cohort.

Table 3.8: Employees' Views on Ways of Taking More Time Off

I would like to get more time off my current job even if this meant a reduction in pay	Agree*	Neither Agree Nor Disagree	Disagree
	(Per Cent of Employees)		
Sex:			
Male	19.3	3.3	77.3
Female	26.3	9.7	64.0
Age:			
<25 years	13.6	2.5	84.0
26–35 years	21.7	8.9	69.4
36–45 years	18.6	3.8	77.6
46–55 years	43.6	1.6	54.1
56+ years	19.8	2.2	77.9
Total	21.6	5.4	73.0
If I was due a pay rise I would prefer to take some or all of it in the form of time-off-in-lieu			
Sex:			
Male	17.0	6.0	77.0
Female	24.0	4.2	71.9
Age:			
<25 years	13.5	1.7	84.9
26–35 years	20.5	5.6	73.9
36–45 years	19.2	3.4	77.4
46–55 years	23.2	18.2	58.6
56+ years	21.9	1.7	76.4
Total	19.4	5.4	75.3

*   Respondents were presented with a five-fold scale: Strongly Agree; Moderately Agree; Neither Agree Nor Disagree; Moderately Disagree; Strongly Disagree.

Finally, Table 3.9 presents information on employees' first preferences for taking extra time off from work. From this it can be seen that just over 53 per cent say that they would prefer to take extra days off during the year, 29 per cent to take the extra free-time in the form of a shorter working week, and 17 per cent in the form of longer holidays. In terms of variations between males and females it is clear that a substantially smaller percentage of females than males would prefer to take the extra time off in the form of holidays (9 per cent compared with 21 per cent respectively). In general, a higher percentage of females would prefer to take the extra free-time in the form of a shorter working week (36 per cent of females compared with 26 per cent for males). The option of a shorter working week also appears to be relatively more attractive as one moves up the age cohorts. Almost 50 per cent of employees aged 56 years or more and 31 per cent aged 46–55 years cite this as their first preference in contrast, for example, to only 18 per cent in the younger age category.

Table 3.9: Main Preferences Among Private Sector Employees for Way of Taking Extra Time Off

	Male	Female	<25 yrs	26–35 yrs	36–45 yrs	46–55 yrs	56+ yrs	Total
	(Per Cent)							
Shorter Working Week	26.2	36.0	17.7	29.2	32.0	30.8	49.7	29.4
Longer Holidays	21.3	9.0	20.1	18.2	18.0	11.3	8.6	17.3
Extra Days to be taken during the Year	52.5	55.0	62.3	52.5	50.0	57.9	41.7	53.3

3.5 STANDARD HOURS IN THE IRISH PUBLIC SECTOR

In this section we consider changes in standard working hours in the relevant public sector organisations included in the survey, as well as managements' perceptions of the effect of such changes on the operation of their organisations. We then briefly outline some of the views of relevant public sector employees on different options for changes in standard working hours.

3.5.1 Present Situation and Extent of Recent Changes

Table 3.10 presents information on average standard working hours for various occupational grades in the public sector, weighted by both the straight enterprise-based weight and the combined enterprise/employee weight which assigns a weight to each firm as the basis of its total employment.

In general, there is little substantial variation between the three occupational grades outlined in the table. There is some limited evidence to suggest that the 'Other Routine' grade has a slightly higher average working week than either of the other two grades. Comparison of the figures in Table 3.10 with those in Table 3.2 suggests that the average hours worked in the public sector are below those in the private sector. The largest gap between the two sectors (of about seven hours per week) is for the Higher Administrative grade.

Table 3.10: Estimated Mean Working Hours Per Week for Various
Grades of Employees

	Higher Admin. / Executive	Routine Clerical	Other Routine
	(Mean Hours / Week)		
Total, All Organisations	36.9	36.0	37.8
Total, Wgt'd by Combined Enterprises/Employees	35.2	34.9	38.8

Table 3.11 provides information on the extent to which there had been a change in the standard working hours of Higher Administrative/Executive workers and Other Clerical/Routine Grades over the five years preceding the survey.

Table 3.11: Extent of Change in Standard Working Hours Over the
Five Years Preceding the Survey

	Enterprise Only Weight			Ent. / Employee Weight		
	Increase	Same	Decrease	Increase	Same	Decrease
	(Per Cent)					
Higher Admin./Exec.	0.0	67.4	32.6	0.0	76.8	23.2
Clerical and Other Routine Grades	0.0	41.5	58.5	0.0	52.0	48.0

From this it can be seen that in a third of relevant public sector organisations the Higher Administrative/Executive staff experienced a reduction in standard hours over the period in question. The comparable figure for Clerical and Other Routine Grades is 58 per cent. When the sample is weighted to account for total number of employees, the figures are 23 per cent and 48 per cent respectively. The fact that the latter pair of figures is lower than those based on the enterprise weight reflects the fact that the reduction in standard hours for both grades was concentrated more in the smaller than larger organisations. As was the case with the private sector, almost 90 per cent of the reductions that occurred were negotiated under the Programme for National Recovery.

Table 3.12 presents information on the impact of the reduction in standard hours on various aspects of their operation. The trends among relevant public sector organisations can be compared with those in the private sector as outlined in Table 3.7 above. Possibly the most interesting feature of this comparison is the extent to which the views of private and public sector management concur on the first six of the eight items listed in the table. About a third of respondents (when adjusted by the combined enterprise/employee weighting factor) in both public and private sectors reported an increase in both overtime hours and costs as a result of the reduction in standard working hours over the five years preceding the survey. Subcontracting was not affected at all in the public sector, whereas 6 per cent of private firms availed of it to compensate for working time reductions. Increases in labour costs were mentioned by 60 per cent of public sector organisations (accounting for 60 per cent of relevant employees). Comparable private sector figures were 48 per cent and 61 per cent respectively. Productivity increases were mentioned somewhat more frequently in relevant public sector organisations than in private sector firms (12 per cent compared with 4 per cent respectively). Expenditure on plant was virtually unaffected in relevant public sector organisations, and only marginally affected among private sector firms (1 per cent and 7 per cent for public and private sectors respectively).

The most striking contrast between the experience of the public and private sectors relates to the effect of reduced standard hours on the change in number of full-time and part-time employees. A third of relevant public sector organisations indicated that they had increased their number of full-time staff in response to the reduction in standard hours. The comparable figure for the private sector was 7 per cent. Almost all of this difference is accounted for by the very high percentage of hospitals and other health service organisations which said that they took on more employees.

Table 3.12: Impact of the Reduction in Standard Working Hours on a Number of Aspects of their Operation Among Relevant Public Sector Organisations Which Experienced a Reduction in Standard Working Hours Over the Preceding Five Years

	Increase	Same	Decrease		Increase	Same	Decrease
	(Per Cent)				(Per Cent)		
Overtime Hours				**Productivity**			
Total All Ents.	23.7	76.3	0.0	Total All Ents.	5.2	88.3	6.5
Total, Wgt'd by Employees	31.2	68.8	0.0	Total, Wgt'd by Employees	11.9	80.8	7.2
Overtime Costs				**Expenditure on Plant etc.**			
Total All Ents.	21.7	78.3	0.0	Total All Ents.	3.5	96.5	0.0
Total, Wgt'd by Employees	31.5	68.5	0.0	Total, Wgt'd by Employees	0.8	99.2	0.0
Subcontracting				**No. Full-Time Employees:**			
Total All Ents.	0.0	100.0	0.0	Total All Ents.	26.0	74.0	0.0
Total, Wgt'd by Employees	0.0	100.0	0.0	Total, Wgt'd by Employees	33.4	66.6	0.0
Labour Costs				**No. Part-Time Employees**			
Total All Ents.	59.2	38.1	2.8	Total All Ents.	41.7	58.3	0.0
Total, Wgt'd by Employees	60.1	39.9	0.0	Total, Wgt'd by Employees	28.3	71.7	0.0

In Table 3.13, the view of public and private sector organisations regarding the effects of a further reduction in standard hours is contrasted. All respondents (including those who had experienced a reduction in standard hours over the preceding five years as well as those who had not) were asked to indicate their level of agreement or otherwise with a number of statements regarding the effects of a (further) reduction in standard hours in the future on their organisation. The table presents figures on the percentage of respondents (managers) who said that they either 'Strongly Agreed' or 'Agreed' with each of the statements in question. The table is adjusted using the enterprise-based weight. From the figures it can be seen that a higher percentage of respondents in the public sector felt that such a reduction would facilitate negotiations on flexible working time (42 per cent compared with 24 per cent), while somewhat fewer felt that such reductions would have a negative effect on productivity (46 per cent compared with 54 per cent). Both sectors were in broad agreement as to the likely impact of any future reduction on the amount of overtime worked, with 58 per cent of private sector firms and 61 per cent of relevant public sector organisations agreeing with this statement. Rescheduling problems were anticipated as a result of a reduction in standard hours by 33 per cent of relevant organisations in the public sector and 45 per cent of private sector firms. As was noted in the discussion of the previous table, the major contrast in perceptions between public and private sector management relates to possible increases in employment. A total of 40 per cent of management in relevant public sector organisations agreed that a (further) reduction would probably result in an increase in full-time employees (compared with 30 per cent in the private sector), while 68 per cent thought that part-time employment would rise (in contrast with 36 per cent in the private sector).

Table 3.13: Firms' Views about the Effect of a Further Reduction in Standard Hours, comparing the views of Public and Private Sector Organisations

Would a further reduction in standard working hours	Private Sector	Public Sector
	(Per Cent of Enterprises / Organisations which Agreed or Strongly Agreed with each Statement)	
Facilitate negotiations on flexible working time	24.5	41.9
Have a negative impact on productivity	53.7	45.9
Probably lead to an increase in the amount of overtime	57.6	60.6
Probably result in serious production rescheduling problems	44.9	33.0
Probably result in an increase in the number of full-time employees	30.2	40.0
Probably result in an increase in the number of part-time employees	35.9	68.2

3.5.2 Employee Preferences for Implementing Changes to Working time Arrangements

Information was collected from public sector employees regarding their perceived trade-off between income and time off work, as well as their preferred option for taking a pay rise. Table 3.14 shows the level of agreements or otherwise among public sector employees with regard to two statements. The first statement asked whether respondents would prefer to get more time off their current job even if that meant a reduction in pay. It can be seen that almost three-quarters of public sector employees would not be in favour of this option, while 21 per cent would support it. The level of support for this statement is almost twice as strong among females as males (26 per cent as compared with 14 per cent respectively).

In the lower section of Table 3.14 we present information of employees agreement or otherwise with the following statement: *If I was due a pay rise, I would prefer to take some or all of it in the form of time-off-in-lieu.* As with the previous statement, there is a high level of disagreement with this proposition — 71 per cent disagreed with it, 26 per cent agreed. There is some evidence to suggest that female employees are slightly more in favour of taking some or all of a pay rise as time-off-in-lieu than are their male counterparts. A comparison of the trends presented in Table 3.14 with those in Table 3.8 shows that there are, in general, no major differences between the responses of public and private sector workers with respect to their attitudes to changes in working time.

Table 3.14: Public Sector Employees' Views on Ways of Taking More Time Off

I would like to get more time off my current job even if this meant a reduction in pay	Agree*	Neither Agree Nor Disagree	Disagree
	(Per Cent of Employees)		
Male	13.8	2.7	83.6
Female	26.2	9.7	64.1
Total	21.0	6.8	72.1
If I was due a pay rise, I would prefer to take some or all of it in the form of time-off-in-lieu			
Male	21.1	7.1	71.8
Female	28.6	1.0	70.3
Total	25.6	3.5	70.9

*   Respondents were presented with a five-fold scale as follows: Strongly Agree; Moderately Agree; Neither Agree Nor Disagree; Moderately Disagree; Strongly Disagree.

Finally, Table 3.15 presents information on public sector employees' first preference for taking extra time off work. In the course of the survey, employees were asked to rank in order of preference the three options set out in the table. From this it can be seen that a total of 30 per cent of relevant public sector employees would opt for a shorter working week; 16 per cent for longer holidays and 54 per cent for extra days off during the year. There is very little difference between these trends for public sector employees and those for the private sector, as outlined in Table 3.10. As was the case for the private sector, it can be seen that a substantially higher percentage of female than male workers were in favour of a shorter working week. In contrast, a lower percentage of females than males said that their preferred option for taking extra time off work was longer holidays (12 per cent and 21 per cent respectively).

Table 3.15: Main Preferences Among Private Sector Employees for Taking Extra Time Off

	Male	Female	Total
	(Per Cent)		
Shorter Working Week	22.9	34.6	29.8
Longer Holidays	21.0	12.3	15.8
Extra Days to be taken during the Year	56.1	53.1	54.4

3.6 SUMMARY

In this chapter a number of aspects of reductions in standard working time in both the private and public sectors were examined from the perspective of management and employee. Issues addressed included the average number of standard hours worked in various occupational grades, as well as the incidence of reductions in those hours over the five years preceding the survey; the effects such reductions had on the operation of private firms and relevant public sector organisations as well as the perceived impact of future reductions; and employees' preferences for implementing changes in working time arrangements.

Significant differences were found to exist between the standard weekly working hours of managerial and professional/administrative on the one hand, and either clerical or manual workers on the other. In general, the standard hours worked in the public sector appear to be below comparable grades in the private sector. The largest gap (of approximately 7 hours) is for the higher administrative grades.

The cut in the standard working hours of all employees working 40 or more hours per week, provided for under the Programme for National Recovery (1987–90), affected substantial proportions of private firms. The standard hours worked by manual workers fell in approximately 48 per cent of private firms (accounting for 65 per cent of the private sector workforce). The hours of non-manual workers fell in just under 30 per cent of firms (accounting for 44 per cent of the private sector workforce). In general, standard hours in the public sector, though lower, did not fall by as much over the five years preceding the survey as did those in the private sector.

The impact of the reductions in standard working hours on private sector productivity; subcontracting activity; expenditure on plant and equipment and full-time employee numbers would seem to be limited. Management in just over 20 per cent of private enterprises (accounting for about a third of relevant private sector employment) said that overtime hours and costs increased. Labour costs were felt to have risen in 48 per cent of companies (accounting for 61 per cent of private employment). Of significance is the fact that in only 8 per cent of companies (employing about 7 per cent of the workforce) did management say that the number of full-time employees had risen as a result of the reduction in standard hours. A total of 3 per cent of companies (accounting for 21 per cent of employees) said that the number of part-time employees increased.[2] Although the general effects of the reduction in standard hours among public sector firms were reported to have been very similar to those of private sector enterprises, the employment impact was reported to have been higher. Just over a quarter of relevant public sector organisations (accounting for a third of relevant employment) reported an increase in the number of full-time staff. Similarly, a total of 42 per cent of relevant organisations (covering 28 per cent of the relevant workforce) reported an increase in the number of part-time employees. When asked about the likely employment effect of a (further) reduction in standard working hours, management in approximately a third of both private and relevant public sector organisations agreed with a statement presented to them to the effect that a (further) reduction would probably result in an increase in the number of full-time employees. A total of 36 per cent of private sector and as many as 68 per cent of relevant public sector organisations agreed with a statement suggesting that a

---

[2] The fact that the percentage of firms reporting an increase in part-time employees is substantially lower than the percentage of the workforce covered by those firms suggests that this trend was concentrated among larger firms.

(further) reduction would possibly result in an increase in the number of part-time employees.

The final aspect of standard hours addressed in the chapter was the likely demand by employees for further reductions. It was noted that only 22 per cent of private sector employees agreed with the statement that they would like to get more time off even if it meant a reduction in pay. The comparable figure in the relevant public sector was 21 per cent. Similarly, only 19 per cent of private sector and 26 per cent of relevant public sector employees agreed with the statement that if they were due a pay rise they would prefer to take all or some of it in the form of time-off-in-lieu. In general, there is clear evidence from the data presented that female employees were more positively disposed than were their male counterparts to taking time-off-in-lieu in preference to financial payments. Although proportions in the order of a fifth in favour of these pay-leisure trade-off options is substantial, they do not suggest an overwhelming demand by employees for further cuts in working time arrangements.

CHAPTER 4

TRADING HOURS FOR JOBS:
THE CONTROL OF OVERTIME

4.1 BACKGROUND

Overtime can be defined as time worked in excess of 'standard' working hours, rewarded at a premium rate or time-off-in-lieu, or occasionally, unrewarded. The continuing presence of overtime work, and its persistence during periods of economic recession and falling employment, has frequently attracted the attention of both employer and union interests. It has invariably been described as 'the curse of the male manual worker', 'a strange scandal' and an 'institution that will not die' (Evans and Curson, 1986: 59). Nevertheless, while various aspects of working time have altered in recent years, levels of overtime continue to display considerable resistance to change.

The maintenance of high levels of overtime work can impact on work sharing developments in two ways (Blyton, 1985). Firstly, a reduction in overtime hours *already being worked* is a possible basis for work sharing. Secondly, and more importantly in the context of the potential for increased employment, is the 'leakage effect' which overtime could have following a round of reduction in standard working hours: the likelihood that such a reduction would be transformed into increased levels of overtime has frequently been put forward as a major critique of the work sharing thesis (Confederation of British Industry, 1980).

Nevertheless, the current scale of overtime working in some European countries (Ireland, France and Britain, in particular) merits attention in itself. Throughout the 1980s, overtime represented a major element (both in terms of time and income) in the typical weekly working time pattern of approximately a third of male manual workers in British manufacturing industry (Blyton, 1989a). From an employer's perspective, overtime can be an expensive component of labour cost, since it is typically remunerated at a premium rate, varying from time-and-a-quarter up to treble or, occasionally, quadruple time. As such, there are several key issues that need to be addressed in any analysis of overtime working, including:

- The reasons for working overtime and the factors that encourage overtime rather than new jobs

- The pattern of overtime working

- The prospects for change and the barriers to such change.

The reasons for working overtime derive from the demands of both management and employees. The degree to which overtime is worked *of necessity,* as against occasions where overtime is used as the most convenient or inexpensive alternative, is an important feature of this debate. From management's point of view, the most significant advantage of overtime is its *flexibility*, with 'emergency' situations such as machine breakdown, unforeseen increases in demand, absenteeism or an important order deadline being the most widely reported factors which make some overtime working *unavoidable* (Carby and Edwards-Stuart, 1981).

However, there is, additionally, a variety of 'non-emergency' reasons that can influence the level of overtime. In particular, reductions in standard working hours can impact upon the economics of continuous shift working so as to increase levels of 'built-in' overtime. Continuous shift systems need to incorporate all of the available 168 hours in a week, and this is typically achieved by employing four shift crews, each working 42 hours per week (Evans and Curson, 1986). With a 40-hour week this arrangement *systematically* provides for two hours overtime per week, and as standard weekly hours begin to fall, further overtime has to be built in to ensure continuity of production. In machine-paced processes, tasks such as maintenance, cleaning and testing (which are routine and predictable rather than 'emergency') are generally allocated to overtime work. The degree to which overtime has become systematic (i.e. to deal with normal operating requirements and demand) is quite endemic, with as many as 51 per cent (NBPI, 1970) citing it as the main reason for overtime.

While overtime is frequently remunerated at a premium rate, there are several factors that can compensate for this extra expense, when compared to the costs of hiring additional labour. An assortment of employer-funded 'non-wage labour costs' such as holiday, pension, maternity and sickness benefits, has grown as a result of collective agreements or legislative measures, to an extent where they now account for anything up to 30 per cent of payroll costs (Hart, 1984a). Since these costs are correlated with levels of employment rather than hours worked, there is a clear incentive for employers to use overtime rather than recruiting additional staff (Smyth and Karlson, 1991). Furthermore, costs associated with recruiting, training and inducting new staff, coupled with redundancy and dismissal payments (statutory or otherwise), serve only to accentuate this incentive.

In times of labour shortages, it has been argued that the availability of overtime is an important factor in attracting a suitable calibre of staff (Evans, 1975). More recently, however, overtime has, on occasion, been used by management to provide employees with the opportunity of increased earnings, particularly where basic rates of pay are low (McNabb, 1989). In addition, many organisations that have introduced downsizing and demanding measures in recent years are reluctant to add high-cost, fixed-labour capacity in the event of an upturn in the business cycle: for example, because 20 per cent of its current production is based on overtime, Ford Motor Company claims that any downturn in market fortunes is unlikely to lead to redundancies or plant closures (Flint, 1988).

From the employees' perspective, the decision as to whether or not to work overtime is largely one of the relative values attached to increased earnings as against increased leisure, and the extent to which it is compulsory or not. International evidence suggests that overtime is worked primarily by prime-age (late 20s to late 40s) male manual workers in the manufacturing, transport and communications sectors (Blyton, 1989a; Katz and Goldberg, 1982; Carr, 1986). In a landmark review of studies of this issue, Whybrew (1968) concluded that not only were large numbers prepared to trade leisure for increased earnings, but also that once the trade-off have been realised for a given period of time, expectations and expenditure patterns rise accordingly: hence, overtime becomes *self-sustaining*. This argument is supported by evidence from Finland where a survey carried out on behalf of the Ministry of Social affairs revealed that only 2 per cent of the respondents valued leisure to such an extent that they were willing to give up their present wage level in favour of shorter working hours (Gröhn, 1979).

In this context, it is important to distinguish between official declarations of intent at national/collective level and rank-and-file preferences at industry and plant level (Hart, 1984b). At local level, there is considerable evidence to suggest that unions respond to members' demands for overtime in order to increase wages. For instance, the UCG (1980) study on overtime practices in Ireland reported that 60 per cent of firms in the production sector indicated that the conditions under which overtime was worked were documented in employee, trade union and management agreements; simultaneously, only 8 per cent of firms reported that employees were reluctant to work, or opposed to working, overtime.

In contrast, at national level, the trade union movement has traditionally argued that overtime increases unemployment during economic recessions, encroaches upon leisure time and supports regimes of low basic rates of pay (ultimately made tolerable by overtime). While recognising that overtime may be necessary in 'emergency' situations, trade unions have taken the view that it is unacceptable that overtime be worked on a systematic basis in periods of high unemployment (ETUI, 1985). The 'official' collective position is exemplified in the resolutions demanding measures to restrict overtime, coupled with compensatory time-off-in-lieu and satisfactory basic pay levels, which were passed at the European Trade Union Confederation's (ETUC) 1979 congress in Munich. For instance, the trade union movement in Norway has claimed that halving overtime levels could cut unemployment by anything up to 20 per cent through the release of between 30,000 and 50,000 full-time jobs (Industrial Relations Europe, 1993e). Thus, at both national and international levels, the issue of overtime provides the trade union movement with a complex dilemma that is inextricably entwined with the individual members' preferences for trade-offs between income and temporal flexibility.

Compensation for overtime ranges from no remuneration at all, all or part paid for (generally at a premium rate), to time-off-in-lieu (or some combination of payment and time off). With regard to pay structures, as already noted, there is some evidence that overtime is more prevalent in industries with lower-than-average rates of pay and among workers on low basic pay rates (Trade Union Research Unit, 1981). In contrast, it has been claimed that while overtime has tended to be endemic in low-pay industries, highly paid skilled craft labour also work, and demand regular, overtime (Carby and Edwards-Stuart, 1981).

Evans (1975) has claimed that trade union arguments for higher rates of basic pay as a deterrent to excessive overtime are not always effective, because higher basic rates tend to be mirrored by increases in overtime rates, thereby prompting further worker demands for overtime. From a statutory point of view, Ehrenberg and Schumann (1982) have suggested that legislating to control overtime premia is a conceivable policy option in order to curb excessive levels of overtime, although they do express the opinion that the employment effects of such a move would only be in the order of between 1 and 3 per cent. Moreover, they caution that offsetting effects such as the capital substitution for labour make this option less attractive. More recently, Trejo (1991) has claimed that there would be no significant employment effects resulting from a statutory overtime premium because firms would react in such a way as to ensure the same package of weekly compensation of hours and work that was initially acceptable to workers. It is in the context of legislation regarding hours restrictions and overtime premia that we review the international experience with regard to overtime.

4.2 THE INTERNATIONAL EXPERIENCE WITH OVERTIME

4.2.1 Country by Country Details

Comparative analyses of international levels of overtime working *per se* are relatively limited (Blyton, 1989b). Variations in country to country definitions of the number of hours in a standard working week directly affect the periods of work that are designated as overtime. In addition, data are frequently incomplete because of a lack of recording of overtime by certain groups (for example, senior managers), whilst the existence of legislative measures to restrict overtime may, inadvertently, have resulted in management and workers colluding to ensure that excess overtime is not recorded (Blyton, 1985).

Belgium

In Belgium, overtime is normally payable for hours worked in excess of the statutory limit of nine hours per day/40 hours per week, or any other limit set by collective agreement at industry or company level (IDS, 1992). Overtime is restricted to two hours per day, 10 hours per week and 130 hours per annum. However, as a result of flexible working time legislation, which in some circumstances allows daily and weekly limits to be exceeded without overtime occurring, the incidence of overtime is relatively low by international standards. In addition, it is a statutory requirement that a 50 per cent premium (100 per cent for Sundays and public holidays) be applied to overtime, with collective agreements sometimes specifying additional supplements or alternative methods of calculation.

Britain

Recent trends in Britain indicate that male full-time employees work 45.3 hours per week on average, compared with 40.3 hours for females (Watson, 1992). A total of 5.9 million employees work a weekly average of 7.1 hours of paid overtime, while 4.5 million work an average of 7.3 unpaid hours. Approximately 17 per cent of employees in coal, oil, gas extraction and nuclear industry work 60 hours a week or more, while the proportion working more than 48 hours per week has risen from 12.2 to 15.5 per cent between 1984 and 1991. Simultaneously, there was a corresponding fall from 41.3 per cent to 36.4 per cent in the proportion working standard hours of between 35 and 40 hours per week. These statistics reinforce both Roche's (1991) claim that the trade union policy of limiting overtime during the 1980s has not met with any significant degree of success, and Hart's (1984b: 44) conclusion that the reductions of working hours in Britain have resulted in 'some workers who lose overtime (and jobs), while the remainder maintain high levels of overtime working'.

France

In France, legislation requires that employees are paid at time-and-a-quarter for the first eight hours of overtime above 39 hours per week. Above this level, rates are at time-and-a-half up to a maximum of nine hours per week, or seven hours per week over a consecutive 12-week period (IDS, 1992). Rates may be improved by collective or plant-level agreement: for example, in the printing industry, the first two hours are paid at 133 per cent, the third and fourth at 150 per cent, and thereafter at 200 per cent. Although relatively higher levels of overtime working have been traditional in France (Blyton, 1989a), reductions in standard working hours since 1945 have resulted in a steady decrease in overtime working amongst manual workers (Jallade, 1991).

Germany

Legislation in Germany, dating from 1938, requires that over-time should be paid at a minimum rate of 125 per cent. Many collective agreements are based on higher premiums, however, and also include provisions for overtime to be compensated for by time-off-in-lieu, and/or with the overtime premium element paid as cash. Hinrichs (1991) has estimated that overtime work-ing in the mid-1980s amounted to the equivalent of about 861,000 full-time jobs. In 1985, employees worked on average 5.6 hours per month (Deutschmann, 1991). There is, however, considerable variation in the distribution of overtime, with many employees working 10 or more hours per week, and others working hardly any at all.

The Netherlands

Overtime is relatively insignificant in the Netherlands (de Neu-borg, 1991). There are no statutory minima laid down concerning pay for overtime work, shift premiums or other supplements for work outside standard hours: collective agreements are used in-stead (IDS 1992). The first half hour is rarely remunerated, and if no provision exists in collective agreements, the employer must pay the basic agreed hourly or piece rate for overtime work: for example, in banking, the rate is calculated on the basis of annual pay divided by a factor of 2,000.

Spain

In Spain, it is a statutory requirement that overtime payments (for work exceeding the maximum 40-hour week) must be at a rate of at least 175 per cent of normal time, irrespective of whether it is worked on a weekday, weekend or a public holiday (IDS, 1992). There is an annual limit of 80 hours overtime per employee, and in an effort to curb overtime and foster job crea-tion, the government ruled in 1981 that overtime pay would at-tract higher rates of social security contributions when worked other than for various 'structural' purposes (i.e. unforeseen in-creases in demand, *force majeure* and other unavoidable in-stances). The rates applying to 'structural' overtime in 1991 were 12 per cent for the employer and 2 per cent for the employee; other (systematic) overtime attracts rates of approximately *double* these levels. In addition, the law permits time-off-in-lieu to be negotiated in place of pay: if this approach is used, employees are entitled to at least 175 per cent of overtime worked.

United States

In the United States, the Fair Labor Standards Acts of 1938 and 1989 provide for overtime rates of 150 per cent. By the early 1980s, almost 60 per cent of the labour force was covered by this legislation. Levels of overtime displayed a rising tendency in the post-war period, stabilised in the 1970s, and increased again in the 1980s. Over the past 20 years, the annual work schedule of Americans increased by about 163 hours per year, or the equivalent of an additional month of work per annum (Volg, 1992). Data from the Current Population Survey have revealed that about 10 per cent of all US workers received overtime pay for a given reference week, with the precision production, craft and repair group and the operators, fabricators and labourers group reporting the highest levels of overtime (Carr, 1986).

Japan

The prevalence of activities such as socialising with colleagues after work, unpaid overtime and small-group activities blurs the issue of overtime working trends in Japan (Deutschmann, 1991). Fixed employment costs are quite significant in Japan because of the traditional emphasis on lifetime tenure jobs: as a result, employers and unions agree to use overtime rather than increased employment in periods of demand fluctuation (Cole, 1972). Furthermore, although a 'dual' economy, with small subcontractors working very long hours, persists in Japan (Sakai, 1990), effective working hours are not significantly different between large and small firms because of the relatively higher amounts of overtime in the former. In 1985, monthly overtime amounted to 14.8 hours per employee, with relatively low overtime premiums (typically of the order of 130 per cent) being one of the most significant contributory factors in this regard. In addition, the emphasis on meeting daily production targets frequently means that workers must stay late to complete their work. Even then, 'irregular' overtime, frequently unpaid, can be scheduled at short notice — this is the case with office workers, who are expected not to leave work until everybody in the group, particularly the supervisor, has finished (Alston, 1986).

Ireland

The most recent review of overtime in Ireland was carried out by the Department of Industrial Engineering at University College Galway (1980). This study addressed five specific issues:

- The extent of overtime in the non-agricultural sectors of the economy

- The reasons for overtime working

- The job-creation potential of a reduction in overtime levels

- How such a reduction might be achieved

- The additional (and perhaps undesirable) consequences of such a reduction.

The review was primarily based on the results of a survey of management in 1,500 firms (with a response rate of 70 per cent) in both the production and service sectors of the economy. In addition, the review elicited the views of both trade union and employer organisations.

The survey revealed that overtime was used quite extensively. For the period of 12 months preceding the survey, 56 per cent of firms in the production sector and 40 per cent of firms in the service sector worked 51 million and 21 million overtime hours respectively. Overtime tended to be concentrated among manual workers in the production sector (particularly in subsectors such as Food, Drink and Tobacco, and Construction) and amongst maintenance personnel in service subsectors such as Transport and Communications. Existing legislation governing working hours permitted (and still does) up to 600 hours annual overtime per employee, with the survey revealing that 11 per cent and 6 per cent of production and service sector firms were close to this level.

The role of overtime in meeting both normal demand and demand variations, combined with its use as a result of the nature of the production process or service activity, were pinpointed as the primary causal factors in overtime levels. In contrast, factors relating to the cost of overtime, the use of overtime to raise levels of earnings, labour shortages, non-wage labour costs, and costs of protective employment legislation did not emerge as significant causal factors in the survey results. For firms that had reduced (or intended to reduce) the level of overtime, the majority indicated that the favoured approach was by way of productivity and efficiency improvements, rather than by increasing employment.

The scope for increased employment as a result of overtime reduction was perceived to be quite limited, with 60 per cent of firms in the production sector and 73 per cent of firms in the service sector indicating little or no potential whatsoever. While the estimated 72 million annual overtime hours could theoretically translate into 37,500 equivalent full-time jobs (assuming that productivity levels were the same), the report concludes that only approximately 12,000 extra jobs could be created as a result of overtime elimination. Furthermore, even more limited scope was anticipated with respect to the creation of extra part-time jobs as a result of reductions in overtime, or for the compensation of overtime working with hours off-in-lieu of payment.

On the basis of survey responses, the report concluded that setting a maximum annual limit of 150 hours overtime per employee would be potentially twice as effective in terms of job creation, when compared to a weekly maximum restriction of a total of 50 hours of work. It was suggested, however, that this form of legislation would probably be most successful if introduced on a gradual, phased basis. Legislation on other aspects of overtime such as statutory controls of overtime rates did, however, prompt a more varied set of replies from the survey respondents: some firms anticipated an increase in overtime hours as a likely result, while others expected decreases. The majority of firms indicated that if overtime rates, were legally controlled at double-time, it would lead to a significant increase in labour costs rather than an increase in employment. The increase in employment arising from such a measure was estimated to be about 1,500 jobs, which is marginal in the light of some respondents predicting an increase in levels of automation and the substitution of capital for labour if such a measure was introduced.

In a micro-level follow-up investigation of the 1,500 firms in the original study, 48 had experienced a pattern of reduced overtime working, coupled with an increase in employment (UCG, 1982). Of these, eight firms were re-examined two years later. It was found that, in all but two cases, employment had *decreased* since the original study. In the two exceptional cases, employment had increased marginally, while overtime had increased in one firm and remained unchanged in the other. Thus, in the face of deteriorating demand conditions, the authors concluded that overtime reduction as a form of work sharing, if anything, 'has proved to be ephemeral' (Hart, 1984b: 50).

4.2.2 Conclusions from the International Experience

The current position with regard to overtime working is one of variation between different groups of workers, different industries and different countries. Many European countries have sought to reduce the level of overtime by enacting legislation on overtime premia, or alternatively to restrict the amount of overtime worked. Although statutory provisions on overtime rates appear to have a very limited effect on reducing overtime, the role of legislation in restricting, the daily, weekly, monthly or annual limits may have some impact in reducing levels of overtime working. The International Labour Organisation (1984) lists a total of 45 countries where overtime is limited by legislation. Such restrictions typically apply to the daily, weekly or annual levels of overtime worked, and are often supplemented by collective or plant-level agreements. In addition, much of the legislation contains provision for 'exceptional circumstances', with the emphasis on the reduction of systematic overtime. In this respect, Blyton (1985: 59) has concluded that:

> it may be that the existence of statutory controls obliges employers and workers to be more conscientious in establishing norms which secure satisfactory output and earnings without resort to overtime.

Furthermore, the absence of statutory control appears to lower the incentive for management to embark on a negotiation process to implement the changes needed to maintain production without using significant amounts of overtime (NBPI, 1970). On the other hand, it has been argued that an accurate assessment of the impact of statutory control is difficult, as both employers and employees may collude to evade restrictive measures (Carby and Edwards-Stuart, 1981). The complexity of drafting legislation to cover a wide variety of operational circumstances, the distinction between what is necessary and what is avoidable, and the 'policing' of such measures could result in what could be described as a major 'bureaucratic nightmare'. Carby and Edwards-Stuart also suggest that employment creation would be better served if legislation on overtime compensation focused on time-off-in-lieu rather than payment rates, although it has been claimed that such measures would essentially only offer limited scope for over-time reduction in the services sector (UCG, 1980).

The employment effects of measures to reduce levels of over-time need to be considered in the context of the recent rounds of cuts in normal working hours. Econometric analyses of working time reductions have generally focused on the employment effects of reduction in standard working hours, rather than *actual* working hours, which includes overtime (Calmfors, 1985; Hoel and Vale, 1986). As previously noted, the employment effect of reductions in standard working hours appears to have been quite marginal. Calmfors (1988), however, comes to the same conclusion when overtime is included in the analysis: because of the 'leakage' effect, a reduction in working time may increase the cost per worker in relation to the cost of overtime, with the result that firms substitute overtime for workers.

One of the traditional arguments put forward by the employer bodies against the principle of a reduction in normal hours has been that it increases standard labour cost per hour, and, consequently, overtime cost per hour. To counteract this, agreements on shorter working hours feature conditions whereby the notional hourly rate is not increased as a result of the shorter working week: for example, the 1980 settlement of the telephone engineers' dispute in Britain, reducing standard weekly hours from 40 to 37.5, was on condition that all payments based on hourly rates would continue to be calculated with reference to 1/40th of basic weekly pay. More recently, the exchange of 'flexibility for reduced standard hours' principle has come to dominate more recent negotiations. Ingram (1991) has estimated that in every year in Britain throughout the 1980s, approximately a third of wage settlements involving trade unions introduced systematic change in the workplace to enhance productivity.

Evans and Curson (1986) have outlined the principal approaches adopted. They include:

- Additional shift crews

- Extension of shift work and part-time work

- Flexible hours arrangements.

As explained above, continuous shift work has traditionally utilised a four-crew system, with three crews working any one day and the fourth enjoying a rest day. Systematic overtime is built into this approach with each crew working an average of 42 (168 weekly hours ÷ 4) hours per week. Since many industries now operate a 35 to 40 hour week, employers are attracted to the concept of introducing a fifth crew in order to reduce overtime levels. Evans and Curson (1986) report instances where the introduction of a fifth crew has cut overtime by as much as 50 per cent and total labour costs by as much as 18 per cent. This is one area where there may be scope for extra employment, which has also found the support of national and international union federations in recent times (Blyton, 1985).

In conjunction with innovations in shift-work systems such as the introduction of fifth crews and the gradual extension of compressed shift-work patterns (for example, individuals working three 12-hour shifts per week), the incidence of shift work has increased substantially in many developed economies in recent years (European Foundation for the Improvement of Living and Working Conditions, 1986). Traditionally, for technical and economic reasons, shift work has been concentrated among male manual workers in continuous production-process industries. More recently, however, there has been a broadening of shift-work arrangements to involve non-manual and female workers in both manufacturing and service sectors. This trend, when coupled with the growth in part-time work (Watson, 1992) and subcontracting (Harrison and Kelley, 1993), is likely to lead to a significant reduction in levels of overtime working in these sectors (Blyton, 1989b).

A variety of flexible hours arrangements has emerged in some industries, with hours fluctuating on a daily, weekly, monthly, annual or seasonal basis, depending on business requirements. Flexitime arrangements tend to be concentrated in large-scale enterprises, generally in the service sector and amongst non-manual workers (Blyton, 1985). The substance of such schemes is that they provide the means for longer hours to be worked during peak periods of demand without the need for overtime, while shorter hours may be worked during quieter periods. The 'flexible rostering' dispute involving the Associated Society of Locomotive Engineers and Firemen (ASLEF) and British Rail is one of the most prominent in recent labour history. The company's objective was the elimination of the fixed eight-hour day and the introduction of rosters varying between seven and nine hours, in order to facilitate a more effective synchronisation of work-time with demand requirements. The union finally acceded to the change, with the net result being that working time above what was previously defined as standard hours, was no longer treated as overtime, but as part of an expandable working day compensated by fewer hours on a subsequent day, rather than by additional payment.

The current trend therefore, seems to be one of eroding the parameters of what has traditionally been considered as overtime work. The 'flexibility for reduction in standard hours' formula that has typified the most recent rounds of hours reductions provides for a much wider classification of what was previously considered standard hours and, consequently, a narrower definition of overtime hours. Similarly, continued growth in shift and part-time work provides management with the opportunity to avoid incurring expensive overtime premia. The product-market characteristics of today's competitive environment, the development of 'high-commitment' work systems, the importance of customer and service quality considerations and the meticulous attention to the *flow* of production that is necessary in just-in-time systems (Klein, 1989; Ingram, 1991; McLaverty and Drummond, 1993), has resulted in an intensification in *effort* levels (Edwards and Whitson, 1991) without gains in employment. All of these trends point to a reduction in the importance of overtime working.

From a trade union perspective, the conclusion is broadly similar to that applying in respect of reductions in standard working hours. Although opposed to overtime at national level, recent achievements in reductions in normal hours have indirectly resulted in increases in overtime because of individual preferences at both local and plant levels. However, as working time negotiations have become more decentralised, employers have continued to strive for (and obtain) increased flexibility in working time arrangements, with overtime frequently becoming the main 'casualty'. Simultaneously, the erosion of traditional overtime arrangements limits the scope for workers to apply the widely used overtime ban in industrial disputes, thereby further weakening their bargaining position. As such, the stated trade union objective of restricting the growth of overtime may have been attained, but not in the manner that the unions would have preferred. Ultimately, while legislative measures restricting overtime levels may have been useful in stemming its growth in a number of countries, market forces may in the long run prove to be equally, if not more, effective.

4.3 MANAGEMENT'S PERCEPTION OF OVERTIME WORK IN THE IRISH PRIVATE SECTOR

In this section management's views and perceptions of overtime work will be considered. In this context, the definition of overtime as discussed in Section 4.1 above is adopted, namely, 'time worked in excess of 'standard' working hours, rewarded at a premium rate or time-off-in-lieu, or occasionally, unrewarded'. Three main areas of interest are examined. First, we consider the extent, incidence and pattern of overtime working; secondly, we look at the reasons for working overtime and the factors that encourage overtime in preference to the creation of new jobs; thirdly, we examine the prospects for change and the perceived potential among private sector management for government intervention to reduce or eliminate overtime working. Because the focus of the study is the potential for redistributing paid work, the emphasis throughout the discussion of the survey results will be on remunerated overtime. This is based on the assumption that, almost by definition, there is no scope whatsoever for redistributing among the unemployed the non-remunerated overtime currently being undertaken and, as such, has relevance in the present chapter only in the degree to which it contextualises the consideration of remunerated overtime.

4.3.1 Extent, Incidence and Pattern of Overtime Work in the Irish Private Sector

Table 4.1A shows the extent to which overtime work, both remunerated and non-remunerated, was undertaken in private sector companies in the 12 months preceding the survey. It can be seen that no overtime of any sort was undertaken in just over 52 per cent of enterprises. In a further 12 per cent only non-remunerated overtime was undertaken; in 16 per cent only remunerated overtime; and in the remaining 20 per cent a combination of both remunerated and non-remunerated overtime was undertaken.

There is some degree of variation within the size/sector categories presented in the table. It is clear that the incidence of overtime work is much lower among small firms than large ones. This is particularly so in respect of the smaller distributive services sector. Just over 19 per cent of companies in this category undertook remunerated overtime, compared with figures of 63 per cent and 34 per cent respectively for small enterprises in the manufacturing/building and non-distributive services sectors.

The propensity of *enterprises* to undertake overtime is only one dimension of the incidence of overtime work. It is relevant to estimate not only how many companies undertake overtime but also what percentage of the *workforce* is employed in those companies.[1] An estimate of the percentage of employees who work in private sector enterprises classified by the nature of overtime undertaken (if any) is provided in column 8 of Table 4.1A. From this it can be seen that although overtime is not worked in 52 per cent of businesses, the employees in such enterprises account for only 12 per cent of the private sector workforce. A further 6 per cent of employees work in businesses in which only non-remunerated overtime is worked. The remaining 81 per cent of the workforce is employed in businesses in which some form of remunerated overtime is undertaken. The very substantial differences in the propensity to work overtime at the level of the firm on the one hand, and at the level of the employee on the other, are a direct function of the higher incidence of overtime work in larger enterprises.

Table 4.1A: The Incidence of Overtime Working (Remunerated and Non-Remunerated) in the Past 12 Months

Overtime Worked	Manuf./Bld.		Distributive Services		Non-distributive Services		Total All Enterprises	Total, Weighted by Employment
	<100 Emps.	*100+ Emps.*	*<20 Emps.*	*20+ Emps.*	*<20 Emps.*	*20+ Emps.*		
	(Per Cent of Employees)							(Per Cent of Employees)
Non-remunerated only	9.0	2.5	9.1	2.3	18.5	6.8	11.7	6.2
Remunerated only	21.2	16.5	10.3	22.7	19.7	15.9	15.7	22.9
Non-remunerated and remunerated	42.0	78.0	8.9	65.9	14.8	70.5	20.4	58.5
None	27.8	3.0	71.7	9.1	47.0	6.8	52.1	12.3
Total	100.0	100.0	100.0	100.0	100.0	100.0	100.0	100.0
Weighted	7,000	500	17,500	900	12,400	1000	39,300	554,600
(Unweighted n)	(75)	(64)	(52)	(44)	(69)	(44)	(348)	(348)

The 81 per cent of the workforce which is employed in companies undertaking remunerated overtime is broken down in Table 4.1B according to the size/sector classification. The figures in this table

---

[1]   This is, of course, different from the percentage of the workforce that undertakes overtime.

show the percentage of the workforce in each size/sector category which is employed in firms that carry out remunerated overtime.[2] From these figures it can be seen, for example, that approximately 92 per cent, 98 per cent and 99 per cent, respectively, of workers in the larger enterprises in the manufacturing/building; distributive services and non-distributive services sectors are employed by companies that undertake remunerated overtime. Comparable percentages in the smaller distributive and non-distributive services sectors are lower (41 and 36 per cent respectively). It is noteworthy that the percentage of workers in smaller manufacturing/building enterprises which work overtime (85 per cent) is more than twice that for smaller firms in the services sector.

Table 4.1B: The Incidence of Remunerated Overtime Working in the Last 12 Months Among Employees Classified by Size/Sector Category

	Manuf./Bld		Distributive Services		Non-distributive Services		
	<100 Emps.	100+ Emps.	<100 Emps.	100+ Emps.	<100 Emps.	100+ Emps.	Total
	(Per Cent of Employees)						
Remunerated Overtime*	85.3	92.3	40.9	98.4	36.0	98.7	81.4

*   Based on the sum of remunerated only + non-remunerated and remunerated.

Table 4.2 considers the concentration within enterprises, according to occupational grade, of both remunerated and non-remunerated overtime work. This shows the average of the percentage of both types of overtime hours accounted for by each of the four grades in question. From Section A of the table it can be seen, for example, that among those firms which undertook non-remunerated overtime, an average of 85 per cent of those non-remunerated hours were worked by the managerial and higher professional grades; 3 per cent were worked by the clerical grades and the remaining 12 per cent by the skilled manual category. No non-remunerated overtime was worked by those in the semi- and unskilled manual grades.

---

[2]   This includes both 'remunerated only' and a combination of 'remunerated and non-remunerated'.

Table 4.2: Average Distribution of the Percentage of Non-Remunerated and Remunerated Overtime Hours Among Occupational Grades

	Manuf. / Bld.		Distributive Services		Non-distributive Services		
Section A							
Non-remunerated Overtime	*<100 Emps.*	*100+ Emps.*	*<20 Emps.*	*20+ Emps.*	*<20 Emps.*	*20+ Emps.*	*Total*
Managerial and Higher Prof.	89	81	91	95	79	94	85
Clerical	1	12	4	5	1	2	3
Skilled Manual	10	7	5	0	18	4	12
Semi-/Unskilled Manual	0	0	0	0	1	0	0
Total	100	100	100	100	100	100	100
Section B							
Remunerated Overtime	*Manuf. / Bld.*		*Distributive Services*		*Non-distributive Services*		
Managerial and Higher Prof.	9	2	13	2	21	13	13
Clerical	5	4	5	17	30	40	15
Skilled Manual	48	30	58	28	30	30	43
Semi-/Unskilled Manual	38	64	24	53	20	18	29
Total	100	100	100	100	100	100	100

In terms of variations across the size/sector classification, it is clear that non-remunerated overtime was universally concentrated in the hands of the managerial and professional group across categories. The data suggest that clerical workers in the larger manufacturing/building sector account for 12 per cent of non-remunerated overtime hours in that sector (compared with an aggregate figure of only 3 per cent). The largest concentration of non-remunerated hours among skilled/manual workers is clearly in smaller-sized enterprises in the non-distributive services sector. A total of 18 per cent of the non-remunerated overtime hours in this size/sector category are accounted for by skilled manual workers.

Section B of Table 4.2 presents information on the distribution of remunerated overtime across the occupational grades. There are clearly substantial contrasts in the distributions of remunerated and non-remunerated hours. It can be seen that on average 13 per cent of remunerated overtime is accounted for by the Managerial and Higher Professional category; an average figure of 15 per cent is attributable to the Clerical group; 43 per cent to the Skilled Manual grades and 29 per cent to the Semi- and Unskilled Manual group. It is clear from the table that there is a concentration of remunerated overtime among Skilled and Semi-/Unskilled Manual workers across all size/sector categories.

Table 4.3 contains details on the frequency of occurrence of the bulk of the remunerated overtime in companies. This is based on responses to a direct question to management which asked respondents whether or not they would describe the bulk of the remunerated overtime worked in their company as: occasional; seasonal; regular monthly (i.e. worked in part of every month); regular weekly (i.e. usually worked 1 to 3 times each week); or regular daily (i.e. usually worked 4 or more days per week). It can be seen that in 58 per cent of enterprises remunerated overtime was described as being worked on an occasional or seasonal basis; in 10 per cent on a regular monthly basis; in 25 per cent on a regular weekly basis and in 8 per cent on a regular daily basis. In general, the data suggest that remunerated overtime is worked most frequently in the larger Manufacturing/Building sector (approximately 52 per cent on a regular weekly or daily basis) followed by the larger Non-Distributive Services sector (49 per cent on a regular weekly or daily basis). These trends contrast with the experience in the smaller Distributive Services sector where it is worked on a regular weekly or daily basis in only 21 per cent of enterprises.

The figures in column 8 of Table 4.3 detail the frequency of occurrence of remunerated overtime at the level of the employee. From these it can be seen that 38 per cent of the workforce are employed in companies in which it is undertaken only on an occasional or seasonal basis; a further 13 per cent work in enterprises in which it is worked on a regular monthly basis; and the remaining 49 per cent are employed in businesses in which remunerated overtime is undertaken on a regular weekly or daily basis.

Table 4.3: Frequency of Occurrence of the Majority of Remunerated Overtime in Enterprises

Frequency	Manuf./Bld.		Distributive Services		Non-distributive Services		Total All Enterprises	Total, Weighted by Employment
	<100 Emps.	100+ Emps.	<20 Emps.	20+ Emps.	<20 Emps.	20+ Emps.		
	(Per Cent of Enterprises)							*(Per Cent Emps.)*
Occasional	32.0	21.3	43.6	25.6	32.7	21.6	33.5	18.1
Seasonal	15.9	17.0	28.2	28.2	32.5	16.2	24.5	19.7
Regular Monthly*	17.2	9.8	7.1	7.7	3.7	13.5	9.8	13.4
Regular Weekly[†]	21.6	30.6	21.2	28.2	27.4	32.4	24.6	31.9
Regular Daily[‡]	13.3	21.3	0.0	10.3	3.7	16.2	7.6	16.9
Total	100.0	100.0	100.0	100.0	100.0	100.0	100.0	100.0
Weighted n	4,300	500	3,100	800	4,100	800	13,600	392,000
(Unweighted n)	(51)	(59)	(13)	(39)	(24)	(37)	(223)	(223)

* Worked in part of every month.

† Usually worked 1-3 times per week.

‡ Usually worked 4 or more times per week.

Information on the way in which remunerated overtime is allocated within enterprises is presented in Table 4.4. This is based on the direct question to Management — 'How is overtime allocated in your company?' Respondents were then asked to indicate whether or not each of five allocative mechanisms was used. The five categories (as outlined in the table) are not mutually exclusive and any combination could be used within a single enterprise. Indeed, it was found in the reweighted sample that 30 per cent of enterprises which undertook remunerated overtime used only one of the allocative mechanisms outlined in the table; 34 per cent used two; a further 7 per cent of businesses used three and the remaining 8 per cent used a combination of four.

Table 4.4: Allocation of Remunerated Overtime

How Overtime is Allotted	Manuf./Bld.		Distributive Services		Non-distributive Services		Total All Enterprises	Total, Weighted by Employment
	<100 Emps.	100+ Emps.	<20 Emps.	20+ Emps.	<20 Emps.	20+ Emps.		(Per Cent Emps.)
	(Percentage of Enterprises Using Each Mechanism for Allocating Overtime)							
1. Employees Volunteer	49.8	52.7	60.5	74.4	64.9	65.8	59.2	66.4
2. Manager/ Supervisor Selects	72.8	59.6	42.3	71.8	48.1	70.3	58.0	76.4
3. Custom and Practice	18.5	27.3	14.1	28.2	26.0	32.4	21.4	42.1
4. Agreements with Employees and Trade Unions	19.4	41.4	29.5	10.3	20.0	35.1	23.0	43.9
5. Other	6.2	14.2	0.0	12.1	21.6	6.9	10.4	7.5
Weighted n	4,000	400	3,100	800	4,100	800	12,000	451,000
(Unweighted n)	(53)	(59)	(13)	(39)	(23)	(37)	(224)	(224)

From Table 4.4 it can be seen that in a total of 60 per cent of companies' employees volunteer to undertake remunerated overtime; in 58 per cent, the manager or supervisor selects who will work remunerated overtime; in 21 per cent of companies it is allocated on the basis of custom and practice; in 23 per cent according to agreements with employees or trade unions; and in just over 10 per cent of companies some other allocative mechanism is adopted.

The final column of the table provides estimates of the percentage of the workforce that works in enterprises in which each of the allocative mechanisms is used. The most significant point to be drawn from these figures is the fact that 42 per cent of the workforce are employed in companies in which overtime is allocated on the basis of custom and practice while 44 per cent work in businesses in which overtime is allocated on the basis of agreements with employees and/or trade unions. These figures, in particular, have obvious implications for any attempt to limit the extent of overtime working or its redistribution in the form of additional jobs.

Management's perception of employees' willingness or otherwise to undertake remunerated overtime is considered in Table 4.5. From this it can be seen that management in 13 per cent of enterprises feels that staff are 'very eager' to undertake remunerated overtime, while in a further 54 per cent of companies they are described as being 'eager'. In only 8 per cent of enterprises are employees felt to be reluctant to carry out overtime. In general, there is relatively little variation as between the six size/sector categories in terms of managements' perceptions of employee willingness to carry out remunerated overtime.

Table 4.5: Management's Perception of Employees' Attitude to Undertaking Remunerated Overtime

Employee Attitude to Remunerated Overtime	Manuf. / Bld.		Distributive Services		Non-distributive Services			
	<100 Emps.	100+ Emps.	<20 Emps.	20+ Emps.	<20 Emps.	20+ Emps.	Total All Enterprises	Total, Weighted by Employment
	(Percentage of Enterprises)							*(Per Cent Emps.)*
Very Eager	17.8	25.3	0.0	10.3	17.3	10.8	12.8	14.6
Eager	58.2	62.3	59.3	56.4	45.7	43.2	53.9	56.9
Indifferent	7.9	12.4	40.7	25.6	29.7	37.8	25.2	25.1
Reluctant	16.0	0.0	0.0	7.7	7.4	8.1	8.1	3.5
Total	100.0	100.0	100.0	100.0	100.1	99.9	100.1	100.1
(Weighted n)	4,400	500	3,400	800	4,100	800	14,000	445,000
(Unweighted n)	(52)	(60)	(14)	(39)	(24)	(37)	(226)	(226)

When the focus changes from enterprises to employees, it can be seen (from the figures in column 8 of Table 4.5) that just over 71 per cent of employees work in companies in which management feels its workforce is 'very eager' or 'eager' to undertake overtime; 25 per cent are employed in firms in which workers are felt to be 'indifferent' to remunerated overtime, and the remaining 3 per cent are in firms in which employees are seen by their management as being 'reluctant' to work remunerated overtime.

The general story told by Tables 4.1–4.5 can be summarised in a number of points. First, remunerated overtime is undertaken in

36 per cent of businesses in Ireland with the incidence being substantially higher in larger than in smaller enterprises. This was
particularly true of the smaller distributive services sector in
which only 19.2 per cent of enterprises carried out remunerated
overtime in the 12 months preceding the survey. These figures on
the incidence of overtime at the level of the firm largely mask the
fact that just over 81 per cent of the workforce work in companies
which undertook some degree of remunerated overtime in the 12
months preceding the survey. This means that remunerated overtime work has the potential to impact on a very substantial proportion of the Irish private sector workforce.

Secondly, the distribution of both remunerated and non-
remunerated overtime between occupational grades is relatively
straightforward. If the average of the percentage of *non-
remunerated* overtime hours worked in each of the four occupational grades discussed in Table 4.2 is considered, it is found that
85 per cent is undertaken by the managerial and professional
group while the majority of the remainder is carried out by the
skilled manual grade (12 per cent in total). There was virtually no
evidence to suggest that the semi-skilled or unskilled manual
group undertook any such overtime.

The obverse trend was apparent in the distribution of *remunerated* overtime. It was seen that the average of the percentages
of remunerated overtime hours worked increased as one moved
from managerial and professional (13 per cent), through clerical
(15 per cent) to skilled manual (43 per cent).

Thirdly, in terms of the frequency of overtime it was found that
remunerated overtime was undertaken on a regular weekly or
daily basis in just under a third of enterprises. When considered
in terms of the percentage of the workforce which worked in such
companies it was seen that these companies employed just under
49 per cent of private sector workers.

Fourthly, most enterprises operate a number of quite different
systems for allocating overtime. These include employees volunteering; manager/supervisor selecting; custom and practice and so
on. At the enterprise level, the most frequently occurring systems
for allocating overtime were: employees volunteering (59 per cent)
and manager/supervisor selecting (58 per cent of companies).
Having said this, however, it was also noted that 42 per cent of
employees worked in companies in which remunerated overtime
was allocated on the basis of Custom and Practice, while 44 per
cent of the workforce was employed in businesses where it was

allocated according to Agreements with Employees and Trade Unions.

Fifthly, in general, a substantial majority of private sector employees are perceived by their management to be 'Very Eager' or 'Eager' to undertake remunerated overtime.

4.3.2 Factors Underlying Overtime Work in the Irish Private Sector

Table 4.6 summarises managements' perceptions of the *single* most important reason for undertaking remunerated overtime. Respondents were presented with a list of 11 reasons (as outlined in the table) for undertaking overtime and asked to state which they felt to be the *single most important* reason for carrying out remunerated overtime in their company.

From the table, it can be seen that the most important factor by far is 'fluctuations in demand'. This was felt by management in 67 per cent of companies to be the single most important factor underlying remunerated overtime work. The importance of this factor to all six size/sector classifications is clear from the table. It was of most relevance to the smaller building sector (cited by just over 78 per cent of enterprises as the most important factor) and was of least relevance to the large non-distributive services sector (mentioned by 42 per cent as the single most important reason).

A further 10 per cent of enterprises cited 'avoiding bottlenecks' as the single most important reason, while just under 7 per cent mentioned 'to meet normal demand' and just over 6 per cent cited 'the continuous nature of the production or service function'. Taken together, these four demand-related factors are viewed by 90 per cent of enterprises as the most important reason for remunerated overtime. Of the other seven potential responses to this question, issues such as 'machine maintenance' were cited by 3.8 per cent of enterprises; 'problems of receiving raw materials' by 2.6 per cent; and 'more economic than increasing employment' by 1.8 per cent.

Table 4.6: Management's Perception of the Single Most Important Reason for Remunerated Overtime

	Manuf. / Bld.		Distributive Services		Non-distributive Services			
	<100 Emps.	100+ Emps.	<20 Emps.	20+ Emps.	<20 Emps.	20+ Emps.	Total All Enter-prises	Total, Weighted by Em-ployment
	(Percentage of Enterprises)							*(Per Cent Emps.)*
A. Fluctuations in Demand	78.2	59.3	64.7	59.0	63.2	42.1	66.6	50.8
B. Avoid Bottlenecks	11.3	4.8	0.0	7.7	14.2	23.7	10.0	5.5
C. Custom and Practice	0.0	0.0	0.0	7.7	3.6	0.0	1.5	8.6
D. Machinery Maintenance	1.7	12.7	7.1	2.6	3.6	0.0	3.8	4.1
E. To Meet Normal Demand	4.0	1.6	14.1	12.8	3.6	5.3	6.6	4.2
F. Shortage of Skilled Labour	0.0	0.0	0.0	0.0	0.0	0.0	0.0	0.0
G. Continuous Nature of Prod/ Service Process	1.7	13.8	7.1	5.1	7.1	21.1	6.3	9.4
H. More Economic than Increasing Employment	0.0	0.0	0.0	2.6	4.8	2.6	1.8	10.8
I. Provide Pay Increases for Employees	0.0	1.6	0.0	0.0	0.0	0.0	0.1	0.1
J. Trade Union Agreements	0.8	1.6	0.0	0.0	0.0	5.3	0.6	1.9
K. Problems of Receiving Raw Materials	2.3	4.8	7.1	2.6	0.0	0.0	2.6	4.5
Total	100.0	99.9	100.1	100.1	100.1	100.1	100.0	100.0
Weighted n	4,400	500	3,100	800	4,300	900	14,200	452,000
(Unweighted n)	(53)	(61)	(14)	(39)	(245	(38)	(230)	(230)

A relatively similar picture is painted by the data when enterprises are weighted in proportion to their total employment (i.e. the figures in column 8). From this one can see, for example, that

51 per cent of employees are in firms which consider 'fluctuations in demand' to be the most important reason for remunerated overtime. A further 11 per cent are employed in firms in which management feels that overtime is 'more economic than increasing employment', while 9 per cent are employed in enterprises which cited 'custom and practice' and 'continuous nature of the production/service process'. Table 4.7 considers the extent to which remunerated overtime is considered to be *essential* to the continued operation of enterprises at current levels of output. From this it can be seen that just over 87 per cent of firms felt that it was essential to their continued operation. The figures in column 8 of the table show that this group of companies employs approximately 84 per cent of the private sector workforce.

Table 4.7: The Extent to Which Remuneration Overtime is Considered to be Essential to the Continued Operation of the Company at Current Levels of Output

Remunerated Overtime Essential?	Manuf./Bld.		Distributive Services		Non-distributive Services			
	<100 Emps.	100+ Emps.	<20 Emps.	20+ Emps.	<20 Emps.	20+ Emps.	Total All Enterprises	Total, Weighted by Employment
	(Percentage of Enterprises)							(Per Cent Emps.)
Yes	91.0	87.3	86.8	79.5	86.9	81.6	87.4	83.7
No	9.0	12.7	13.2	20.5	13.1	18.4	12.6	16.3
Total	100.0	100.0	100.0	100.0	100.0	100.0	100.0	100.0
Weighted n	4,300	500	3,400	800	4300	900	14,100	450,000
(Unweighted n)	(52)	(61)	(14)	(39)	(25)	(38)	(229)	(229)

Enterprises which said that remunerated overtime was necessary for their continued operation were asked to give their reasons for saying this. The results are presented in Table 4.8. This table is based on information collected in an open-ended question in which respondents were given the opportunity to express spontaneously their views on the reasons for the necessity of overtime. Because this sort of multiple response was possible, column totals are in excess of 100 per cent.

From the table it can be seen that four main reasons are given as to why enterprises consider remunerated overtime to be essential to the continued operation of their business. These are:

1. *To Meet Fluctuations in Demand:* this is cited by 48 per cent of enterprises. This reason was given by a large percentage of firms in all size/sector categories. In the manufacturing/ building sector it was cited by a total of 49 per cent of large firms and 38 per cent of smaller ones. Comparable figures for the distributive services sector were 52 per cent and 62 per cent respectively. Among the non-distributive services sector it was mentioned by 48 per cent of both large and small firms.

2. *The Nature of the Business:* this is mentioned by 28 per cent of companies and appears to be of relatively greater relevance to smaller enterprises in the distributive and non-distributive services sectors.

3. *To Meet Deadlines / Targets:* this response was given by 19 per cent of businesses. It was of particular significance for smaller enterprises in the manufacturing/building sector (mentioned by 42 per cent of firms).

4. *Company Operates Outside Normal Hours:* this answer was given by 11 per cent of companies and was mentioned by an above-average percentage of smaller distributive service companies as well as by firms of all sizes in the non-distributive sector.

Other issues were raised only on an infrequent basis. For example, 2.2 per cent of companies mentioned that overtime was more economic than part-time employees. This response was largely confined to the larger manufacturing/building companies and to all companies (i.e. both large and small) in the distributive services sector. Employees' expectation of overtime to augment their wages was mentioned in only 3.6 per cent of enterprises. As with the previous response, this reason was largely confined to the manufacturing/building sector as well as the larger distributive services sector.

The final column in the table suggests that at the aggregate level the distribution of response categories is not substantially changed when the unit of analysis is shifted from the enterprise to the employee. The table shows, for example, that 55 per cent of the private sector workforce are employed in firms which feel overtime is essential to their continued operation so that they can meet fluctuations in demand. A further 19 per cent are in companies which cite 'meeting deadlines/targets' and 16 per cent each in companies which gave 'nature of the business' and the 'company operates outside normal hours' as a reason for considering remunerated overtime to be essential to their continued operation.

Table 4.8: Reasons Given by Those Enterprises Which Consider Remunerated Overtime to be Essential to the Continued Operation at Current Levels of Output

	Total Enterprises (per cent employees)	Total, Weighted by Employment (per cent employees)
To Meet Ongoing/Current Output	1.1	4.8
To Meet Deadlines/Targets	19.5	19.5
To Meet Fluctuations in Demand	48.0	55.2
Company Operates Outside Normal Hours	10.9	15.7
Nature of Business	28.3	15.9
To Fully Utilise Plant	1.8	3.8
Employees Expect Overtime to Improve Their Wages	3.6	5.0
More Economic than Part-time Employees	2.2	2.1
Plant Maintenance	1.1	3.0
Other	3.4	3.4
Total	109.0	128.4
Weighted n	12,300	373,000
(Unweighted n)	(196)	(196)

From Table 4.7 it was seen that just under 13 per cent of firms which undertook overtime said that they did not consider remunerated overtime to be essential to their continued successful operation. The firms in this small subgroup were asked why they had not eliminated it from their company. Their responses are presented in Table 4.9. The reader's attention is drawn to the particularly small number of reweighted firms upon which the table is based. Because of these small numbers we present a breakdown only for the larger enterprises in each of the three sectors.

It can be seen that, in aggregate, approximately two-thirds of this subgroup of enterprises cite peaks in demand as their reason for continuing with some degree of remunerated overtime even though management does not consider it to be essential to the continued operation of the company. A further 20 per cent mentioned the 'nature of the business', and just over 10 per cent said that it was related to tradition and employee expectations.

The final column of the table presents comparable figures based on the workforce. The importance of these estimates lies in the virtual reversal of the relative importance of 'peaks in demand' and 'tradition/employees expect overtime'. The figures in column 8 of the table show the relative significance (in terms of employees) of tradition and employee expectation among this small subset of companies (13 per cent of all enterprises) which continued to work overtime but which felt that such overtime was not essential to their continued successful operation. Because multiple responses to this question were possible, the total columns are in excess of 100 per cent.

Table 4.9: Reasons Given by Those Enterprises Which Did Not Consider Remunerated Overtime to be Essential to the Continued Operation of Their Businesses as to Why They Had Not Eliminated it From Their Company

Reasons for Not Eliminating Remunerated Overtime	Manuf. / Bld.		Distributive Services		Non-distributive Services		Total All Enterprises	Total, Weighted by Employment
	<100 Emps.	100+ Emps.	<20 Emps.	20+ Emps.	<100 Emps.	100+ Emps.		
	(Percentage of Enterprises)							*(Per Cent Emps.)*
Peaks in Demand	—	57.1	—	50.0	—	16.7	63.1	19.0
Nature of the Business	—	14.3	—	0.0	—	16.7	20.3	6.5
Traditional Employees Expect Overtime	—	14.3	—	50.0	—	16.7	10.4	65.7
Other	—	14.3	—	16.7	—	50.0	7.8	9.7
Total	—	100.0	—	116.7	—	100.1	101.6	100.9
Weighted n	100	100	200	100	600	100	1,200	67,000
(Unweighted n)	(2)	(7)	(1)	(6)	(3)	(6)	(25)	(25)

Overall, therefore, the information contained in Tables 4.6–4.9 strongly suggests that in managements' view the most important reasons underlying remunerated overtime are related to fluctuations in demand or the avoidance of bottlenecks in their output. When a series of 11 pre-coded factors was put to management it was found that these two demand-related issues were identified by 77 per cent of companies as being the single most important reason for undertaking remunerated overtime. A further 7 per cent related remunerated overtime to the meeting of normal or ongoing demand, while 6 per cent mentioned the continuous nature of the production/service function.

When the focus was changed from the enterprise to the employee it was found that, in general, the perceived relativities of the reasons for overtime did not change very substantially. For example, 51 per cent of the workforce was employed in companies which mentioned fluctuations in demand, while 5 per cent of employees worked in companies which said that their most important reason for working overtime was to avoid bottlenecks. Two notable changes in the relative importance of reasons for undertaking remunerated overtime were 'overtime is more economic than increasing employment' (11 per cent of the workforce worked in firms which gave this reason) and 'custom and practice' (just under 9 per cent of the workforce was employed in firms which mentioned this issue).

In Table 4.7, it was seen that 87 per cent of enterprises which undertook remunerated overtime felt that it was essential to the continued operation of their company. When those firms were asked to say why they thought so, the overriding response was, once again, related to fluctuations in demand or the meeting of deadlines and targets. These two factors were spontaneously mentioned by two-thirds of firms which felt that overtime was essential to the continued operation of the company.

4.3.3 Government Incentives or Schemes to Reduce or Eliminate Overtime

Firms which undertook remunerated overtime were asked whether or not they felt that the government could introduce any schemes or incentives which would encourage them to reduce or eliminate their current level of overtime work. The responses to the question are shown in Table 4.10. From this it can be seen that just over 30 per cent of all companies in aggregate felt that the government could take action. The data suggest that an above-average percentage of firms in the distributive services sector (particularly among small companies) did not think that government intervention could reduce overtime.

Table 4.10: Management's View as to Whether or Not the Government Could Introduce Any Schemes or Incentives Which would Encourage Enterprises to Reduce or Eliminate Current Levels of Overtime Work.

Government could introduce scheme or incentive to cut overtime?	Manuf./Bld.		Distributive Services		Non-distributive Services		Total All Enterprises	Total, Weighted by Employment
	<100 Emps.	100+ Emps.	<20 Emps.	20+ Emps.	<100 Emps.	100+ Emps.		
	(Percentage of Enterprises)							*(Per Cent Emps.)*
Yes	46.3	47.8	7.1	21.1	28.4	42.1	30.3	37.7
No	53.7	52.2	92.9	78.9	71.6	57.9	69.7	62.3
Total	100.0	100.0	100.0	100.0	100.0	100.0	100.0	100.0
(Weighted n)	4,400	500	3,100	800	4,300	900	13,900	430,000
(Unweighted n)	(51)	(60)	(13)	(38)	(25)	(38)	(225)	(225)

Note: Table based only on companies which have undertaken *remunerated* overtime in the past 12 months.

Those firms which thought that government intervention would be possible were further asked to say spontaneously what the government could do to reduce or eliminate remunerated overtime work. Information on their responses is shown in Table 4.11.

From this it can be seen that the answers given were of a fairly generic nature. Interviewers had difficulty in eliciting responses that were clearly and unambiguously targeted at the issue of reducing overtime. The most frequently occurring response is the reduction in employer's PRSI (mentioned by 51 per cent of enterprises). The employers' view is clearly that a reduction in PRSI would potentially eliminate or reduce at least one perceived barrier to increased employment and thus enhance the potential for replacing remunerated overtime with increased employees. This, however, should be interpreted within the context of the reasons given by firms for undertaking overtime. It was clear in the discussion of Table 4.6 that the most important factors seemed to be fluctuations in demand. It is hard to see how a reduction in employers' PRSI would have a major impact on the amount of remunerated overtime worked when such a large percentage of firms state that a substantial proportion of that overtime is a response to demand fluctuations.

Table 4.11: Management's View on What the Government Could Do to Reduce or Eliminate Current Levels of Overtime Work

Nature of Government Incentive	Manuf./Bld.		Distributive Services		Non-distributive Services			
	<100 Emps.	100+ Emps.	<20 Emps.	20+ Emps.	<100 Emps.	100+ Emps.	Total All Enter- prises	Total, Weighted by Em- ployment
	(Percentage of Enterprises)							*(Per Cent Emps.)*
Relax labour protection legislation	3.7	13.9	—	0.0	0.0	23.1	4.2	9.8
Offer financial incentives for employment and training	24.7	13.9	—	12.5	37.5	15.4	25.5	14.1
Reduce Employer's PRSI	59.3	30.3	—	25.0	37.5	38.5	50.7	28.9
Reduce employee tax and PRSI	14.1	13.9	—	62.5	12.5	7.7	14.3	12.8
Introduce legislation to ban overtime	1.8	17.4	—	0.0	0.0	23.1	3.4	10.8
Other	10.4	20.9	—	25.0	37.5	15.4	19.3	36.6
Total	114.0	110.3	—	125.0	37.5	123.2	117.4	113.0
(Weighted n)	2,000	200	200	200	1,200	300	4,100	156,000
(Unweighted n)	(21)	(28)	(1)	(8)	(8)	(13)	(79)	(79)

The next most frequently occurring response was that the government should offer financial incentives for employment and training (mentioned by 25 per cent of respondents). The nature and scale of such incentives were not, however, well thought through or elaborated upon by the respondents. The only other issue to be raised by more than 10 per cent of respondents was a reduction in employee tax and PRSI (mentioned by just over 14 per cent of firms). The 'Other' category in the table (with just under 20 per cent of responding enterprises) was made up of responses which were very specific to the needs of the individual firm rather than sector-wide initiatives which could be applied in broad terms across the labour market.

Overall, therefore, the information in Tables 4.10 and 4.11 suggests that although the managements in 30 per cent of enterprises feel that government intervention could reduce or eliminate current levels of remunerated overtime, there were relatively few well-formulated suggestions or proposals as to what government could or should do in practice to implement any such policy.

4.4 THE EMPLOYEES' RESPONSE TO OVERTIME WORKING

In the previous section, the extent, incidence, motivation and managements' views on overtime work were examined. In this section, the reactions and views of employees are considered. The data are presented in two sections. The first issues to be considered are the extent to which employees undertook overtime in the 12 months preceding the survey; the regularity of that overtime and its nature (remunerated; non-remunerated; and time-off-in-lieu as opposed to cash payment etc.) Secondly, there is a discussion of employees' attitudes to overtime and their perception of the importance of income from overtime in maintaining their standard of living etc.

4.4.1 Incidence, Regularity and Nature of Overtime Work — The Employee View

Table 4.12 shows the percentage of employees who worked overtime (remunerated and non-remunerated) over the 12 months preceding the survey, classified by size/sector category, occupational grade and gender. From this it can be seen that a total of 78 per cent of employees said that they had worked some form of overtime in the 12 months preceding the survey. The incidence was lowest in the distributive services sector (particularly in the smaller service enterprises). In terms of occupational grade, the incidence was relatively lower among the clerical group than either the managerial/professional or manual workers. Finally, higher percentages of males (80 per cent) than females (74 per cent) had undertaken overtime in the period in question.

Table 4.12: Percentage of Employees Who Worked Overtime in the Previous 12 Months, Classified by (a) Sector; (b) Occupational Grade and (c) Sex

	Worked Overtime	Did Not Work Overtime	Weighted N	(Unweighted N)
Size/Sector	*(Per Cent)*			
Manufacturing/Building (<100 Employees)	83.8	16.2	86,000	(133)
Manufacturing/Building (+100 Employees	84.8	15.2	179,000	(173)
Distributive Services (<20 Employees)	60.7	39.3	32,000	(38)
Distributive Services (+20 Employees)	83.1	16.9	55,000	(88)
Non-distributive Services (<20 Employees)	83.6	16.4	27,000	(59)
Non-distributive Services (+20 Employees)	63.4	36.6	98,000	(110)
Occupational Grade	*(Per Cent)*			
Managerial/Professional etc.	76.8	23.2	175,000	(191)
Other Clerical	64.4	35.6	125,000	(203)
Manual	89.5	10.5	172,000	(204)
Gender	*(Per Cent)*			
Male	80.5	19.5	329,000	(323)
Female	73.8	26.2	153,019	(278)
Total	78.3	21.7	477,000	(601)

Note: Table based only on employees in those firms which undertook overtime.

Table 4.13 outlines the regularity with which overtime was worked by employees over the reference period.[3] It can be seen that, in aggregate, just over 26 per cent of employees who worked in firms which did overtime undertook some such overtime work on three or more days per week, while a further 24 per cent undertook overtime on one or two days each week. A total of one-third of those who undertook overtime did so only on an occasional basis. The table shows that males have a higher propensity to carry out overtime on a regular basis than do females.

---

[3]   By definition this table relates only to the 78 per cent of employees who undertook some overtime in the year preceding the interview.

Table 4.13: Regularity With Which Overtime was Worked by Employees in the Previous 12 Months, Classified by Sex

Regularity of Overtime Worked	Male	Female	Total
	(Per Cent)		
3+ days/week	28.0	22.3	26.3
1–2 days/week	25.4	20.3	23.9
Once per fortnight	11.9	10.9	11.6
Once per month	4.8	6.0	5.1
Occasional basis	29.9	40.5	33.1
Total	100.0	100.0	100.0
Weighted n	261,000	113,000	369,000
(Unweighted n)	(281)	(203)	(484)

Note: Table based only on employees who worked overtime in the 12 months preceding the survey.

Section A of Table 4.14 considers the usual form of remuneration received by employees for the overtime that they worked in the 12 months preceding the survey. It can be seen that in aggregate terms just over 50 per cent were remunerated in the form of a cash payment; 10 per cent by time-off-in-lieu; 7 per cent by a combination of cash and time-off-in-lieu; while just under a third (31 per cent) were mostly non-remunerated.

In general, females have a lower propensity than males to receive cash payments for overtime and, accordingly, a higher propensity to be remunerated either in the form of time-off-in-lieu or a combination of both cash payment and time-in-lieu. A higher proportion of males than females were not remunerated for the overtime that they worked in the year preceding the survey (35 per cent compared to 24 per cent).

The variations in type of remuneration within occupational grade are also outlined in Section A. These tend to reflect the trends discussed in relation to the management survey as outlined in Table 4.2 above. In general, it can be seen that almost two-thirds of those in the managerial/professional grades who undertook overtime were not remunerated for it. This is in stark contrast to the manual grades where there was only minimal evidence of working non-remunerated overtime. A total of 89 per cent of those in the manual grades who undertook overtime were exclusively paid in cash, while another 4 per cent were remunerated for their overtime with a combination of cash payments and time-off-in-lieu. It is clear from the table that the clerical grades fall between the two extremes of managerial/professional, on the one hand, and manual on the other.[4]

Table 4.14: (A) Usual Form of Remuneration Received by Employees for Overtime Worked in the 12 Months Preceding the Survey and (B) Preferred First Choice of Remuneration

A. Usual Form of Remuneration						
	Male	*Female*	*Managerial/ Professional*	*Other Clerical*	*Manual*	*Total*
	(Per Cent)					
All cash payment	54.5	43.8	18.3	34.8	89.1	51.3
All time-in-lieu	8.5	13.4	10.8	17.1	5.7	9.9
Combined cash/time-in-lieu	2.4	19.1	7.2	13.4	4.5	7.7
Mostly unremunerated	34.6	23.8	63.7	34.7	0.7	31.4
Total	100.0	100.0	100.0	100.0	100.0	100.0
Weighted n	259,000	109,000	131,000	80,000	154,000	368,000
(Unweighted n)	(277)	(199)	(163)	(135)	(176)	(476)
B. Preferred Form of Remuneration						
	Male	*Female*	*Managerial/ Professional*	*Other Clerical*	*Manual*	*Total*
	(Per Cent)					
All cash payment	44.8	32.0	32.0	26.9	54.5	40.9
All time-in-lieu	15.4	21.3	23.4	31.6	4.4	17.2
Combined cash/time-in-lieu	39.8	46.7	44.6	41.5	41.1	41.9
Mostly unremunerated	—	—	—	—	—	—
Total	100.0	100.0	100.0	100.0	100.0	100.0
Weighted n	259,000	113,000	132,000	81,000	154,000	371,000
(Unweighted n)	(277)	(204)	(167)	(138)	(176)	(481)

Section B of Table 4.14 presents information on the preferred first choice of remuneration for overtime. This table is based on answers to a direct question to employees asking: 'If you had a choice, which method of remuneration would you prefer for

---

[4] The relationship between gender and grade are clearly reflected in the relevant percentages of overtime propensities.

working overtime?' Respondents were then asked to rank 'all paid'; 'all time-off-in-lieu'; and 'a combination of paid and time-off-in-lieu' as 1, 2 or 3 in terms of preference.

In aggregate terms, the figures suggest that 17 per cent of employees would prefer their overtime to be completely remunerated by time-off-in-lieu, while approximately equal proportions of the remainder opted for remuneration in the form of cash payments and a combination of both cash and time-off-in-lieu (representing 42 per cent of all those who undertook remunerated overtime).

In terms of variations by sex, it is clear that a substantially higher than average figure among females than males would opt for all remuneration in the form of time-off-in-lieu or a combination of time-off-in-lieu and cash payment. For example, 21 per cent of females compared with 15 per cent of males would prefer all remuneration in the form of time-off-in-lieu. Comparable figures for a combination of time-in-lieu and cash payment are 47 per cent and 40 per cent respectively. Section B of Table 4.14 also shows that manual grades would seem to prefer all remuneration in the form of cash payments (approximately 55 per cent) while time-off-in-lieu seems acceptable to higher percentages of the managerial/professional and clerical grades. Some of this variation (particularly in the clerical group) will be related to the gender composition of the grades in question.

A number of general points emerge from the information in Table 4.11–4.14. First, overtime work does affect the majority of employees. Approximately 78 per cent of employees who work in the 48 per cent of firms which undertook overtime (see Table 4.1a) did some such work in the 12 months preceding the survey. In terms of frequency of this work it was seen that a quarter of employees did overtime work on three or more days each week, while a further quarter had undertaken overtime on one or two days each week. Secondly, almost exactly half of employees who worked overtime were remunerated in cash; 7 per cent by a combination of cash and time-off-in-lieu; 10 per cent by time-off-in-lieu; and 31 per cent were mostly unremunerated. Thirdly, the preferred first choice of remuneration for overtime among employees who undertook some overtime in the 12 months preceding the survey was cash payments or a combination of cash and time-off-in-lieu (approximately 41 per cent of those who worked overtime expressed a preference for each of these methods). The remaining 17 per cent of employees stated that their first choice would be time-off-in-lieu. These figures clearly indicate that substantial percentages of the workforce undertake overtime, many on a regular basis, and that the vast majority of those who do work overtime (about 83 per cent) would prefer to receive either a straight cash payment or a combination of cash and time-off-in-lieu. Such trends have clear implications for the implementation of any scheme to reduce overtime. In the next section, employees' perception of the importance of overtime is briefly considered.

4.4.2 Employee Perception of the Importance of Overtime

In the course of the employee questionnaire a number of statements on various aspects of overtime were put to employees who were then asked to state their level of agreement or otherwise with each. The results are presented in Table 4.15.

1. *Overtime is Important in Maintaining my Standard of Living:*
   Overall, a total of 15 per cent of employees strongly agreed with this statement, while a further 16 per cent moderately agreed. Just under 40 per cent strongly disagreed, while 12 per cent moderately disagreed. Given the lower incidence and frequency of overtime work among females (as seen in the previous section) gender differentials in terms of levels of agreement are as one would expect. The level of agreement was lowest among workers in the small distributive services sector where, as was seen from earlier tables, the incidence of remunerated overtime is lowest. Similarly, agreement among staff in the managerial/professional and (to a slightly lesser degree) clerical grades was substantially below the aggregate figure. A total of 59 per cent of manual workers agreed (either strongly or moderately) that overtime was important in maintaining their standard of living.

2. *There is No Point in My Doing Overtime Because of Tax:* just over a quarter of employees strongly agreed with this statement, while a further 27 per cent moderately agreed. A total of 28 per cent disagreed, 13 per cent strongly disagreeing.

3. *Reducing the Amount of Overtime Could Significantly Reduce the Number of Unemployed:* from the table, it can be seen that 22 per cent of employees strongly agreed with this statement, while a further 35 per cent moderately agreed. A total of 31 per cent disagreed (either moderately or strongly). The reader should note, of course, that a high level of agreement with a

statement like this does not, of itself, imply that employees would be willing to redistribute the overtime that they currently undertake so as to help reduce unemployment. The next section of the tables goes some way towards identifying whether or not this is so.

4. *I Would Gladly Give Up My Overtime if it Helped in the Creation of Jobs for the Unemployed:* the figures suggest that 42 per cent of employees strongly agree and a further 28 per cent moderately agree with this statement. Only 13 per cent disagree (moderately or strongly). There is some evidence to suggest that a slightly higher percentage of females than males agree with this proposal.

Table 4.15: Employees' Agreement or Otherwise with Seven Statements Measuring their Reception of Overtime Work

	Strongly Agree	Moderately Agree	Neither Agree or Disagree	Moderately Disagree	Strongly Disagree	Total	Weighted n
A. Overtime is Important in Maintaining My Standard of Living							
Male	20.9	17.6	15.8	11.9	33.8	100.0	2,585,000
Female	2.0	11.9	22.5	11.1	52.6	100.0	1,120,000
Total	15.2	15.9	17.8	11.7	39.5	100.0	3,703,000
B. There is No Point in My Doing Overtime Because of Tax							
Male	25.3	27.6	18.3	17.9	10.9	100.0	2,590,000
Female	24.7	24.5	24.3	8.9	17.5	100.0	1,120,000
Total	25.1	26.6	21.0	15.2	12.9	100.0	3,710,000
C. Reducing Amount of Overtime Could Significantly Reduce the Number of Unemployed							
Male	23.8	36.1	8.9	18.7	12.5	100.0	2,600,000
Female	17.2	34.0	17.4	15.6	15.8	100.0	1,120,000
Total	21.8	35.5	11.4	17.8	13.5	100.0	3,720,000
D. I Would Gladly Give Up My Overtime if it Helped in the Creation of Jobs for Unemployed							
Male	37.5	30.9	16.1	9.4	6.1	100.0	2,600,000
Female	53.4	22.1	15.7	3.3	5.6	100.0	1,120,000
Total	42.3	28.2	16.0	7.5	6.0	100.0	3,730,000

The reader is cautioned not to over-interpret the story told by Section D of Table 4.15. Inferring *actual* future behaviour from hypothetical proposals of this sort is fraught with difficulties. Nevertheless, it is encouraging to note that just over 70 per cent of employees would agree in principle that they would be happy to give up their overtime if it helped in the creation of jobs for the unemployed.

Overall, the data in Table 4.15 suggest that approximately a third of employees felt that overtime was important in maintaining their standard of living. This would clearly have implications for any measures aimed at placing restrictions or limitations on the degree of overtime undertaken. In this context, just over 57 per cent of employees felt that by reducing the amount of overtime carried out, the level of unemployment could be significantly reduced.

Furthermore, 70 per cent of employees agreed that they would gladly give up their overtime if it helped to create jobs for the unemployed. It was noted, however, that it would be extremely dangerous to base strong policy recommendations on this sort of hypothetical option to respondents.

4.5 OVERTIME IN THE IRISH PUBLIC SECTOR

In this section, the focus shifts from private to public sector, concentrating in particular on contrasts between public and private sectors in the incidence, motivations and consequences of overtime work. Managements' perceptions of overtime work are first considered, before turning in section 4.5.2 to an examination of the employees' reactions.

4.5.1 Incidence and Pattern of Overtime Working

In general, the incidence of overtime working in those sectors of the public sector sampled was slightly higher than in the private sector. A total of 2.5 per cent of organisations[5] said that they did not work any overtime. This compares with a figure of 12.3 per cent for the private sector. The incidence of the combined operation of remunerated and non-remunerated overtime in public sector organisations is substantially higher than their private sector counterparts (75.7 per cent compared to 58.5 per cent), while approximately equal percentages of enterprises in both sectors only

---

[5]   These figures are based on the results re-weighted in proportion to the total number of employees.

operate a remunerated system to the exclusion of non-remunerated overtime (21 and 23 per cent in the public and private sectors respectively). In aggregate, only 0.5 per cent of the public sector organisations operate only a system of non-remuneration overtime, compared with 6.2 per cent in the private sector.

The distribution of both non-remunerated and remunerated overtime hours by occupational grade largely conforms to what might be expected. For example, 88 per cent of the non-remunerated overtime hours worked are undertaken by Higher Administrative/Executive workers, a further 9 per cent by Routine Clerical Staff, and the remaining 3 per cent by Other Routine Grades. In contrast, the distribution of remunerated overtime hours shows a clear concentration in the Other Routine Grades (61 per cent), with substantially lower percentages in the Routine Clerical and Higher Administrative/Executive grades (24 and 15 per cent respectively). These trends are entirely consistent with those in the private sector, as outlined in Table 4.2 above.

Table 4.16 presents a summary comparison of the frequency of occurrence of remunerated overtime work between public and private sectors. From this it can be seen that in approximately 16–18 per cent of organisations in both sectors it is undertaken on an occasional basis, while in 18–20 per cent of enterprises it is carried out on a seasonal basis. There are clearly substantial differences between public and private sectors in the frequency of occurrence of remunerated overtime in the other two categories. It can be seen that it is worked on a regular monthly basis in 13 per cent of private sector companies. This compares with 31 per cent for the public sector. Comparable figures for regular weekly or more frequent occurrence of remunerated overtime are 49 per cent and 35 per cent for private and public sectors respectively. In the aggregate, therefore, it would appear from the data presented that remunerated overtime is worked on a slightly more regular basis in the private sector as compared to the public sector.

Table 4.16: A Comparison of the Frequency of the Majority of Remunerated Overtime in Public and Private Sector Organisations

	Private Sector	Public Sector
	(Per Cent of Enterprises / Organisations)	
Occasional	18.1	15.7
Seasonal	19.7	18.4
Regularly monthly*	13.4	31.2
Regularly weekly or more frequently**	48.8	34.7
Total	100.0	100.0

*   Worked in part of every month.

** Includes worked 1–3 times per week and worked 4 or more times per week.

Managements' perception of employees' willingness or otherwise to undertake remunerated overtime in both sectors is contrasted in Table 4.17. At first sight, it appears that there are very substantial differences in the attitudes of public and private sector employees to carrying out remunerated overtime. It can be seen, for example, that in the public sector 55 per cent of employees work in organisations in which management feels that the workforce is 'very eager' to work overtime, while a further 15 per cent work in organisations in which management feels that the workforce is 'eager' to undertake overtime work on a remunerated basis. Comparable figures for the private sector are 15 and 57 per cent.

Table 4.17: A Comparison of Management's Perception of Employees' Attitude to Undertaking Remunerated Overtime in Public and Private Sector Organisations

Employee Attitude to Remunerated Overtime	Private Sector	Public Sector
	(Per Cent of Enterprises / Organisations)	
Occasional	18.1	15.7
Seasonal	19.7	18.4
Regularly monthly*	13.4	31.2
Regularly weekly or more frequently**	48.8	34.7
Total	100.0	100.0

*   Worked in part of every month.

** Includes worked 1–3 times per week and worked 4 or more times per week.

There appear to be similar, though less substantial, contrasts in the percentages of public and private sector employees who are considered by their management to be 'indifferent' or 'reluctant' to undertake overtime.

The reader should note, however, that the story told by these figures changes quite dramatically if the four-fold classification of employee attitude is reduced to a two-fold classification of 'very eager/eager' and 'indifferent/reluctant'. When this is done, the percentage of employees in private sector organisations which fall into the 'very eager/eager' group is 71.5 per cent. This compares with 70.3 per cent for the public sector. Comparable figures for the 'indifferent/reluctant' category are 28.6 and 29.6 per cent respectively. By redefining the response groups, therefore, it is clear that there is actually a much greater degree of similarity among public and private sector enterprises than may at first be apparent.

4.5.2 Factors Underlying Overtime Work

Table 4.18 provides a comparison between the public and private sectors of managements' perceptions of the *single most important* reason for undertaking remunerated overtime. Respondents were presented with the 11 statements contained in the table, and asked to say which was the *single* most important reason for undertaking remunerated overtime.

It is clear from the data that there are some quite substantial differences between public and private sector organisations in terms of their perceptions. Four factors stand out as being relatively more important in the private sector as compared to the relevant public sector. These are: fluctuations in demand (mentioned by 51 per cent of private sector companies compared with 41 per cent of public sector organisations); custom and practice (8.6 and 1.3 per cent respectively); more economic than increasing employment (10.8 and 1.4 per cent respectively); and problems of receiving raw materials (4.5 and 0.0 per cent respectively). In contrast, two reasons are very substantially more important to the public than private sector, namely, to meet normal demand (13.7 per cent among public sector organisations and 4.2 per cent among private sector companies); and continuous nature of the production/service process (30.9 and 9.4 per cent respectively).

Table 4.18: A Comparison of Managements' Perception of the Single *Most Important Reason for Working Remunerated Overtime in Public and Private Sector Organisations*

Single Most Important Reason	Private Sector	Public Sector
	(Per Cent Enterprise / Organisation)	
A. Fluctuations in Demand	50.8	41.3
B. Avoid Bottlenecks	5.5	7.9
C. Custom and Practice	8.6	1.3
D. Machinery Maintenance	4.1	3.5
E. To Meet Normal Demand	4.2	13.7
F. Shortage of Skilled Labour	0.0	0.0
G. Continuous Nature of Prod./Service Process	9.4	30.0
H. More Economic and Increasing Employment	10.8	1.4
I. Provide Pay Increases for Employees	0.1	0.0
J. Trade Union Agreements	1.9	1.0
K. Problems of Receiving Raw Materials	4.5	0.0
Total	100.0	100.0

The general picture painted by these figures is that remunerated overtime in the private sector is largely driven by *fluctuations* in demand or the continuous nature of the production/service process, along with issues related to the cost-base of production ('more economic than increasing employment') and various aspects of industrial relations ('custom and practice'). In the public sector, overtime is largely seen as a response to fluctuations in demand, the *continuous* nature of the production process or the need to meet *normal*, ongoing demand. The probability of each of these latter two reasons being cited as the *single* most important factor in undertaking remunerated overtime among public sector organisations is just over three times that of their counterparts in the private sector. This pattern among public sector organisations and its contrast with the private sector reflects delivery of health care and related services in the public sector. Delivery of such care was clearly interpreted by respondents as an aspect of the continuous nature of their function or quite simply as part of their 'normal demand' by public sector respondents.

In the course of the management survey, respondents were asked whether or not they considered remunerated overtime to be essential to the continued operation of their organisation/ enterprise at its current levels of output. From Table 4.7 above, we saw that 84 per cent of private sector enterprises answered in the affirmative — that remunerated overtime was essential to their continued operation. The comparable figure among public sector organisations was 89 per cent, suggesting relatively little difference between public and private sectors as regards this aspect of their operation.

A final aspect of overtime working in the public sector considered whether or not management felt that central public sector employment practice should attempt to eliminate overtime in State-funded organisations. Exactly two-thirds (66.1 per cent) of firms responded in the affirmative to this question.

4.5.3 The Employee Response to Overtime Work in the Public Sector

In this section, aspects of the reaction of public sector employees to overtime work are considered. As in the previous section, the primary focus is on the extent to which their reaction differs from that of their private sector counterparts.

Incidence, Regularity and Nature of Overtime Work —
The Employee View

The survey estimates suggest that a total of 71 per cent of public sector employees worked some form of overtime in the 12 months preceding the interview. This compares with a figure of 78 per cent for the private sector. A total of 79 per cent of workers in each of the higher administrative/executive and other routine grades had worked some overtime in the period in question, compared with 59 per cent in the routine clerical grades. These differences between grades in the propensity to work overtime are roughly comparable with those in the private sector. In that sector, it was found that 77 per cent of those in the managerial/ professional grade, 64 per cent in the other clerical grade and 89 per cent in the manual grade had undertaken some overtime work in the 12 months preceding the survey.

Table 4.19 summarises information on the regularity of overtime worked in both public and private sectors. It is clear from this that, in general, the frequency of employees in the public sector undertaking overtime is lower than that for employees in the private sector. For example, a total of 52 per cent of public sector employees carry out overtime work only on an occasional basis or once per month. This compared with a figure of 38 per cent among private sector employees. Similarly, 50 per cent of private sector employees undertook overtime on at least a weekly basis, while the comparable figure for public sector employees was 43 per cent.

Table 4.19: Regularity With Which Overtime Was Worked by Public Sector Employees in the 12 Months Preceding the Survey

	Private Sector	Public Sector
	(Per Cent of Employees)	
Occasional basis	33.1	47.9
Once per month	5.1	4.0
Once every two weeks	11.6	4.7
1–2 days per week	23.9	23.7
3+ days per week	26.3	19.8
Total	100.0	100.0

Table 4.20 presents details on the usual form of remuneration for overtime work in both public and private sectors. The picture painted by this information is that there is a much higher probability in the public sector of overtime either being non-remunerated or being remunerated by time-off-in-lieu rather than by cash payments. It can be seen from the table that just over 38 per cent of employees in the public sector who did overtime were usually not remunerated for it. This compares with 31 per cent in the private sector. A further 18 per cent of public sector employees were remunerated by time-off-in-lieu, compared with 10 per cent of those in the private sector. As a consequence of the higher probability of non-remuneration or remuneration in the form of time-off-in-lieu there is a substantial differential (of 16 percentage points) in the percentage of public and private sector employees who receive cash payments (35 compared with 51 per cent).

Table 4.20: Usual Form of Remuneration Received by Public and Private Sector Employees Respectively for Overtime Worked in the 12 Months Preceding the Survey

Usual Form of Remuneration	Private Sector	Public Sector
	(Per Cent of Employees)	
All paid	51.3	35.4
Time-off-in-lieu	9.9	18.2
Combined (time off and paid)	7.4	8.1
Unpaid	31.4	38.3
Total	100.0	100.0

The preferred first choice of remuneration for overtime is summarised in Table 4.21. From this it can be seen that approximately equal percentages of employees in both the public and private sectors would like to be fully remunerated for overtime in cash payments (44 and 41 per cent respectively). Some differences between public and private sectors can be observed, however, as regards the other two types of remuneration. For example, 36 per cent of public sector employees said that they would prefer all remunerated overtime to be compensated for by time-off-in-lieu. The comparable figure for private sector employees is 17 per cent. As a corollary to this, more than twice the proportion of private as of public sector employees (42 and 20 per cent respectively) said that they would prefer a combination of cash payment and time-off-in-lieu.

Table 4.21: Preferred First Choice of Remuneration for Overtime Among Public and Private Sector Employees

Preferred Choice of Remuneration	Private Sector	Public Sector
	(Per Cent of Employees)	
All Cash Payment	40.9	44.4
All Time Off in Lieu	17.2	35.5
Combined Cash and Time Off in Lieu	41.9	20.1
Total	100.0	100.0

4.5.4 Employee Perception of the Importance of Overtime

Respondents were asked to state their level of agreement or otherwise with a number of aspects of overtime. A comparison of the perceived importance of each to both private and public sector employees is outlined in Table 4.22.

Table 4.22: Public and Private Sector Employees' Agreement or Otherwise With a Number of Statements on Overtime

	Strongly Agree	Moderately Agree	Neither Agree nor Disagree	Moderately Disagree	Strongly Disagree
A. Overtime is Important in Maintaining My Standard of Living					
Public Sector	3.7	10.6	21.3	21.3	43.0
Private Sector	15.2	15.9	17.8	11.7	39.5
B. There is No Point in My Doing Overtime Because of Tax					
Public Sector	33.3	26.9	15.6	16.1	8.0
Public Sector	25.1	26.6	21.0	15.2	12.9
C. Reducing Amount of Overtime Could Significantly Reduce the Number of Unemployed					
Public Sector	20.0	41.0	13.2	15.4	10.5
Public Sector	21.8	35.5	11.4	17.8	13.5
D. I Would Gladly Give Up My Overtime if it Helped in the Creation of Jobs for Unemployed					
Public Sector	34.2	37.0	16.6	8.0	4.1
Public Sector	42.3	28.2	16.0	7.5	6.0

Section A of the table suggests that there are quite substantial differences between public and private sector employees in terms of their perception of the importance of overtime in maintaining their standard of living. A total of only 14 per cent of public sector employees either 'strongly' or 'moderately' agreed with the statement, compared with 31 per cent of their counterparts in the private sector.

Section B suggests that just over 60 per cent of public sector and 51 per cent of private sector employees either 'strongly' or 'moderately' agree that there is no point in their doing overtime because of the effect of income tax.

Section C indicates that there is relatively little difference between public and private sector employees in terms of their agreement or otherwise with the statement that 'a reduction in the amount of overtime could significantly reduce the number of unemployed'. On the whole, such differences as are apparent from the table could be attributed to sampling variances.

Section D suggests that employees in both sectors differ only slightly in terms of their levels of agreement with the statement that 'I would gladly give up my overtime if it helped in the creation of jobs for the unemployed'.

4.6 SUMMARY

In this chapter, a range of aspects of overtime work in both private and public sectors has been examined from the perspectives of both employer and employee. In the course of the chapter, the extent, incidence and pattern of overtime work were considered; together with managements' interpretation of the factors underlying overtime as well as their views on any government incentives or schemes that could be introduced to reduce or eliminate the amount of overtime worked. To counterbalance managements' views, the incidence, regularity and nature of overtime as seen by the employee were also discussed, including such important issues as employees' perceptions of the importance of overtime work in maintaining living standards.

The data presented suggest that the levels of overtime work in Ireland are high by international standards. As many as 81 per cent of private sector employees work in companies in which overtime is undertaken on a regular weekly or daily basis. A total of 82 per cent of employees said that they had worked some form of overtime during the 12 months preceding the interview. Similarly, as many as 97.5 per cent of public sector workers covered in the survey were employed in organisations where some remunerated overtime was worked. The significance of these figures is the extent to which policy changes in this area could potentially impact on substantial numbers of companies and employees.

The responses emerging from a series of questions aimed at eliciting information on why overtime work is undertaken in companies seems to suggest strongly an economic or business rationale. As many as 84 per cent of private sector workers and 89 per cent of relevant public sector employees work in organisations which reported that remunerated overtime was necessary if they were to continue in business at current levels of output. In general, the principal reasons given by management for continuing to carry out overtime work would appear to be largely demand-driven: to meet fluctuations in demand, to meet ongoing demand; to remove bottlenecks, and so on. Issues such as custom and practice or employee agreements do not seem to have a significant influence in determining overtime work in Irish business life.

CHAPTER 5

SHARING JOBS

5.1 BACKGROUND

There has been widespread experimentation with job sharing schemes in the United States, Scandinavia and Europe. The practice is particularly operated in the US by employers (Losey, 1992; Marinelli and Berman, 1991; Bahls, 1990), where they form part of what is termed 'family-friendly policies' (Losey, 1992). Many organisations implement forms of job sharing — from federal and state institutions to large multinationals. Alternatives to the traditional working day were found in seven out of 10 organisations surveyed by Losey, with working part-time and job sharing the most frequently mentioned by both men and women who want to balance work and family commitments. While it may be said that job sharing has only recently gained prominence as an alternative to full-time working, the concept is not new. In the 1940s, Barclay's Bank employed administrative and secretarial staff on a week-on, week-off basis (Syrett, 1983).

Job sharing involves dividing one former full-time position into two or more positions *while retaining all the rights and privileges attached to the full-time position.* It is this latter point which differentiates job sharing from part-time work, in that many, if not all, part-time jobs do not carry *pro rata* terms and conditions, and they are very often low-paid and low-status jobs. The most common way in which jobs are divided under a job sharing scheme is by two equal periods of two and a half days per week each. A survey by the Equal Opportunities Commission in Britain found that this was the most popular method used (1981). Division by alternate weeks or by morning and afternoon is also used. The latter is least often used since travel time and cost may be prohibitive. The Equal Opportunities Commission also reported a number of job sharing arrangements where there was no fixed schedule. Working patterns were arranged according to the needs of the individual or organisation. The demand for job sharing has grown from the needs of individuals, and the feminist movement looking for patterns of work less suited to the interests of male workers (Arkin and Dubrofsky, 1978). Job sharing has also been experimented with in relation to phased early retirement, where older workers share their jobs while phasing out of the workforce.

The literature on job sharing stresses the element of employee demand and employee preference in the growth of job sharing. Blyton (1985) claims that job sharing is a more flexible work arrangement where both employer and employee needs can be accommodated. More recently, some governments have looked upon job sharing as a means of reducing unemployment (Syrett, 1983; Humphreys, 1986).

Many claims have been made for the *advantages* of job sharing for employers (Syrett, 1983; Evans and Attew, 1986). Chief amongst these are:

- *Improved Productivity*: A study of 35 German firms using job sharing found on average, a 33 per cent productivity gain where job sharers replaced full-time employees (Walton, 1985).

- *Reduced Turnover*: This can happen for a number of reasons: firstly, full-time working may not suit certain types of employees, so employers can retain staff by offering flexible working arrangements — for example, women who wish to combine work with other options; secondly, job sharing can be used to reduce pressure in highly pressurised or monotonous work situations with high turnover levels.

- *Reduced Absenteeism*: As there is more time off during the week, personal and domestic issues can be dealt with during that time.

- *Greater Efficiency*: As there are two people in the one job, it is possible to cover two events simultaneously; peaks of work can be handled more efficiently; greater effort can be put into the job by both incumbents because the job sharer's work day or week is shorter than the full-timer's.

- *Greater Continuity*: Holidays or sick leave are covered on a part-time basis by the other sharer, so that the work continues, whilst the job sharer may cover for absences of their partner on a temporary basis.

- *Greater Creativity*: 'Two brains are better than one.'

- *Wider Range of Skills*: With two sharers there will be a wider pool of skills to draw on, as each will have their own strengths and weaknesses.

- *Wider Pool of Potential Employees*: Job sharing may attract people into employment who might not otherwise seek employment.

- *Eases Older Workers into Retirement*: Older workers may prefer a gradual transition from work to retirement, while younger workers are enabled to be recruited simultaneously and trained alongside the older worker.

- *Training Opportunities for Younger People*: Employers can take advantage of job sharing to double the number of young people being trained without doubling the associated cost.

On the other hand, job sharing schemes also have potential *disadvantages*, including:

- *Administration Costs*: There will be some increased costs caused by processing the payroll, training, recruitment and selection procedures, although routine administration, if computerised, may not add significantly to overall costs.

- *Communication*: With job sharing there is more need for good internal communication and communication between the job sharers during work and at handover periods.

- *Management*: There will be an increase in effort required for the managers of job sharers in terms of supervision, work allocation and so forth.

- *Division of Responsibility*: How the work is divided up and the competencies of job sharers may cause problems.

- *Time Delays*: This can happen where tasks have to wait for one member of the job sharing team to return and deal with them.

Some employers may perceive that job sharers are less committed to their jobs than full-time employees. Syrett (1983) argues, however, that this may be an erroneous perception and cites evidence from his case analysis of Sheffield City Council that in fact job sharers may exhibit more commitment. Other studies confirm some of the advantages cited above (McCarthy and Rosenberg, 1981; Verespej, 1989; Anon, 1989). These studies have found that job sharers are more enthusiastic about their work, suffer from less burn-out and are more creative. From the cost point of view, there is evidence to suggest that even though an employer may have to pay more in social security and employment tax, there are cost savings in terms of reduced unemployment costs, less turn-over and higher productivity. McCarthy and Rosenberg's (1981) study of 100 job sharers in the Wisconsin civil service found that the cost of employing two job sharers was similar to the cost of employing one full-time person. They also found that productivity was higher while absenteeism and turnover were lower.

From the employees' perspective, job sharing has a number of advantages. Arkin and Dubrofsky's (1978) study of job sharing couples in the United States (sharing the same or different jobs) found positive reactions from participants. The kinds of improvements cited were increased leisure time, increased work flexibility and shared child-care and home responsibilities. Blyton (1985) highlights another advantage of job sharing as that it gives access to potentially more fulfilling work with higher status than part-time work traditionally does. A Swedish study (Fredericksson, 1988) of job sharers also found that the majority were women with young children. The major advantage to them was the ability to schedule working hours in ways that best suited their needs. Some disadvantages cited in this study included lower income levels and lower income-related benefits, such as sickness benefit and parental leave allowance, which indicates that job sharing in that study did not have all the attendant *pro rata* benefits which differentiate job sharing from other forms of part-time work.

5.2 THE INTERNATIONAL EXPERIENCE

5.2.1 Country by Country Details

The experiences of a number of countries adopting job sharing practices will now be discussed.

Belgium

In Belgium, job sharing initially was combined with early-retirement schemes and sabbatical leave, whereby unemployed people were recruited to fill the posts on a part-time basis (Humphreys, 1986). Between 1977 and 1983, part-time work increased from 5 to 10 per cent of the labour force. There were increases in the number of men working part-time also, from 0.7 to

3 per cent (De Rongé and Molitor, 1991). While not job sharing as such, part-time workers are entitled to the same social security rights as full-time workers. This partly explains the rise in its popularity in Belgium. The promotion of part-time working was aimed at reducing the levels of unemployment, particularly among young people. There was also a demand from women for part-time work. The trade unions were opposed to part-time work even though they admitted that they had underestimated the level of demand for it (De Rongé and Molitor, 1991). The Belgian government promoted a number of job sharing initiatives in the public sector in order to reduce the impact of unemployment, rather than in an attempt to create additional jobs. Recruits to public administration work a reduced week in their first year of employment, while existing employees could opt for a reduction of their working week to 50 per cent. In the education sector, staff could work part-time prior to retirement. Employees over 50 years of age received a proportionate reduction in their salary, along with a bonus of 25 per cent of their remaining salary if they were not employed during the time off work. In local authorities and social-assistance centres staff could also opt for part-time early retirement if they had been employed for at least 20 years and were over 55. They received 75 per cent of their salaries for half of their original time, and they had to retire at 60.

Britain

As stated earlier, job sharing was first in evidence in Britain after the Second World War at Barclay's Bank. Other banks followed suit. The schemes operated to entice women back into the work-force and were primarily in the administrative and clerical areas. Later, in 1969, the Department of Health and Social Security sought ways of encouraging married women back through job sharing. Job sharing has expanded in the public sector with many local and health authorities, government departments and education and community services promoting job sharing. A number of private sector establishments have also promoted job sharing, including GEC Telecommunications, the Stock Exchange, and Fox's Biscuits. The range of jobs has been wide, while the majority have been in administrative and clerical areas. Blyton (1985) lists some of the jobs where job sharing has taken place. They include administration, clerical work, journalism, social work, research, teaching, medicine, the legal profession and librarianship. Most of these are clearly *non-manual* occupations.

Job sharing has been introduced for a variety of reasons. Evans and Attew (1986) group them as follows: firstly, the creation of new employment opportunities; secondly, the retention of existing employees; thirdly, to achieve more effective work patterns for the organisation and finally, as part of an Equal Opportunities Programme, encouraging women returnees.

Local government has been to the forefront in using job sharing as a means of generating employment opportunities. Authorities (mainly Labour) such as Sheffield City Council, Camden, Hackney, Lewisham, Lambeth and Brent — all in London — have significant job sharing policies (Syrett, 1983; Curson and Palmer, 1986). Nearly 1,000 employees at the Department of Health and Social Security were involved in a scheme of job sharing and part-time working (Evans and Attew, 1986). Under this scheme, job sharing was open to all levels of employee and they also had the option of returning to full-time employment in the future if they wished. The BBC also has posts shared to retain valuable staff who can only work part-time. The arrangements are initiated by the staff themselves and job sharers must be willing participants. In their policy statement about job sharing, the BBC made explicit reference to the fact that their scheme was not a form of 'job splitting' (a government-initiated programme that met with opposition from unions and the Equal Opportunities Commission, as it did not grant benefits on a *pro rata* basis as does job sharing), and also distinguished it from part-time working. Their definition reads as follows:

> Job sharing is a working arrangement whereby two or more people share the duties of a full-time post and the various components of the work, though divided, are still regarded as constituting one job (Evans and Attew, 1986: 109).

The Job-Splitting Scheme, referred to above, was introduced by the government in 1982 to encourage employers to create additional employment through offering a subsidy to split existing jobs. The jobs could be filled in a variety of ways — for example, by two unemployed people, by an existing employed and an unemployed person or by two existing full-timers changing to part-time working. It has been criticised for a number of reasons. Firstly, it only allowed employers to take on unemployed people for less than 16 hours per week, the limit above which they become entitled to legal protection against unfair dismissal; secondly, because there was no pension rights protection; and finally, because the scheme offered incentives to employ unemployed people, it may have indirectly discriminated against those who voluntarily wished to work part-time.

The Part-Time Job Release Scheme, an allied scheme to the Job Release Scheme, introduced in 1983, allowed early retirees to phase their retirement by sharing their jobs with an unemployed person. The employer was given a grant to recruit that person. Participation in the government schemes was disappointing for some of the reasons cited above. Also it appeared that there was a lack of interest in job sharing by British employers, and that, coupled with a lack of enthusiasm on the part of trades unions, has rendered job sharing less than a successful option in Britain.

Germany

In 1982, Germany introduced a job sharing scheme which allowed public sector employees to convert from full-time to part-time working, while maintaining their pension rights (Humphreys, 1986). With the introduction of job sharing, nearly all civil servants were entitled to opt for part-time working for up to 10 years. Also, the educational sector operated a system of training to promote part-time work. In 1980, five regions carried out, on an experimental basis, a scheme subsidising employers to hire additional part-time employees from the ranks of the unemployed. The size of the subsidy varied between the regions and in two of them it was paid for additional jobs created. The take-up was disappointing and the experiment was discontinued (Humphreys, 1986). The German government also encouraged the creation of part-time employment.

Italy

In Italy, regulations were introduced to give part-time workers equal treatment to full-time workers and enable movement from full-time to part-time work. For example, between May and December of 1984, Humphreys (1986) reveals that there were 50,897 part-time contracts and 8,137 full-time/part-time contracts signed in Italy.

The Netherlands

The rise in part-time employment was significant in the Netherlands during the 1970s (de Neuborg, 1991). By 1981, a fifth of the workforce worked part-time. In the Netherlands, the government stressed the role of part-time working in job creation. In 1982, in its Employment Plan, it aimed to create 39,000 jobs through the conversion of full-time jobs. These were to be done on condition that there would be no reduction in overall hours worked. Employers were also encouraged to create part-time jobs. In the public sector, part-time working was also promoted through government agreements whereby a proportion of jobs was to be converted into part-time jobs. In 1984, 9 per cent of central government employees worked part-time. By the end of 1985, the government estimated that an additional 150,000 jobs had been created during the period since the introduction of work sharing schemes. De Neuborg (1991) argues, however, that part-time working would have increased anyway and cannot be attributed to government intervention. He concludes on a pessimistic note, stating that the various work sharing policies, including job sharing, did not create an overall growth in employment in the Netherlands. He also states that work sharing contributed to social inequality caused by imbalances between those remaining in the labour force versus those who decided to leave, but it did help to reduce the imbalance between male and female workers. Other experiments in the Netherlands show how new management styles have been developed in the school system through the shared leadership scheme (Blase, 1992). Shared and part-time management has been promoted to improve the quality of life and to meet the challenge of the 1990s. Part-time leadership experiments reveal a number of advantages associated with productivity gains, quality of working experiences, more flexibility and job satisfaction.

United States

Job sharing has been more widely practised in the United States, especially in the public sector (McCarthy and Rosenberg, 1981). Christopherson (1991) notes that the widespread increase in part-time working was primarily caused by the entry into the workforce of married women who had reached the end of their childbearing years. Many of these women were married to male full-time workers and Christopherson argues that they returned to work on a part-time basis to supplement total income and increase household consumption. Many of the part-time jobs were unregulated and had non-standard hours. Between 1950 and 1960, participation of women in the 45–54-year age group increased from 34 to 48 per cent. In the 1970s, employment increased in the service sector of the US economy and those years witnessed a large growth in the numbers of women entering the labour force to take up these jobs. Women in the 25–44-year age group joined the labour force in increasing numbers, and by 1985 had risen from 48 to 71 per cent of all women in this age category. At the same time, women with young children also entered in large numbers, while the participation of men started to fall, so that the nature of labour supply changed dramatically. Currently, most women are in the labour force and in more 'flexible' jobs.

More recently, a number of commentators (Christopherson 1991; Moss Kanter, 1986) have pointed to the growing numbers of women moving back into full-time employment from part-time work. This is seen as choosing consumption over reduced hours and private consumption over social consumption — Americans viewing health-care and welfare provision as more of a private business. As a consequence, women tend to work more full-time to provide for household consumption, while their responsibilities for domestic work have not decreased. Christopherson claims that this phenomenon is the source of the contemporary time crisis in the US. Thus, as the burden of waged and domestic work is falling more to women, there is no evidence of any decrease in domestic work time to compensate for this increase in waged working time. Women have, on average, five to six hours less free time per week than men; they engage less in educational pursuits than men, and they spend more time on caring and domestic work. There is, therefore, a growing concern about the need to balance work and family responsibilities, which is not only a primary consideration for women themselves, but also for employers who are concerned about productivity.

The move towards more 'family-centred' work in contemporary United States business has its roots in the concern for the impact of women working full-time. This has led to increases in absenteeism and decreased productivity, because of family responsibilities. Changes in the workforce therefore have prompted many firms to seek alternatives to the traditional 9.00–5.00, 5-day, working week. A survey of 348 companies in 1987 revealed that flexitime had doubled in use in the previous 10 years, 30 per cent of the companies surveyed in the US and Canada used flexitime, and about 10 per cent of companies had job sharing schemes (Thomas, 1987). Losey's (1992) survey of human resources professionals revealed that eight out of 10 offer at least one family-friendly personnel policy, while seven out of 10 offer alternatives to the traditional working day. Working part-time and job sharing are becoming increasingly popular for men and women who wish to balance work and family needs. Another study carried out in 1989 discovered that there were 7 per cent more firms employing staff on a flexible basis than in the previous year (McKendrick, 1989). The number of firms using job sharing had increased by 1 per cent while a further 2 per cent were considering the option. According to Lee of Workshare Inc. (Bahls, 1989), job sharing is considered an acceptable form of part-time working by traditional corporations. The benefits considered by employers were: firstly, valuable employees were retained during personal transition periods; secondly, employees did not conduct personal business during office time; and finally, a broader range of abilities was brought to the position.

Job sharing is also reported as a small but growing trend in the hotel and catering sector (Seal, 1991). The Marriott Corporation has initiated a job sharing scheme as has Westin Hotels and Resorts. The schemes are being launched in response to the acute shortage of skilled labour in the sector. It is anticipated that this trend will continue. Current participants are women, wishing to combine family and work commitments.

In the public sector, many experiments with job sharing have been documented (Marinelli and Berman, 1990; Anon, 1990; Parr, 1988; Humphreys, 1986). One of the first job sharing experiments was in the Department of Public Welfare in Massachusetts. Other states followed and job sharing is practised in many state and federal institutions. For example, in Boulder, Colorado, Boulder Valley School District Principals devised a comprehensive plan to job share. A one-year pilot project was agreed and evaluated at the end of the year. Results indicated that job sharing can benefit employers, as it reduces the high cost of turnover and can also be used as a training ground for future managers and as an alternative to total retirement (Marinelli and Berman, 1991). New York State introduced a range of work sharing options in 1984 as a result of a major survey of its employees. The survey discovered that women especially preferred more flexible working arrangements. A two-year pilot programme commenced in 1984, with the agreement of the union. This allowed up to 200,000 employees the opportunity of reducing their working hours along agreed criteria. At the end of 1988, New York state agencies had 7,000 salaried employees sharing jobs. The Department of the Civil Service set up a Part-Time/Shared Job Office to provide information and support to employees wishing to job share.

A number of factors have contributed to the use of job sharing in the US, from the initial demands of employees to the employer experimentation with alternative work sharing measures to ameliorate the impact of women working full-time. Very few of the studies addressed the issue of creating additional employment. In fact, in many instances, job sharing has been introduced to cope with skill shortages, to retain skilled employees or to deal with conflicting pressures of home and workplace.

5.2.2 Conclusion: The International Experience of Sharing Jobs

Several factors have been identified which contributed to the introduction of job sharing schemes. In the US, for example, they were introduced in response to employee demand, but a number of employers also experimented with them. Blyton (1985) evaluates the impact of job sharing and concludes that the practice of job sharing has progressed very slowly despite the claims made for it. The numbers involved represent a small proportion of the total employed on a part-time basis. Drèze (1985) also concludes that job sharing has not developed in Europe as a means of dealing with unemployment, nor has it spread among men, except for the examples of early retirement discussed. High incidence of part-time work in general is associated with above-average participation of women in the labour force, thus indicating that promoting part-time work and job sharing may also increase the participation of women in the workforce, and not reduce unemployment levels.

Blyton (1985) looks at the reasons for this slow uptake in job sharing. From the employer's perspective, job sharing has been slow to develop for two main reasons: inertia and cost. Job sharing is a different way of working and requires thought and energy to implement effectively. It is also a form of part-time working, which is not enthusiastically welcomed by employers. If employers use job sharing to retain existing skilled staff or to fill vacancies, then in times of high labour supply, they may be less inclined to use job sharing as a means of doing so. Indeed, there may be more of an argument for promoting job sharing during times of labour shortages, thus limiting the role of job sharing in employment generation. Companies experiencing difficulties may turn to job sharing as a means of introducing short time. Here the stimulus is to avoid further unemployment, not to create additional jobs. Management attitudes may militate against the introduction of job sharing. Supervisors can also exert a negative influence. In a study carried out in the US (McCarthy and Rosenberg, 1981), the role of supervisors was seen as very important to the success of job sharing schemes. In fact, the supervisors in the study claimed that if they had to replace the job sharers, they would do so with full-time replacements.

Unions also have negative attitudes to job sharing. This may be for a variety of reasons. Unions themselves do not promote job sharing, possibly because they are dominated by men. Part-time working is viewed with suspicion and is linked to attempts to undermine collective bargaining. Roche (1988: 139) asserts that the Irish trade union movement is 'sceptical' of job sharing. The job sharing schemes in the Irish context have been introduced into the state and semi-state sector through pressure from employees, not unions or management. The take-up of these schemes is low, with the majority being availed of by married women with children. The union view of this is that job sharing is a poor substitute for proper child-care provision, and that job sharing itself may perpetuate inequality between male and female workers (despite the evidence cited by de Neuborg above). Wickham (1993: 86), states that Irish trade unions are perhaps the least likely (apart from Spain) to support the introduction of part-time working and are more likely to 'oppose it under all circumstances'. Drew (1990: 231) goes further in trying to explain the antipathy to part-time working. She states that, as part-time work has been traditionally associated with women's work and with low pay and conditions, it is therefore seen as 'a departure from the 'male' full-time norm of a 40-hour week for life'. In other words, forms of part-time work are 'women's work' and therefore not real jobs. There are some exceptions to this general rule. In the UK, the National Association of Local Government Officers (NALGO) has negotiated job sharing agreements in local authorities for its members in response to pressure from those members (Equal Opportunities Commission, 1981). The Equal Opportunities Commission (1981: 11) in the UK has stated that trade unions need to take a much more positive role in promoting job sharing to overcome employer resistance:

The current experience of trade union involvement in job
sharing indicated that unions can play an important positive
role in initiating and taking part in negotiations for an or-
ganisation-wide job sharing policy; in assisting individuals
negotiating from full-time work to job sharing; and in ensuring the best possible terms and conditions for job sharers.

In relation to costs, there are national differences on whether it is
more expensive to hire one full-time person as opposed to two
part-time people. Costs include national social insurance contributions, which differ from country to country. For example, in Canada (Meltz et al., 1981) it has been estimated that employers' contributions to statutory benefits would add 2 per cent to the cost of
job sharers as opposed to full-time employees. Other types of costs
discussed are administrative and developmental costs. Those who
advocate job sharing counter with benefits accruing through job
sharing, such as greater productivity and lower turnover.

Employees themselves appear to be the main promoters of job
sharing. In an MRBI survey in Ireland, 62 per cent of respondents
favoured the use of job sharing in combating unemployment (*Irish
Times*, 1987). The Wisconsin study (McCarthy and Rosenberg,
1981) revealed high levels of interest in job sharing, especially
among older employees. A number of organisational and governmental obstacles conspire to reduce the take-up of job sharing, however. These include rigidities in pension schemes and the difficulty
in developing career paths for job sharers. Government measures
which would provide a more favourable climate for the improved
take-up of job sharing schemes include the protection of pension
rights, changes in the laws relating to social security payments
and entitlements, and subsidies to overcome transition costs.

Finally, until there is a change in the perception of part-time
working, and by inclusion job sharing, as being somehow an infe-
rior form of work, the potential for job sharing will not be more
fully realised. Indeed, it can be argued that unless sex discrimination is comprehensively tackled, this perception will continue to
be the main reason for the unfair treatment of those whose hours
are shorter.

5.3 JOB SHARING IN THE IRISH PRIVATE SECTOR

In this section, the results from the management questionnaire
concerning issues related to job sharing will be discussed. Five
main topics are considered. First to be looked at will be the

incidence and extent of job sharing options offered in private sector firms. Secondly, the origins and current organisation of job
sharing schemes (including aspects of the terms and conditions
offered to employees who work on a job sharing basis) will be examined. Thirdly, managements' view of the prospects for extending job sharing schemes in the future will be considered. Fourthly,
what managements see as the advantages and disadvantages of
job sharing work arrangements will be discussed.

5.3.1 Extent and Incidence of Job Sharing in Private Firms

Table 5.1 presents information on the extent to which companies
offer a job sharing option to their staff. From this it can be seen
that, when weighted in terms of enterprises only, just over 5 per
cent of all firms offer this facility to their staff. This represents
just under 2,000 companies.

*Table 5.1: Estimated Number of Employers Currently Offering the
Opportunity to Work on a Job Sharing Basis*

Does your company offer job sharing?	Manuf. / Bld		Distributive Services		Non-Distributive Services			
	< 100 Emps.	100+ Emps.	< 20 Emps.	20+ Emps.	< 20 Emps.	20+ Emps.	Total, All Enter-prises	Total, Weighted by Em-ployment
	(Per Cent of Enterprises)							*(Per Cent of Employees)*
Yes	4.5	18.0	5.3	11.4	3.3	16.3	5.1	31.2
No	95.5	82.0	94.7	88.6	96.7	83.7	94.9	68.8
Total	100.0	100.0	100.0	100.0	100.0	100.0	100.0	100.0
Wgt'd	7,000	500	17,500	900	12,400	1,000	39,300	554,600
(Unwgt'd n)	(75)	(64)	(52)	(44)	(69)	(44)	(348)	(348)

In general, job sharing is offered in a substantially higher percentage of larger firms in each of the three sectors outlined in the
table. This highest incidence is in the large manufacturing/
building and non-distributive services sectors (18 and 16 per cent
respectively). Comparable figures for smaller firms in these sectors are 4.5 and 5.3 per cent respectively.

To obtain an indication of the number of employees working in
companies offering job sharing schemes, the final column of Table

5.1 presents data weighted by the combined enterprise/employee weight.[1] Because the earlier data in the table indicate that work sharing schemes are largely concentrated in larger firms, it is not surprising that there is a substantial difference between the percentage of firms offering this option (50 per cent) and the percentage of workers covered by it. It can be seen that just over 31 per cent of private sector employment (or over 170,000 employees) is accounted for by firms offering job sharing arrangements. The reader should note, however, that such arrangements may not be offered to all employees in all grades or sections within the 5 per cent of firms in question.

Table 5.2 provides details of the estimated number of private sector employees who were working on a job sharing basis at the time of the survey.[2] This shows that the estimate of employees who were then availing of job sharing is just over 5,300. This represents only 3 per cent of those who could potentially avail of existing schemes and only 1 per cent of private sector employment.

Table 5.2: Estimated Number of Employees Currently Working on a Job Sharing Basis

	Manuf. / Bld		Distributive Services		Non-Distributive Services				
	< 100 Emps.	100+ Emps.	< 20 Emps.	20+ Emps.	< 20 Emps.	20+ Emps.	Total, All Enterprises	Total No.	As Per Cent of all Employees
	(Per Cent)								
Male	0.0	0.0	5.6	0.9	2.8	16.9	26.3	1,400	0.4
Female	13.6	5.6	30.0	1.4	8.4	14.6	73.7	3,925	2.2
Total	13.6	5.6	35.7	2.3	11.3	31.5	100.0	5,325	1.0
As percentage of all employees in sector	0.7	0.2	2.9	0.2	1.1	1.6	1.0	—	—
(Unwgt'd n)	(8)	(12)	(3)	(5)	(2)	(7)	(34)		

[1]   The figures in the last column of the table are adjusted by assigning to each company a weight which is proportional to its number of employees.

[2]   Given the low incidence and take-up rates of job sharing schemes, the reader is advised that Table 5.2 is based on a small absolute number of respondents.

From the table, it can be seen that almost three-quarters of those working on a job sharing basis were female. Just over a third were in the smaller distributive sector, while a further third were in the larger non-distributive sector. The relative importance of job sharing to the smaller distributive sector is shown in the second last row of Table 5.2. This provides details of the number of job sharers as a percentage of each size/sector's total employment. From this it can be seen that 2.9 per cent of employees in the smaller distributive services sector were on a job share arrangement. This was followed by the larger non-distributive services sector (1.6 per cent) and the smaller non-distributive sector (1.1 per cent).

5.3.2 Origin and Implications of Job Sharing

Information on four aspects of the origin and organisation of job sharing were collected in the course of the management questionnaire. First, details were collected on the year in which job sharing was initiated, at whose initiative it was initiated and the main reasons for its introduction. Secondly, information on the employment effect of job sharing was recorded. Thirdly, the extent to which the terms and conditions of job sharers are the same as (or differ from) those of other workers was examined.

Information from the management survey confirms that job sharing is a relatively recent working arrangement. In exactly 50 per cent of the firms which offered this option to staff it was introduced over the period 1991–94, while in a further 15 per cent of firms it was introduced in the period 1985–90.

In 72 per cent of all firms offering job sharing, its introduction seems to have been initiated by local management, while in a further 5 per cent it was introduced on the initiative of head office management. In contrast, in only 19 per cent of firms was the idea suggested by the employees, and in only 3 per cent of firms by trade unions. In just over 1 per cent of enterprises the initial suggestion originated from some 'other' source.

The managerial motives behind the introduction of job sharing appear primarily to have involved the facilitation of employees. This was cited as the reason for its introduction in 73 per cent of enterprises. It seems somewhat strange that management in almost three-quarters of firms mentioned this as the reason for the introduction of job sharing arrangements, given that there is relatively little evidence from the same survey to suggest any strong employee pressure for its introduction. A further aspect of employer motives for bringing in job sharing which was mentioned by management in 14 per cent of enterprises was an attempt to 'generate employment'.

Firms which said that they offered job sharing arrangements to staff were asked whether or not its introduction had increased the number of staff employed. A total of 61 per cent of relevant firms which offered the job share option said that its introduction had resulted in an increase in employment. The aggregate estimate of the numbers of jobs that had resulted from its introduction was 1,200.

One particularly important aspect of job sharing is the effect it might have on the terms and conditions of employment of those availing of it. To assess this issue, managements were asked whether job sharers had the same terms and conditions of employment as other workers in six specified areas as listed in Table 5.3 below. From this it can be seen that annual and other leave is enjoyed (on a *pro rata* basis) by the vast majority of job sharers. Promotional prospects appear to be the same as between job sharers and other employees in approximately 73 per cent of firms. Tenure is enjoyed to an equal degree in 60 per cent of companies. Training and development is equally available to job sharers in 88 per cent of firms. Retirement benefits and pensions are enjoyed *(pro rata)* in 64 per cent of enterprises. Other benefits (such as health insurance, etc.) are also available to job sharers in 87 per cent of firms.

Table 5.3: Extent to Which Job Sharers Have the Same Terms and Conditions of Employment as Other Workers

Job Sharers Have Same Conditions Regarding:	Total, All Enterprises (Per Cent Enterprises)	Total, Weighted by Employment (Per Cent Emps.)
	(Per Cent Saying 'Yes')	
Annual and other leave	97.1	98.6
Promotion	73.2	96.2
Tenure	60.5	96.1
Training and development	87.9	98.4
Retirement benefits/pensions	64.3	96.0
Other benefits	87.1	98.3
(Unweighted n)	(34)	(34)

Note: Unweighted sample N upon which table is based is particularly small.

As in other tables, the second column of Table 5.3 presents an estimate of the percentages of employees in firms where job sharers enjoy the same conditions as other workers. It can be seen that the percentages derived from a reweighting of the data by the combined enterprise/employee weight are larger than those based solely on an enterprise weight. This reflects the fact that conditions are equalised as between job sharing and other employees to a greater degree in larger firms than in small ones. In other words, the percentage of larger firms which say that job sharers have the same conditions as their full-time counterparts is higher across all sectors for each of the six benefits listed in the table. The figures in the second column of Table 5.3 suggest that over 96 per cent of the estimated 170,000 employees (see Table 5.1 above) who work in firms offering job sharing could benefit from this work arrangement without disadvantaging themselves in career terms. Overall therefore, the data in Table 5.3 would seem to suggest that, especially in larger firms, job sharers cannot be viewed as a 'marginal' work-force which is offered appreciably poorer terms and conditions of employment than full-time workers. Having said this, however, the data would suggest that there are some disadvantages for job sharers in some of the smaller firms with respect to terms and conditions of employment. Thus, any attempt to extend the popularity of job sharing must seek to ensure that the terms in smaller firms do not disadvantage job sharers relative to their full-time counterparts. In the absence of any attempt to equalise the terms and conditions of employment as between job sharers and full-time workers, the extension of job sharing among smaller firms threatens to open up a gap between the two sectors of the labour force.

5.3.3 Future Prospects for Job Sharing

In the course of the employer questionnaire, managements were asked about their intentions regarding the extension (where relevant) or introduction of job sharing. The responses are presented in Table 5.4.

As can be seen from the table, a total of 27 per cent of firms currently operating job sharing arrangements (accounting for 38 per cent of the private sector workforce) said that they intended to extend this at some time in the future. Column 8 of the table shows that 38 per cent of the workforce in firms currently offering job sharing arrangements work in firms which actually intend to extend these arrangements at some point in the future. Differences of intent between size and sectors emerge: 60 per cent of the larger firms in the distributive services sector said that they intended to extend job sharing. This compared with between 24 and 50 per cent of firms in other size/sector categories. Once again it emerges that larger firms in all sectors are more interested than smaller ones in extending job sharing. In aggregate, companies which express a willingness or intention to extend job sharing employ approximately 66,000 private sector employees.[3]

Table 5.4: Future Intentions of Firms Currently Operating Job Sharing

Do You Intend to Extend Job Sharing?	Manuf./Bld		Distributive Services		Non-Distributive Services			
	< 100 Emps.	100+ Emps.	< 20 Emps.	20+ Emps.	< 20 Emps.	20+ Emps.	Total, All Enterprises	Total, Weighted by Employment
Yes	44.2	50.0	24.0	60.0	—	42.9	26.8	38.1
No	55.8	50.0	76.0	40.0	—	57.1	73.2	61.9
Wgt'd	300	100	900	100	0	200	1,600	
(Unwgt'd n)	(5)	(12)	(3)	(5)	(0)	(7)	(32)	

The companies which did not operate job sharing arrangements at the time of the survey were very definite in their views and intentions. A total of 99 per cent of such companies (accounting for 91 per cent of relevant employees) said that they had never been approached by staff with a request for job sharing. Just under 4 per cent of firms not operating job sharing (accounting for 16 per cent of relevant employees) had ever seriously considered at management or board level its introduction. Such consideration was substantially concentrated in larger companies. Finally, just under 3 per cent of firms (employing 9 per cent of relevant employees) said that they intended to introduce job sharing at

---

[3]   From Table 5.1 it can be seen that 31.2 per cent of the private sector workforce is employed in firms currently operating job share arrangements. Table 5.4 indicates that approximately 38.1 per cent of those employees are in firms which intend to extend job sharing arrangements.

some point in the future. This would represent approximately 34,000 employees.[4]

5.3.4 Perceived Advantages and Disadvantages of Job Sharing

Table 5.5 presents details of managements' views of the advantages of work sharing schemes. In the first column, aggregate estimates are provided for all firms, adjusted by the enterprise weight. In column two, the combined enterprise/employee weight is used. From this it is clear that almost three-quarters of all companies saw no advantage to job sharing. These companies accounted for just over half (53 per cent) of the private sector labour force. The fact that the figure in the second column is 20 percentage points lower than the corresponding figure in the first column indicates that smaller firms were more likely than their larger counterparts to see no advantages to work sharing. Of the 25 per cent of firms which did see some possible benefits, the advantages ranged fairly evenly across a number of response categories such as: the retention of workers who would otherwise be lost (3.3 per cent of firms); the balancing of employers' and employees' needs (4.5 per cent); increased productivity (3.9 per cent) etc.

Columns 3 to 5 of Table 5.5 provide a breakdown of firms' perceptions of the advantages of work sharing arrangements classified by their situation regarding job sharing at the time of interview. A threefold classification of firms regarding their job sharing status was used, namely: (i) currently offers job sharing; (ii) intends to offer job sharing in the future; (iii) does not intend to offer job sharing in the future. This information allows us to consider whether or not there are differences between the perceptions of firms according to their then current or stated future intentions regarding job sharing activity. The figures suggest that there is more emphasis on issues such as the 'balancing of employer/employee needs' or 'improves motivation' among those firms which currently operate job sharing arrangements. Those intending to introduce job sharing were much more likely to

---

4   Table 5.1 shows that 66.8 per cent of the private sector workforce was employed in firms which did not offer work sharing arrangements. Approximately 9 per cent of these employees worked in firms which said that they intended to introduce job sharing at some time in the future. This represents approximately 34,000 from a workforce of 554,600.

mention the 'retention of experienced staff who would otherwise be lost to the firm'; 'improvements in staff motivation'; 'employment creation and enhanced flexibility in the workplace'.

Table 5.5: Advantages of Job Sharing, Classified by Whether Firm Currently Offers Job Sharing, Intends to Offer it or Does Not Intend to Offer it

Advantage Mentioned	Total, All Enterprises	Total Weighted by Employment	Firm's Situation Regarding Job Sharing		
			Currently offers Job Sharing	Intends to offer Job Sharing	Does not intend to offer Job Sharing
			(Per Cent of Enterprises)		
None	74.5	53.3	9.7	11.2	79.7
Retains experience which would otherwise be lost	3.3	11.1	7.3	25.7	2.5
Allows balancing of employer and employee needs	4.5	12.4	44.9	0.7	2.5
Employees more productive	3.9	9.4	12.8	15.3	3.1
Less sick leave, absenteeism etc.	3.4	9.4	7.9	—	3.2
Improves motivation	6.7	7.3	27.2	23.1	5.1
Reduces costs	3.1	19.8	4.3	3.0	3.0
Creates employment	4.6	1.9	11.7	22.3	3.7
Greater flexibility	1.8	2.3	2.3	22.3	1.2
Wgt'd	39,300	554,600	1,900	100	37,300
(Unwgt'd n)	(348)	(348)	(17)	(9)	(322)

* Note that, since firms may mention more than one advantage, columns may sum to more than 100 per cent.

Table 5.6 presents details on managements' perceptions of the disadvantages of job sharing. From this it can be seen that 21 per cent of companies (accounting for some 23 per cent of the private sector workforce) said that there were no disadvantages to job sharing. These figures are in stark contrast to the significantly higher proportion of firms (74 per cent) which said that there were no *advantages* to job sharing arrangements. The data suggest that employers are better able to see the disadvantages of job sharing than they are to see its advantages. The main disadvantages mentioned mostly relate to the lack of continuity it brings to the workplace (mentioned by 28 per cent of firms) and its cost to the company (mentioned by 24 per cent of respondents).

Table 5.6: Disadvantages of Job Sharing, Classified by Whether Firm Currently Offers Job Sharing, Intends to Offer it or Does Not Intend to Offer it

Disadvantage Mentioned	Total, All Enterprises	Total, Weighted by Employment	Firm's Situation regarding Job Sharing		
			Currently offers Job Sharing	Intends to offer Job Sharing	Does not intend to offer Job Sharing
			(Per Cent of Enterprises)		
None	26.6	23.0	45.4	26.1	25.5
Loss of efficiency	3.0	7.4	—	24.6	2.6
Lack of continuity	27.7	28.5	21.4	41.4	27.6
Too costly	23.7	28.0	20.4	9.7	24.3
Demotivates employees	2.7	10.8	3.1	—	2.7
Adversely affects pro- ductivity	1.3	10.8	12.0	—	0.7
Not feasible in our business	20.1	7.1	0.8	—	21.7
No single worker responsible for work	4.8	7.1	1.2	3.0	5.0
Difficult to get two workers equally matched in skills etc.	1.0	1.1	0.4	—	0.4
Wgt'd	39,300	224,600	1,900	100	37,300
(Unwgt'd n)	(348)	(348)	(17)	(9)	(322)

*   Note that, since firms may mention more than one disadvantage, columns may sum to more than 100 per cent.

As in the previous table, columns 3 to 5 of Table 5.6 provide a breakdown of responses classified by the firm's status regarding job sharing activity. It can be seen that those intending to introduce job sharing were much more likely to refer to the loss of efficiency or continuity, while those with actual experience of the system mentioned a wider range of problems, including costs and adverse effects on productivity. The main disadvantages cited by firms which did not intend to bring in job sharing were: lack of continuity; cost; and the unsuitability of job sharing to their specific business.

5.3.5 Government Incentives to Promote the Introduction of Job Sharing

Managements were asked whether they felt that the government could introduce any scheme or initiative that would encourage the firm to introduce or extend (as relevant) job sharing arrangements in their company. A total of 27 per cent of firms answered in the affirmative. Because a higher percentage of larger firms felt that government initiatives could encourage them to make job sharing work arrangements available to employees, the 27 per cent of firms in question employ 39 per cent of relevant private sector employees.

Firms which felt that the government could act in this area were asked to outline what types of schemes or incentives it could introduce. On the whole, it was found that the responses given tended to be extremely broad and generic. A number of the inducements mentioned did not seem to be specifically related to job sharing and corresponded to the sort of answers given to general questions about what the government could or should do to help industry. Thus, for example, a reduction in employers' PRSI headed the list of support mechanisms (mentioned by 40 per cent of firms which felt that the government could introduce some incentives in this field). A total of 17 per cent said 'general support' from the government and 9 per cent said 'less bureaucracy'. Issues which seem to be specifically oriented towards job sharing included general financial support for training (mentioned by 17 per cent of firms) and changes in the tax and social welfare codes to favour part-time workers (cited by 8 and 9 per cent of firms respectively).

5.4 EMPLOYEES' EXPERIENCE AND PERCEPTIONS OF JOB SHARING

In this section the emphasis turns to employees' experiences and perceptions of job sharing. Issues considered include incidence and coverage of job sharing schemes; employees' views on its advantages and disadvantages, as well as potential demand for this working time arrangement.

5.4.1 Incidence and Coverage of Job Sharing Schemes

A total of 24 per cent of employees said that the job sharing option was available to them. This figure can be compared with the response from the management questionnaire when adjusted by the combined enterprise/employee weight which suggested that 31 per cent of the relevant private sector labour force worked in companies which offered job sharing facilities to staff. Much of the 7 percentage point difference between the two estimates may be the result of ignorance on the part of employees regarding the availability of work sharing in their firm.

The number of employees sampled who worked on a job sharing basis was very small indeed. Only 11 out of the 759 private sector employees who were successfully interviewed were working on this basis. It is not, therefore, feasible to present any weighted estimates relating to all job sharing employees. Instead, some of the characteristics of the 11 job sharers who successfully completed the employee questionnaire are described as an illustration of the situation of those currently working on this basis.

All of the 11 job sharers who were interviewed were female. A total of five were in the age range 26–35 years; two were 36–45 years; three were aged 46–55 years and one was aged 55 years or more. The majority of the job sharers were employed in a clerical capacity (six out of the 11) while a further four were manual workers and one was in a managerial grade. A total of seven worked on a split-week basis; two on a week-on/week-off basis and the remaining two on the basis of a morning/afternoon split. When asked why they had taken up job sharing arrangements, four said that they had done so for family reasons; three mentioned 'the nature of the business'; two felt that they had no option; one cited health reasons and the final job sharer said that she was 'tired of full-time work'. In terms of previous work experience, six of the job sharers interviewed said that they had worked full-time (either in their current job or elsewhere) immediately before taking up the job share option.

5.4.2 Employee Views on Advantages and Disadvantages of Job Sharing

All employees were asked about their views on the advantages and disadvantages of job sharing. The information on *advantages* is presented in Table 5.7 below. This classifies responses in terms of gender, age cohort and occupational grade. From this it can be seen that a total of 24 per cent of all employees said that they could see no advantages to work sharing. The most frequently mentioned advantage was 'time off for family' (mentioned by 46 per cent), followed by 'time off for leisure' (mentioned by 21 per cent) and 'job creation' (13 per cent).

Table 5.7: Employee Perception of the Advantages of Job Sharing, Classified by Gender, Age and Occupational Grade

	Sex		Age Cohorts					Total
	Male	Female	<25 yrs.	26–35 yrs.	36–45 yrs.	46–55 yrs.	56+ yrs.	
	(Per Cent)		(Per Cent)					
None	30.7	11.3	28.3	9.4	31.7	44.4	52.4	24.3
Time off for leisure	23.4	14.6	23.7	29.0	12.4	6.1	14.2	20.5
Time off for family	34.9	68.2	38.5	54.2	44.5	39.7	22.3	45.9
Time off for study	1.0	4.5	3.5	3.0	0.3	0.8	3.2	2.7
Allows one to maintain a good income	0.9	1.9	1.0	0.6	2.1	0.8	3.2	2.1
Creates jobs	13.3	11.3	10.8	14.4	13.8	6.4	9.3	12.6
Net hourly pay is higher	0.8	1.6	0.3	1.0	2.2	0.0	0.0	1.1
Other benefits to employee*	2.1	6.9	4.1	3.5	5.7	0.8	0.0	3.7
Other benefits to employers**	5.4	4.7	1.6	6.3	5.1	6.2	3.8	5.2

*   e.g., 'less stress' 'more content' etc.
**   e.g., 'better productivity' 'greater flexibility' etc.

A breakdown by gender shows that males are much more likely than females to see no advantage to job sharing work arrangements (31 per cent compared with 11 per cent). Males are also more likely to stress the advantage of 'time off for leisure' than are females (23 per cent compared with 15 per cent respectively). In contrast, females are twice as likely as males to mention 'time off for family' (with 68 per cent and 35 per cent respectively). Both sexes seem to be equally of the view that job sharing can create jobs (13 per cent of males cite this as an advantage compared with 11 per cent of females).

The second section of Table 5.7 looks at the perceived *advantages* of job sharing classified by employee's stage in the life cycle.

From this it can be seen that, as would be expected, 'time off for family' was most often mentioned by employees in the 26–35-year and 36–45-year cohorts. 'Time off for leisure' was most often mentioned by people in the 16–25-year and 26–35-year age categories.

Information on employees' views on the *disadvantages* of job sharing are presented in Table 5.8. From this it can be seen that a total of 13 per cent of respondents said that they could see no disadvantage to job sharing schemes. By far the most frequently mentioned disadvantage was 'lower pay' (cited by 54 per cent of employees). This was followed by 'break in continuity of work' (18 per cent) and problems relating to the sharing of a job — mostly communications problems which were mentioned by 17 per cent of respondents. Just over 9 per cent of employees mentioned the potentially damaging effect that job sharing might have on their career development. Perhaps surprisingly, only a relatively small percentage of employees mentioned potential problems with either pension or social welfare entitlements (1.4 per cent and 0.5 per cent respectively).

Table 5.8: Employee Perception of the Disadvantages of Job Sharing, Classified by Gender and Age

	Sex		Age Cohorts					Total
	Male	Female	<25 yrs.	26–35 yrs.	36–45 yrs.	46–55 yrs.	56+ yrs.	
	(Per Cent)		(Per Cent)					
None	10.7	16.2	15.7	9.8	17.6	4.5	13.3	12.6
Lower Pay	58.1	44.5	26.3	27.8	49.3	42.4	51.9	53.6
Work load would increase	1.8	3.6	3.6	2.4	2.1	2.9	0.0	2.4
Poor career development	9.7	8.3	8.0	14.0	4.6	3.3	8.4	9.2
Less job satisfaction	2.3	1.1	1.0	0.7	4.6	1.8	0.0	1.8
Breaks continuity of work	17.5	19.5	16.6	16.5	21.0	15.8	25.4	18.0
Affects pension	1.7	0.7	0.8	0.7	3.1	0.0	1.8	1.4
Problems with sharing my job	13.8	22.5	8.6	12.3	22.6	36.7	11.8	16.8
Would affect SW entitlements	0.7	0.0	0.0	0.2	1.1	0.9	0.4	0.5
Other disadvantages to employee	4.2	2.2	2.9	2.2	3.3	11.2	3.3	3.6
Other disadvantages to employer	1.8	2.5	1.3	2.6	1.5	3.5	0.0	2.1

When the responses were broken down by gender, it was clear that, in general, there were few substantial differences between male and female attitudes to the disadvantages of job sharing. Females, on the whole, seemed to hold a slightly more positive attitude than males to this form of work arrangement, with 16 per cent saying that they could see no disadvantage to it compared with 11 per cent of their male counterparts. Females were also apparently less concerned than males about the impact of job sharing on their pay (44 per cent of females mentioned this as a problem compared with 58 per cent of males). Finally, female workers seemed to see more communications and related problems with job sharing than did male employees (23 per cent compared with 14 per cent).

The breakdown of responses by age category indicates that lower pay seems to be of greatest concern to people in the 26–35-year age category, where financial commitments are likely to be heaviest. Poorer career prospects were also identified by a substantially above-average percentage of respondents in this age category.

5.4.3 Potential Demand for Job Sharing Arrangements

In an attempt to measure the potential demand for job sharing, employees were asked whether or not they would like to work on this basis. If so, information was recorded on their main reason for wanting to job share; as well as whether or not it would be financially feasible for them to do so. The responses to these questions are presented in Table 5.9.

From this it can be seen that 18 per cent of respondents said that they would like to job share. This option is clearly favoured by a substantially larger percentage of females than males (36 per cent compared with 10 per cent). Although 18 per cent of employees said that they would like to do so, many may find that this would not be financially feasible. Indeed, only 43 per cent of those who said that they would be interested in this working time arrangement felt that they could afford to choose it as an option. This means that a total of 7.5 per cent of employees said that they would like to work on a job sharing basis *and* could afford to do so. As can be seen from Table 5.9, the imposition of a financial consideration substantially increases the male/female differential. Only 2 per cent of males said that they were interested in job sharing *and* could afford to avail of it. The comparable figure for females was 20 per cent.

Table 5.9: Potential Demand, Financial Feasibility and Motivation for Job Sharing Among Employees, Classified by Gender

		Males	Females	Total
		(Per Cent)		
(i)	Would you like to Job share?			
	Yes	9.6	35.6	17.6
	No	90.4	64.4	82.4
(ii)	Would you like _and_ could you afford to job share?			
	Yes	2.0	19.9	7.5
	No	98.0	80.1	92.5
(iii)	Main reason why employee would like to job share			
	Family commitments	15.0	61.2	44.1
	Want more time off work	45.5	15.7	26.8
	Educational/Training opportunity	6.6	5.0	5.6
	To take another job	7.3	13.4	11.2
	Reduce work stress	14.9	2.4	7.0

The primary motivation for wanting to job share is family commitments (44 per cent), followed by a general desire to take more time off work (27 per cent). It is noteworthy that more than one in 10 of those who expressed an interest in job sharing mentioned taking another job as the main reason for wanting to do so. In general, family commitments were mentioned more frequently by females than males (61 per cent and 15 per cent respectively). The same was true of a desire to take another job (which was mentioned by 13 per cent of females and 7 per cent of males. On the whole, males who wanted to job share said that their primary motivation for doing so was that they 'wanted more time off work'.

5.4.4 Resistance to Job Sharing by Employees

Respondents who said that they were not interested in working on a job sharing basis were presented with five pre-coded reasons and asked to state which was their main reason for not wanting to do so. The responses are classified by gender in Table 5.10. From this it can be seen that 39 per cent of relevant respondents expressed a simple preference for full-time work. A total of 35 per cent were discouraged because of the loss of take-home pay. A further 19 per cent felt that their particular job would not lend itself to job sharing. It is noteworthy that only 2 per cent of those who said that they would not be interested in job sharing mentioned a deterioration in terms or conditions of employment as being their main reason for a lack of interest in the job sharing option. It can be seen from the figures that the main gender differential relates to a preference for working full-time. A total of 48 per cent of females who were not interested in job sharing cited this as their main reason, compared with only 36 per cent of males.

Table 5.10: Main Reason Given by Those who Do Not Want to Job Share

Main Reason Given for Not Wanting to Job Share:	Males	Females	Total
	(Per Cent)		
Prefer full-time work	36.3	48.5	39.3
Loss of take-home pay	34.5	34.4	34.5
Deterioration in terms or conditions	2.3	0.4	1.8
My job would not be suitable	19.5	15.6	18.6
Other	7.4	1.1	5.9

5.5 JOB SHARING IN THE IRISH PUBLIC SECTOR — THE MANAGEMENT VIEW

In this section the experience of job sharing in the relevant public sector is considered from the managements' perspective. Issues covered include prevalence and nature of job sharing as well as managements' views on its advantages and disadvantages.

5.5.1 Prevalence and Nature of Job Sharing

Job sharing appears to be much more prevalent in the public sector than in the private sector. The survey found that some 79 per cent of organisations (accounting for well over 90 per cent of relevant public sector employment) reported that they offered at least some of their employees the opportunity of working on a job sharing basis.

Using the survey responses an estimate could be made of the number of job sharers in the relevant public sector. This is broken down in Table 5.11, by gender and grade of employee. Although the figures are based on a small sample[5] they none the less emphasise two points. First, job sharers account for a much higher proportion of total employment in the public than in the private sector. It was

---

[5]   Because these estimates are based on interviews with only 59 public sector organisations they will obviously be subject to wide margins of error.

estimated in Section 5.3.1 above that there are approximately 5,300 job sharers in the relevant private sector with its total workforce of just over 0.5 million. In contrast, Table 5.11 shows that the estimated number of job sharers in the relevant public sector is of the order 6,500 in a workforce of approximately 200,000.

Table 5.11: Estimated Number and Breakdown of Employees Who Work on a Job Sharing Basis in the Relevant Public Sector

	Male	*Female*	*Total*
Total Number	30	6,525	6,555
	(Per Cent of Total)		
Higher/Administrative/Executive	0.3	56.8	57.1
Clerical	0.0	40.1	40.2
Other Routine Grades	0.0	2.7	2.7
Total	0.4	99.6	100.0

Secondly, only a trivial percentage of jobs sharers in the relevant public sector are male. This is in marked contrast to the situation in the private sector where it was found that up to 26 per cent of job sharing employees were male. It should further be noted that less than 3 per cent of relevant public sector job sharers come from other routine grades. A total of 57 per cent come from the higher administrative/executive grades and 40 per cent from clerical grades.

When account is taken of those sectors of the public sector not included in our survey sample (for example, the gardaí, defence forces, central civil service and teachers) it is estimated, on the basis of information available from other sources, that total job sharing in the public sector as a whole is of the order of 8,000.

Job sharing appears to be much longer established in the public sector than in the private sector. Over 20 per cent of the relevant public sector organisations which offered employees the opportunity to share jobs said that this had been introduced prior to 1985. This compared with the private sector experience of only 2 per cent of firms which offered such arrangements before the mid-1980s. A total of 65 per cent of the organisations which offered job sharing said that it had been introduced in response to public policy, while about 20 per cent said that it had been introduced in response to requests from employees.

As shown by Table 5.12, almost all job sharing in the relevant public sector appears to be on either a split week or week-on/week-off basis (54 per cent and 40 per cent respectively. As can be seen from the table, this contrasts quite substantially with the situation in the private sector where split days (mornings/afternoons) or other forms of sharing arrangements assume a greater significance.

Table 5.12: Estimated Proportions of Employees in the Public and Private Sectors Working on Different Types of Job Sharing Bases

Basis of Job Sharing	Private Sector	Public Sector
Split week	67.2	53.5
Week on/week off	4.4	40.2
Mornings/afternoons	13.8	5.6
Other basis	14.6	0.7
Total	100.0	100.0

Slightly higher proportions of public sector organisations than of commercial ones felt that job sharing had led to an increase in the number of employees (69 per cent as compared with 61 per cent in the private sector). The public sector organisations felt that about 2,500 extra jobs had been created by work sharing. This compared with 1,200 among relevant private sector companies.

As in the private sector, practically all employees who job shared enjoyed the same terms and conditions as full-time employees with respect to leave; tenure; training and development; and retirement benefits and pensions. There was, however, something of a divergence between the sectors in respect of promotion. As was shown above (Table 5.3), some 96 per cent of private sector job sharers were reported by their employers as enjoying the same promotional opportunities as full-time employees. This contrasts with 83 per cent of employees in the public sector organisations interviewed. In general, however, persons involved in job sharing cannot be regarded as suffering from substantially more disadvantageous terms and conditions than their counterparts.

Of the relatively small number of relevant public sector organisations not now offering some form of job sharing, most had not seriously considered it and few intended to introduce it.

5.5.2 Advantages and Disadvantages of Job Sharing — Public sector Management

Section A of Table 5.13 provides a comparison of the advantages of job sharing as perceived by management in both private and relevant public sector organisations. From this it can be seen that public sector organisations are less likely than commercial bodies to say that there are no advantages to job sharing (40 per cent as compared with 75 per cent respectively). Among the main advantages cited were: retention of experienced employees (16 per cent); improved productivity (13 per cent); lower absenteeism (10 per cent) and greater flexibility (10 per cent).

Table 5.13: Advantages and Disadvantages of Job Sharing as Perceived By Private and Public Sector Management

Section A			Section B		
Advantages	Private Sector	Public Sector	**Disadvantages**	Private Sector	Public Sector
	(Per Cent)			(Per Cent)	
None	74.5	39.8	None	20.6	13.3
Retains experience which would other wise be lost	3.3	15.7	Loss of efficiency	3.0	3.8
Allows balancing of employer and employee needs	4.5	7.3	Lack of continuity	27.7	62.3
Employees more productive	3.9	13.1	Too costly	23.7	23.0
Less sick leave, absenteeism etc.	3.4	10.2	Demotivates employees	1.3	0.0
Improves motivation	6.7	16.0	Adversely affects productivity	1.3	0.0
Reduces cost	3.1	1.7	Not feasible in our business	4.8	2.9
Creates employment	4.6	7.1	No single workers responsible for the work	4.8	3.3
Greater flexibility	1.8	10.2	Difficult to get two workers equally matched in skills, etc.	1.0	3.1

Note: Because firms/organisations could mention more than one advantage/ disadvantage, column totals may add to more than 100 per cent.

Section B of the table compares managements' views on the disadvantages of job sharing. It can be seen that relevant public sector bodies were less likely than their private sector counterparts to see no disadvantages in job sharing. It could be speculated that this might possibly be the result of the greater experience of job sharing among relevant public sector organisations. It is clear from the table that the most frequently mentioned difficulties were associated with ensuring continuity of work (62 per cent) and the costs involved in job sharing (23 per cent).

5.6 EMPLOYEES' PERCEPTIONS OF JOB SHARING — THE PUBLIC SECTOR

In this section, two main aspects of the views and experience of public sector employees as regards job sharing are considered. First, the incidence of job sharing is looked at, as well as perceived advantages and disadvantages. Secondly, demand for job sharing in the public sector is considered together with the reasons underlying this demand.

5.6.1 Views and Experience of Job Sharing — Public Sector Employees

The effective sample of 270 public sector employees contained interviews with only 17 respondents who worked on a job sharing basis. It is not possible to provide weighted estimates for the totality of public sector job sharers based on such a very small sample. As for the private sector, a few of the main characteristics of the 17 individuals in question will instead be described to serve as an illustration of the situation of those currently working on a job sharing basis in the public sector.

All the job sharers interviewed in the survey were female. In general, the age profile was quite similar to that found among job sharers in the private sector. Of the 17 public sector employees in question, eight were aged 26–35 years; eight were aged 36–45 years and one was aged 46–55 years. A total of seven were in the higher administrative/executive grades, eight were in the clerical grades and two were in the other routine grades. In terms of motivation for job sharing, 14 mentioned family commitments, one said that she had no other job option and two gave 'other personal reasons'.

Table 5.14 provides information on the advantages and disadvantages of job sharing as seen by employees in both the public and private sectors. From Section A of the table it can be seen that almost a quarter of private sector employees said that they could see no advantages to work sharing. This contrasts with a figure of 6 per cent for the public sector. In terms of actual advantages mentioned, it can be seen that the greatest sectoral contrasts relate to 'time off for family'. This was mentioned by over 80 per cent of public sector workers, compared with 46 per cent of private sector employees. In general, there is little sectoral difference in terms of responses relating to perceived disadvantages of job sharing. The data suggest that public sector employees are less concerned about the effects that job sharing may have on pay than are their private sector counterparts.

Table 5.14: Advantages and Disadvantages of Job Sharing as Perceived By Private and Public Sector Employees

Section A			Section B		
Advantages	*Private Sector*	*Public Sector*	**Disadvantages**	*Private Sector*	*Public Sector*
	(Per Cent)			(Per Cent)	
None	24.3	5.9	None	12.6	15.9
Time off for leisure	20.5	13.8	Lower pay	53.5	40.1
Time off for family	45.9	81.8	Work load would increase	2.4	1.5
Allows one to maintain a good income	1.2	2.0	Poor career development	9.2	16.6
Creates jobs	12.6	13.8	Less job satisfaction	1.9	4.3
Net hourly pay is higher	1.1	0.9	Breaks continuity of work	18.2	10.8
Other benefits to employee*	3.7	11.0	Problems with sharing my job	16.7	27.7
Other benefits to employer**	5.2	7.8	Would affect SW entitlements	0.5	2.2
			Other disadvantage to employee	3.5	4.1
			Other disadvantage to jobs	2.0	7.9

*   Includes 'less stress', 'more content', etc.
** Includes 'greater flexibility', 'better productivity' etc.

5.6.2 Potential Demand for Job Sharing in the Public Sector

When asked whether or not they would be interested in job sharing, a total of 17.4 per cent answered in the affirmative. As shown in Table 5.9 above, the comparable private sector figure was 17.6

per cent. Although in aggregate terms employee interest in job sharing is the same in both sectors, it is noteworthy that the differential between the responses of males and females was much less marked in the public sector. A total of 15 per cent of males and 19 per cent of female employees in the public sector expressed an interest in job sharing. Comparable figures for private sector employees were 10 per cent and 36 per cent respectively.

When the 17 per cent of the public sector employees who said that they would like to work on a job sharing basis were asked whether they could afford to do so, 35 per cent replied that they could. This means that a total of 6 per cent said that they would like *and* could afford to change to working on a job sharing basis. When presented with six pre-coded options from which respondents were asked to select the main reason they had for wanting to work on a job sharing basis, the most frequently mentioned reason was simply 'wanted more time off work'; (said by 32 per cent to be the main reason why they would wanted to job share). This was followed by 'family commitments' (28 per cent); 'to engage in further education or training' (15 per cent); 'to reduce work-related stress' (13 per cent) and 'to take another job' (3 per cent). The remaining 8 per cent cited 'other' reasons as their main motivation for wanting to take on a job sharing option.

5.7 SUMMARY

This chapter examined a wide range of topics relating to job sharing, from the perspective of both management and employees, and also in respect of both the public and private sectors. Issues addressed included the incidence of job sharing options offered by firms; estimates of the number of employees availing of job sharing options at the time of interview; perceptions of the advantages of job sharing; the potential (from both demand- and supply-side perspectives) for extending job sharing schemes and the effect of job sharing on career development.

In terms of incidence, it was shown that only about 5 per cent of private sector companies operated job sharing schemes at the time of interview. Because such options were more commonly available in larger firms, the companies offering such facilities account for approximately a third of the private sector workforce. The incidence of such schemes among relevant public sector organisations is much higher. A total of 70 per cent of organisations (accounting for well over 90 per cent of relevant public sector employees) offer some employees the opportunity to work on a job sharing basis.

Estimates of the actual numbers of employees involved in job sharing suggested that approximately 8,000 people are involved throughout the entire public sector, and a further 5,300 in the private sector. This latter accounts for about 1 per cent of the relevant private sector workforce.

In the private sector, a total of 26 per cent of job sharers are male. The gender differentials in the public sector, however, are much more marked, where almost all job sharers are female.

In terms of managements' perception of the advantages of job sharing, it was shown that 75 per cent of private sector companies saw no advantages. A considerably lower percentage of relevant public sector organisations said that they could see no advantages. Among the main advantages cited by management were the retention of experienced employees who would otherwise be lost; improved productivity; lower absenteeism and greater flexibility. In general, public sector organisations were more likely to mention disadvantages than were private sector firms. A total of 13 per cent of public sector organisations (compared with 21 per cent of private companies) said that they could see no disadvantages in job sharing. By far the most frequently mentioned difficulty was the problem of ensuring continuity when staff involved were changing (mentioned by 62 per cent of respondents). The other main disadvantages mentioned related to the costs involved (cited by approximately a quarter of both public and private sector bodies).

In view of the particularly small percentage of the workforce currently working on a job share basis, it can justifiably be asked what the scope would be for extending this work option and how well proposals for such an extension would be received by both employers and employees. A total of 27 per cent of private sector firms (accounting for approximately 66,000 workers) which currently operate job sharing said that they intended to extend it. On the whole, larger firms in all sectors seemed more interested than smaller ones in extending job sharing options. The supply-side prospect for extending job sharing among companies which did not operate it at the time of interview was not so optimistic. Just under 3 per cent of such firms (accounting for only 9 per cent of relevant employees) said that they intended to introduce job sharing at some time in the future.

On the demand side, just over 17 per cent of both public and private sector employees said that they would like to job share at some time. It is noteworthy, however, that gender differentials in responses were less marked in the public sector than among those in private companies. A total of 15 per cent of male and 19 per cent of female employees in the public sector expressed an interest in job sharing. Comparable figures in the private sector were 10 per cent and 36 per cent respectively. When financial constraints were introduced into the question, it was found that approximately 5–6 per cent of employees in both sectors said that they would like to job share *and* could afford to do so.

Finally, of particular importance was the potential effect that working on a job sharing basis could have on the career development prospects of employees in question. It was found that, in general, as regards the conditions of employment in both the public and private sectors, the job sharer did not appear to be disadvantaged in career terms relative to full-time workers. Although job sharers in smaller firms may have been at a slight disadvantage, the data seem to suggest that job sharers as a whole could not be viewed as a marginalised segment of the workforce, offered poorer terms and conditions of employment than full-time workers.

CHAPTER 6

TRADING JOBS: EARLY RETIREMENT

6.1 ISSUES

Blyton (1985) claims that, for a variety of reasons, retirement is a key issue in working time patterns. There has been a decrease in retirement age, while, at the same time, life expectancy has been increasing and older age-groups are becoming more active. Retirement is also viewed as a major transition in life, with attendant contradictory experiences ranging from depression to relief. There are economic costs to the individual as well as the society, especially where there are significant drops in income for the individual and high dependency ratios, as in Ireland's case. Drèze (1985) believes that early retirement is one of the simplest forms of work sharing to operate, in that it does not impact on the organisation of work in the same way that other methods do. The notion of choice is considered to be important in most early retirement schemes, as is the inclusion of compensatory incentives such as supplementing of income and the retention of pension rights. For early retirement schemes to have an effect on unemployment levels there must be a replacement policy. Blyton (1985) highlights the difference between public and private schemes, whereby the former tend to emphasise job replacement, while the latter emphasise reductions in the workforce. In addition, there is considerable variation in retirement ages in the countries researched. In the Scandinavian countries, retirement ages are higher than in the EU generally. In the US, compulsory retirement age is 70, while it is 55 in Japan. In many countries there is a difference between male and female retirement ages, with women retiring earlier than men. A number of countries have promoted early retirement policies and these are examined below.

6.2 THE INTERNATIONAL EXPERIENCE WITH EARLY RETIREMENT SCHEMES

6.2.1 Country by Country Details

Belgium

In 1987, the number of people on early retirement pensions in Belgium was 197,247 (De Rongé and Molitor, 1991). The age for eligibility was 60 for men and 55 for women. There was mandatory replacement by unemployed individuals under 30 years of age. A replacement rate of 83 per cent has been quoted (Drèze, 1985). Once more, those affected were laid-off workers. The age was later reduced to 58, and in some cases firms in economic difficulties could lower it to 50. This system has been widely availed of since its introduction and has resulted in a number of significant outcomes. The Belgian rate of participation of the over 55s is the lowest in the EU. This has resulted in the loss of older expertise in favour of younger people. The scheme has also been expensive for both the state and employers, who subsidise the scheme. A further problem is that there is a widespread feeling that the scheme does not meet the needs of employers or employees on it. There is also an 'ageism' which has developed in the world of work.

To combat some of these issues, more flexible and phased approaches, whereby early retirement was be phased in, were tried in 1985. However, even these have proven to be unsuccessful, as the benefits were considered too low. A more recent initiative, (European Industrial Relations Review, 1993c) has tried to combine the two approaches, involving phased early retirement and part-time working, with support from the state and employers. This scheme has a replacement condition where unemployed job-seekers are to be recruited.

Britain

In Britain, the Job Release Scheme (JRS) was introduced in 1977. It was a voluntary retirement scheme and included mandatory replacement with an unemployed person. A replacement had to be found for the same job, or for a job arising indirectly from the voluntary retirement. Men aged 64, women aged 59 and disabled men aged 60 were eligible. Between 1976 and 1984, 272,100 participated in the scheme, with a replacement rate of 92 per cent. According to Metcalf (1982), the JRS has the lowest cost in terms of cost per job created, at approximately £1,650 in 1985 prices (after adjusting for savings in unemployment benefits). Government evaluations (Department of Employment, 1980) indicated that the majority of applicants were from semi-skilled and unskilled, lower income groups with no access to company pension schemes. Therefore, it can be assumed that the replacements were recruited from these groupings also. Blyton (1985) asserts that the age limit plus the relatively low payment rates restricted its take-up. If these factors had been addressed, he claims, more would have availed of the scheme.

Another method for reducing official unemployment is to include the older unemployed among the retired category. Regulations for including unemployed older men changed in 1983, with the result that 160,000 men were removed from the unemployment register, reclassified as retired, and received pensions instead of unemployment benefit, and were no longer required to sign on (Blyton, 1985). According to Roche (1991), rather than resulting from the need to create additional employment, the growth of early retirement schemes in Britain had its origins in the development of 'internal' labour markets and formed part of employee fringe-benefit programmes. Thus, they tended to occur in administrative and managerial grades and in certain types of industry and in the public sector. A study carried out in manufacturing companies (White, 1980) found that nearly a third of the respondents used early retirement as a means of reducing labour. Indeed, voluntary retirement programmes are considered as 'soft' options when considering reducing labour, and in some cases are in fact redundancies by another term. Older employees may prefer the label 'retired' to 'unemployed'. Inducements such as lump sums, retained pension rights and other benefits are often incorporated into early retirement schemes. Schemes for gradual retirement are other forms of innovative measures used to ease people gradually out of the workforce.

Denmark

In Denmark, the Voluntary Early Retirement Pay Scheme (VERPS) was introduced in 1979 and had a higher than expected take-up. Under the scheme, workers over 60 years of age were entitled to an early retirement wage until they reached retirement age.

France

In 1972, the first early retirement scheme was established in France. This was the result of a tripartite agreement between the unions, employers and the government. The measure was a response to the need to lay off workers. All workers to be laid off who were over 60 years could benefit. The benefit entailed receiving 70 per cent of their wages up to the official retirement age of 65. This scheme was expanded in 1977 to include all involuntary and voluntary resignations at 60 years of age. Manufacturing sectors which adopted these schemes included those experiencing difficulties during the 1970s, such as the coal and steel industries. For instance, in the steel industry, workers can 'retire' at 56 and receive augmented unemployment benefit until 60, early retirement benefit until 65, and pension thereafter.

In 1982, the 'Contrats de Solidarité' stipulated that retirees must be replaced by new workers on a one-to-one basis. Estimates have been made of its beneficiaries in its two years of operation (Jallade, 1991; Marchand, 1984). According to Marchand, nearly 700,000 people benefited in one way or another from early retirement schemes: 180,000 through the 'Contrats de Solidarité', with up to 95 per cent replacement rates, while the previous retirement schemes involved almost 520,000 people retiring (these however, were not replaced). In addition, Jallade concluded that 330,000 'potential' early retirees had been identified under the replacement scheme, while the number who effectively retired at the end of the period was 210,000, most of whom were replaced. In fact, Jallade asserts, by the end of 1983, 60 per cent of all workers over 60 years of age had effectively retired under one guise or another.

One of the most significant features of the take-up of early retirement programmes was the attraction of the benefits package. When, in 1982, the benefits were reduced somewhat, the take-up tapered off. Employers were also motivated to sign up under the 'Contrats de Solidarité', even though they had to replace older workers with younger workers who were considered to be more flexible and less costly. One survey carried out with employers involved in the scheme (Galand et al., 1984) found that firms became involved not because they were in difficulties, but because they required more flexibility. Hence the needs of the flexible firm were satisfied through early retirement with replacement. This is an interesting finding for a number of reasons. First, there is a perception among employers that older employees are less flexible and more resistant to changes and redeployment policies. Secondly, and the corollary of the first reason, is that younger employees are more adaptable and more open to change. Thirdly, at a time of change, where rapid response and flexible operations are required in order to maintain competitiveness, this approach seems to be workable, certainly from the employer perspective. Finally, the contracts were agreed between employer and union organisations, which further facilitated their implementation.

One of the downsides to this scheme in terms of employment generation is that upwards of 50 per cent of those replaced did not come from the ranks of the unemployed but from new entrants to the labour market. Nonetheless, the contribution to reducing unemployment is still significant in that unemployment figures were prevented from rising even higher, through capturing new entrants who might otherwise have become unemployed (Jallade, 1991). Another feature is that the costs of the scheme were largely borne by the state, which, in effect, subsidised employment through the payment of benefits. Eventually the cost became so great that, by 1983, 50 per cent of state unemployment benefit was going towards early retirement payments. As a result, the French government discontinued the scheme in 1983. Ultimately, Jallade questions the widespread effectiveness of early retirement schemes. Valuable human resources and skills can be lost and, in situations without replacement, those left behind to do the work may become overburdened, while, at the same time, a large cohort can be without work.

Germany, Greece and Luxembourg

National schemes in Germany, Greece and Luxembourg allow workers to retire at 60. The schemes have been introduced with the intention of dealing with youth unemployment. At the time of writing, there is little evidence of their impact on employment.

United States

By contrast, in the US, the growing lobby of older people (for example, 'The Gray Panthers') has led to the opposite effect. In 1978, an amendment to the Age Discrimination in Employment Act of 1967 allowed for workers in firms of 20 or more employees to retain employment up to the age of 70. There is no maximum compulsory retirement age for federal employees.

6.2.2 Conclusion: Early Retirement

Early retirement schemes have been designed with different agendas in relation to employment. The first is in response to the reduced demand for labour. These schemes allow for reduced supply through shedding jobs of older workers and allowing older workers to opt for early retirement as opposed to lay-off or redundancy in many cases. Firms in difficulty or firms seeking flexibility have tended to use this option. By re-designating those laid off as retired, the spin-off effect is to retain unemployment levels, while reducing employment levels. In this scenario there is usually no replacement of workers, and while there may be in a minority of cases, replacement is generally not mandatory. Therefore, these schemes contribute little to reducing current unemployment levels, although they may retain current levels through redefining those as retired.

The second approach is in response to high levels of unemployment. Here, there is usually state intervention and union agreement. Retirees are replaced by either full-time or part-time young unemployed. Estimates vary on the impact of these schemes in terms of their overall effect on unemployment levels, and there is little information on their longer-term impact. Moreover, most of the schemes outlined involved high subvention costs, the effect of which is also difficult to measure in the longer term. An additional view is that even with replacement, there may be no net increase in jobs, but rather a redistribution of existing jobs.

Drèze (1985: 28) raises a number of pertinent questions as to the use of early retirement:

1. What proportion of the effectively eligible population has joined programmes of early retirement, and how has that proportion varied with age, with sex, with qualifications or occupations and with income-maintenance provisions of the programmes? It is to be hoped that there is enough variation in the provisions, both across countries and within countries across specific groups, to throw some light on this issue.

2. What is the net impact of early retirement programmes on labour supply, taking into account natural attrition of the labour force in the relevant age groups?

3. What is the net impact of these programmes on employment taking into account normal replacement ratios at the time of normal retirement? (This is a much more problematic calculation, requiring new micro data on replacements).

4. How are the answers to questions 1. and 3. affected by mandatory replacement provisions?

5. What are the budgetary costs of alternative programmes?

He concludes from examining the British, French and Belgian experiences that mandatory replacement is crucial to job creation and that the reduction in the supply of workers under contract is substantial.

Further issues relevant to early retirement practices concern the wider social and economic implications. These in turn relate more closely to life-style concerns and questions of choice and flexibility. For instance, will older people become more demanding, as in the US, or will they readily accept lowering of retirement ages? What will be the impact on society of larger numbers of old people, out of the workforce and dependent on pensions of one sort or another? What will be lost to employers in terms of experience? What quality of life will prevail in the longer term and how can the easing out of employment be managed without producing just another disadvantaged group economically and socially? What are the equality implications, not only between women and men, but also between the young and the older worker?

6.3 THE IRISH EXPERIENCE OF EARLY RETIREMENT — THE PRIVATE SECTOR MANAGEMENT VIEW

This section considers the responses given by management to questions on early retirement. There are three subsections as follows: first, the extent of early retirement is considered, and whether firms believe that it has the potential to generate employment. Secondly, the perceived advantages and disadvantages of early retirement schemes are examined. Thirdly, there is an examination of whether companies which do not currently operate an early retirement scheme feel that the government could introduce some incentive or inducement to encourage them to do so.

6.3.1 Extent and Perceived Advantages/Disadvantages of Early Retirement Schemes

Section A of Table 6.1 presents information on enterprises classified by whether or not they offer special arrangements for early or phased retirement. From this it can be seen that a total of only 6 per cent of companies provide this sort of facility for their employees. The rates are highest in the larger enterprises in each of the three sectors — 35 per cent in the larger manufacturing/ building sector; 18 per cent in the larger distribution services sector; and 27 per cent among larger non-distributive firms.

Table 6.1: Enterprises Classified by Whether or Not They Offer Special Arrangements for Early Retirement or Phased Retirement — (A) Weighted by Enterprise Weight Only; (B) Weighted by Combined Enterprise / Employee Weight

Offer Special Arrangements?	Manuf. / Bld		Distributive Services		Non-Distributive Services		Total All Enter-prises
	< 100 Emps.	100+ Emps.	< 20 Emps.	20+ Emps.	< 20 Emps.	20+ Emps.	
Section A: Adjusted by Enterprise Weight	*(Per Cent of Enterprises)*						
Yes	8.1	35.0	5.5	18.2	2.5	27.3	6.2
No	91.9	65.0	94.5	81.8	97.5	72.7	93.8
Total	100.0	100.0	100.0	100.0	100.0	100.0	100.0
Weighted N	7,000	500	17,500	900	12,400	1,000	39,300
Section B: Adjusted by Enterprise/Employee Weight							
Working in Companies Offering Early Retirement	6.6	43.4	1.0	19.2	1.7	28.1	38.1
(Unweighted N)	(75)	(64)	(52)	(44)	(69)	(44)	(348)

In Section B of the table, the focus changes from the enterprise to the employee. This section presents information on enterprises reweighted in line with their total number of employees. From this it can be seen that a total of 38 per cent of the private sector workforce is employed in companies which offer these arrangements.[1] Trends in the percentage of the workforce covered by early retirement arrangements are very similar to those apparent

---

[1]   The disparity between the percentage of firms on the one hand and employees on the other reflects the higher than average propensity among larger firms to offer these arrangements to their workforce.

for the enterprises level as outlined in Section A of the table. Thus, for example, 43 per cent of those working in larger manufacturing/ building enterprises can avail of those facilities, as can 19 per cent of those in the larger distributive services sector and 28 per cent in the larger non-distributive services sector.

Those firms which do not currently offer any early or phased retirement arrangements were asked whether they felt that their introduction had the potential for employing new staff whom they would not otherwise employ. The results are shown in Table 6.2.

Table 6.2: Enterprises Which Do Not Currently Offer Early Retirement Arrangements, Classified by Whether or Not They Think that the Introduction of an Early retirement Scheme has the Potential for Employing New Staff Whom They Would not Otherwise Employ

Do Not Offer Special Arrangements?	Manuf. / Bld		Distributive Services		Non-Distributive Services			
	< 100 Emps.	100+ Emps.	< 20 Emps.	20+ Emps.	< 20 Emps.	20+ Emps.	Total All Enterprises	Total, Weighted by Employment
	(Per Cent of Enterprises)							(Per Cent Employees)
Yes	23.7	48.3	10.7	44.4	16.8	37.5	16.5	31.1
No	76.3	51.7	89.3	55.6	83.2	62.5	83.5	68.9
Total	100.0	100.0	100.0	100.0	100.0	100.0	100.0	100.0
Weighted N	6,300	300	16,500	700	12,100	700	36,700	(338,100)
(Unweighted N)	(67)	(40)	(50)	(36)	(67)	(32)	(292)	(292)

From this it can be seen that a total of 16 per cent of firms which do not currently offer such schemes felt that their introduction had the potential for employing new staff. This view was held on an above-average basis by larger enterprises in each of the three sectors. Column 8 of the table shows that just under a third of the private sector workforce was accounted for by the 16 per cent of firms in question.

Managements' perceptions of the advantages of early retirement are examined in Table 6.3. From this it can be seen that exactly two-thirds of companies felt that it had no advantages, while a further 8 per cent felt that it had no relevance to their particular firm because of the age of people on their staff — their employees were too young. This was the view of much higher percentages of smaller firms in each of the three sectors. Almost exactly two-thirds of *smaller* companies in each sector felt that early retirement schemes offered no advantages for their companies. Only two definitive responses occurred with any significant degree of regularity. These were 'assists manpower planning' (20 per cent of firms) and 'allows new ideas/young blood' to be introduced into the company (6 per cent of companies).

Table 6.3: Percentage of Enterprises in Each Size / Sector Category, Classified by the Advantages (if any) of an Early Retirement Scheme in their Company

Advantages of Early Retirement Scheme	Manuf. / Bld		Distributive Services		Non-Distributive Services			
	< 100 Emps.	100+ Emps.	< 20 Emps.	20+ Emps.	< 20 Emps.	20+ Emps.	Total All Enterprises	Total, Weighted by Employment
								(Per Cent Employees)
	(Per Cent of Enterprises)							
None	65.2	31.8	69.3	36.6	67.5	36.4	66.1	34.9
N.A./staff too young	12.8	6.6	8.0	4.5	7.8	6.8	8.3	3.8
Allows new ideas/ young blood	3.9	23.1	5.5	15.9	5.3	22.7	6.2	31.0
Assists manpower planning	16.2	31.8	15.8	38.6	22.2	43.2	19.6	42.4
Facilitates employees	1.0	5.0	1.3	2.3	1.7	0.0	1.4	0.0
Other	3.7	16.5	0.0	13.6	1.2	6.8	1.5	9.8
Total	102.8	114.8	100.0	111.5	105.7	115.9	103.1	121.9
Weighted N	3,800	400	17,500	900	12,400	1,000	36,100	551,800
(Unweighted N)	(72)	(64)	(52)	(44)	(69)	(44)	(345)	(345)

Note: This table is based on an open-ended question in which respondents were given the opportunity to express their views spontaneously on the advantages (if any) of an early retirement scheme in their company. Because multiple responses were possible, the column totals are in excess of 100 per cent. The table is based on all enterprises (i.e., both those that currently operate an early retirement scheme and those that do not).

In terms of employees, it can be seen from column 8 of the table that 35 per cent of the workforce is employed in companies which feel that there is no advantage to early or phased retirement schemes. A total of 42 per cent of employees work in businesses which feel that such schemes assist in manpower planning, while a total of 31 per cent work in companies which cited 'new ideas/ young blood' as an advantage of these schemes.

In contrast to the advantages of early retirement schemes, Table 6.4 provides information on managements' perceptions of the *disadvantages* of such schemes. From this it can be seen that just over 60 per cent of firms felt that there were no disadvantages to such schemes, while 9 per cent felt that they were not applicable to their company because of the age profile of their workforce (i.e., 'staff too young'). Of the other reasons mentioned, the most frequently occurring were associated with loss of experienced staff and related retraining costs (mentioned by 25 per cent of firms). The issue of funding early retirement schemes was raised by 7 per cent of enterprises.

Table 6.4: Percentage of Enterprises in Each Size / Sector Category Classified by the Disadvantages (if any) of an Early Retirement Scheme in their Company

Disadvantages of Early Retirement Scheme	Manuf. / Bld		Distributive Services		Non-Distributive Services			
	< 100 Emps.	100+ Emps.	< 20 Emps.	20+ Emps.	< 20 Emps.	20+ Emps.	Total, All Enterprises	Total, Weighted by Employment
	(Per Cent of Enterprises)							*(Per Cent Employees)*
None	50.7	34.4	68.3	46.5	56.1	34.9	60.4	44.8
N.A./Staff too young	15.5	3.4	5.3	4.7	13.1	4.7	9.0	5.0
Too expensive to fund	6.8	27.6	7.1	11.6	5.0	14.0	6.9	21.1
Lose experienced staff/retraining costs	30.7	38.0	22.2	41.9	24.4	44.2	25.2	31.7
Other	1.0	5.1	0.0	0.0	1.4	2.3	0.7	2.2
Total	104.7	108.5	102.9	104.7	100.0	100.1	102.2	104.8
Weighted N	3,800	400	16,800	900	11,300	1,000	34,200	540,202
(Unweighted N)	(71)	(62)	(50)	(43)	(63)	(43)	(332)	(332)

Note: See footnote to Table 6.3.

The final column of the table shows that when considered in terms of employees, just under 45 per cent worked in companies which said that there were no advantages to an early or phased retirement scheme. Just under a third were employed in companies which mentioned the problems associated with the loss of experienced staff and related training costs of replacements, while 21 per cent worked in companies which mentioned that such schemes were too expensive to fund.

An interesting aspect of management views on early retirement schemes is the extent to which firms felt that there were neither advantages nor disadvantages to such schemes. A total of 42 per cent of all companies said that such schemes had neither any advantages nor any disadvantages. The incidence of this apparent indifference to early retirement schemes seems to be higher among smaller than larger enterprises in each of the three sectors. For example, 25 per cent of firms in the smaller manufacturing/building sector felt that there were neither advantages nor disadvantages to such schemes, compared to 10 per cent of their larger counterparts. Comparable figures for the distributive services sector are 54 per cent and 23 per cent; and 39 per cent compared with 20 per cent for the non-distributive sector.

6.3.2 The Potential for Government Intervention in Early Retirement Schemes

In the course of the management questionnaire, firms which did not at the time operate an early retirement scheme were asked whether they felt that the government could introduce any incentive which would encourage them to introduce one into their company. Firms responses to this question are presented in Table 6.5.

Table 6.5: Enterprises Which Do Not Currently Operate an Early Retirement Scheme, Classified by Whether They Believe that the Government Could Introduce Some Scheme or Incentive to Encourage Them to Introduce One into Their Company

	Manuf. / Bld		*Distributive Services*		*Non-Distributive Services*			
	< 100 Emps.	*100+ Emps.*	*< 20 Emps.*	*20+ Emps.*	*< 20 Emps.*	*20+ Emps.*	*Total, All Enterprises*	*Total, Weighted by Employment*
	(Per Cent of Enterprises)							*(Per Cent Employees)*
Yes	33.1	61.4	38.0	58.3	30.4	62.5	35.8	54.5
No	66.9	38.6	62.0	41.7	69.6	37.5	64.2	45.5
Total	100.0	100.0	100.0	100.0	100.0	100.0	100.0	100.0
Weighted N	6,200	300	16,500	700	11,900	700	36,500	335,100
(Unw'd N)	(65)	(41)	(50)	(36)	(66)	(32)	(290)	(290)

From this it can be seen that just over a third of enterprises (36 per cent) felt that government intervention in this area would be feasible. The table shows that this view was systematically held by a higher percentage of large than small firms across the three broad sectors. Between 58 and 62 per cent of large firms felt that the government could introduce some such incentive(s). This trend contrasts with 30–38 per cent of smaller firms which considered that direct government intervention in this field was not a realistic proposition.

Those firms which believed that the government could offer incentives to encourage enterprises to provide early retirement facilities to their staff were asked to specify what form such incentives should take. From Table 6.6 it can be seen that just over a third of firms (34 per cent) mentioned cutting tax on pension payments and retirement lump sums.

This view was expressed by a greater percentage of small than large firms in the manufacturing/building and distributive services sectors. Approximately 30 per cent of both large and small companies in the non-distributive sector cited this as an example of possible government intervention in this area. A third of firms also mentioned subsidising pension schemes or some form of financial grant to the employer to offer early retirement schemes. The only other points raised by a substantial number of enterprises was a reduction in the State retirement age — mentioned by management in 15 per cent of firms; an improvement in State pension provision — cited by 10 per cent of firms; and tax relief for employer and employee contributions to pension schemes (mentioned by 7 per cent of firms).[2] It is clear that there is a strong compensatory element in most of the interventions suggested by managements (reduction in tax premiums; subsidisation of schemes; tax relief for contributions to schemes etc.). These obviously have substantial implications for tax receipts and social welfare payments.

---

[2] The fairly substantial percentage of firms which believe that the government could help to encourage early retirement by cutting tax on pension payments and retirement lump sums seems a little strange given that lump sums are already exempt from tax, and pensions are taxed in the same way as other income. The fact that around 15 per cent of firms in the non-distributive services sector suggested tax relief on pension schemes is surprising since employer and employee contributions to pension schemes benefit from favourable tax arrangements. It may be that many of these firms do not provide pension schemes for their employees, and consequently are not familiar with the relevant tax arrangements.

Table 6.6: Government Schemes/Incentives Suggested by Enterprises Not Currently Offering Early Retirement Which Feel that the Government Could Encourage Such Programmes by Offering Schemes or Incentives

Suggested Government Schemes/Incentives	Manuf./Bld		Distributive Services		Non-Distributive Services			
	< 100 Emps.	100+ Emps.	< 20 Emps.	20+ Emps.	< 20 Emps.	20+ Emps.	Total, All Enterprises	Total, Weighted by Employment
	(Per Cent of Enterprises)							(Per Cent Employees)
Provide training grants	12.7	4.2	9.9	4.8	4.4	10.0	8.4	4.8
Cut tax on pension/ retirement lump sums	25.2	16.7	43.2	23.8	29.4	30.0	34.2	20.3
Subsidise pension schemes/grants to employer to offer early retirement	30.7	33.3	33.3	42.9	36.8	5.0	33.2	21.1
Cut State retirement age to 60 years	26.0	45.8	9.1	23.8	14.7	25.0	15.5	28.3
Tax relief for employer and employee contribution to pension schemes	0.0	4.2	4.5	0.0	14.7	15.0	7.1	21.3
Improve state pensions	5.3	8.3	9.9	14.3	10.3	20.0	9.8	11.1
Total	100.0	112.5	109.9	109.6	110.3	105.0	108.2	106.9
Weighted N	1,900	200	4,900	400	3,500	500	11,400	167,000
(Unweighted N)	(22)	(24)	(15)	(21)	(20)	(20)	(122)	(122)

6.4 THE EMPLOYEES' EXPERIENCE OF EARLY RETIREMENT

In this section, the employees' views and experience of early retirement are considered. Issues discussed include an estimate of the numbers who might seriously consider this as an option at some stage; the extent to which demand and supply for early retirement are matched in the workplace; and future work intentions of those who would be interested in early retirement.

6.4.1 Demand and Supply of Early Retirement Among Private Sector Workers

In the course of the employee questionnaire, respondents were asked the direct question: 'Would you yourself be seriously interested in taking early retirement at some stage?' The responses are outlined in Table 6.7. From this it can be seen that a total of 68 per cent replied in the affirmative.

Table 6.7: Employees Classified by Whether They Might Seriously be Interested in Taking Early Retirement at Some Stage (Table is based on All *Responding Employees, Irrespective of Whether or Not Management in the Firm in Which they Currently Work Actually Offer Early / Phased Retirement Arrangements)*

	Early Retirement Some Time?			Weighted N	(Unweighted N)
	Yes	No	Total		
	(Per Cent of Employees)				
Gender					
Male	69.8	30.2	100.0	371,000	(399)
Female	63.2	36.8	100.0	182,400	(358)
Employee's Age					
0–25 years	45.9	54.1	100.0	87,000	(170)
26–35 years	72.6	27.4	100.0	228,000	(282)
36–45 years	77.3	22.7	100.0	153,000	(192)
46–55 years	69.5	30.5	100.0	55,000	(76)
56+ years	39.5	60.5	100.0	30,000	(37)
Total	67.6	32.4	100.0	553,000	(757)

The most interesting employee characteristic to consider in this context is age. It can be seen that employees in the three central age cohorts (26–55 years) had the highest probabilities of considering early retirement at the same future date — 73 per cent; 77 per cent; and 69 per cent respectively. The percentage expressing an interest in this option falls to 39 per cent for the 56+ age category. This may, at least in part, reflect the fact that for some in this age group retirement may no longer be perceived as being 'early'.

When disaggregated by occupational grade (not shown in the table), it would appear that the percentages of employees in the managerial/professional grades (78 per cent) who express an interest in early retirement at some stage in the future are slightly higher than the percentages of their counterparts in either the other clerical (63 per cent) or manual (61 per cent) grades who express an interest.

At least two important points should be made in regard to the interpretation of these figures. First, as noted in several sections throughout this report, it is dangerous and could be potentially misleading to infer actual future behaviour from hypothetical scenarios such as that reported in Table 6.7 on employees' future intentions regarding early retirement schemes. The most that can be said is that respondents in the older age-cohorts presented in Table 6.7 are probably in a better position to provide a meaningful focus on the realities of early retirement than are their counterparts in the three younger cohorts reported. Secondly, Table 6.7 is based on *all* respondents so as to give an overview of future potential for this form of job sharing.[3] It does not take account of the extent to which demand and supply are equated in the labour market. Even if full replacement could be assumed, the employment impact of early retirement schemes would be substantially limited if all of those who would at some stage aspire to taking early retirement were employed in enterprises which did not offer any such arrangement to staff. Table 6.8 attempts to quantify the degree to which supply and potential demand are matched in the marketplace.

Table 6.8: Employees Who Might Seriously be Interested in Taking Early Retirement at Some Stage, Classified According to Whether or Not Such Arrangements are Offered in the Company in Which They Currently Work

Management Offers of Early Retirement	Employee's Age Cohort					Total
	<25 yrs	26–35 yrs	36–45 yrs	46–55 yrs	56+ yrs	
	(Per Cent)					
Yes	5.0	49.9	30.5	39.0	49.6	41.0
No	95.0	50.1	69.5	61.0	50.4	59.0
Total	100.0	100.0	100.0	100.0	100.0	100.0

This table classifies those employees in each age cohort who said that they might be seriously interested in taking early retirement at some stage according to whether or not they currently work in

---

[3]   This, of course, presupposes replacement among those who take early retirement.

a company that offers such arrangements.[4] From the results it can be seen, in aggregate terms, that a total of 41 per cent of employees who felt that they might at some stage like to take early retirement actually worked in organisations which provided such facilities to staff. It is obvious from the table that there is a considerable degree of variation in this figure across the age cohorts. For example, only 5 per cent of those aged 25 years or less who answered the early retirement question in the affirmative actually work in companies that offer some form of early retirement arrangements. This may reflect a 'young company syndrome' where the age profile of staff is such that management does not yet offer early retirement arrangements. Tables 6.3 and 6.4 showed, for example, that approximately 9 per cent of enterprises effectively disqualified themselves from answering questions relating to the advantages or disadvantages of early retirement on the grounds that the question was not applicable to them in view of the age profile of their staff.[5] The importance of this group in the context of a discussion of the employment-generation potential of early retirement schemes is obviously limited, and in this respect whether the percentage for the youngest age cohort is a 'young company syndrome' or not is largely of academic interest. It can be seen from the table, however, that only 39 per cent of those in the 46–55-year age category who express the view that they might possibly in the future consider an early retirement option actually work in companies offering such an arrangement. This is possibly the prime age cohort for take-up of early retirement schemes (and hence the age group that has maximum potential for consequent job redistribution). In this regard, it is disconcerting to note that as many as 61 per cent of those who express some interest in early retirement schemes would effectively be prevented from participating in them.

---

[4] Respondents could clearly change jobs prior to retirement. This cannot be controlled for in Table 6.8 and would have most relevance for those in the younger cohorts.

[5] This does not imply that only 9 per cent of companies would be thus defined. It simply says that 9 per cent of companies chose to self-define themselves in this way in relation to questions on advantages/disadvantages of early retirement. In the present discussion, therefore, the 9 per cent should be seen as a lower bound.

6.4.2 Future Work Intentions of Employees Considering Early Retirement

A further aspect of the efficacy of early retirement schemes in the context of potential job creation is the future work intentions (if any) of those who express an interest in taking early retirement. If a large proportion of those who would consider taking early retirement from a long-standing career did so with a view to taking up a subsequent job as an employee, this would inhibit the role that such schemes could play in redistributing current positions in the labour market. To address this issue those employees who said that they would be seriously interested in such an option at some time in the future were asked whether they would consider (a) full-time employment; (b) part-time employment; (c) self-employment; or (d) never working again after taking early retirement. The results are presented in Table 6.9. From this it can be seen that a negligible percentage said that they would like to work on a full-time basis after early retirement. It is noteworthy, however, that as many as 54 per cent would like to undertake part-time work, while 32 per cent would like to work on a self-employed basis. Only 14 per cent (in aggregate) said that they would like never to work again.

Table 6.9: Employees Who Stated that they Would be Seriously Interested at Some Stage in Early Retirement, Classified by Work Intentions on Taking up Early Retirement

	Full-time Employment	Part-time Employment	Self-Employment	Never Work Again	Total	Weighted N
	(Per Cent of Employees)					
Gender						
Males	0.5	50.8	36.5	12.2	100.0	257,700
Females	0.3	59.9	21.1	18.8	100.0	114,400
Employee's Age						
<25 years	0.4	49.1	40.8	9.6	100.0	39,800
26–35 years	0.4	54.8	34.8	10.0	100.0	164,200
36–45 years	0.7	55.6	29.1	14.6	100.0	118,200
46–55 years	0.0	46.1	24.6	29.3	100.0	37,900
56+ years	0.0	55.6	8.3	36.1	100.0	11,900
Total	0.4*	53.6	31.7	14.2	100.0	372,100

* The absolute number of cases opting for 'Full-time Employment' is particularly small.

It can be seen that a higher percentage of males than females consider the self-employment option after early retirement, In contrast, a higher percentage of females than males would consider part-time work (60 per cent compared with 51 per cent respectively). A higher percentage of females would also consider never working again (19 per cent compared with 12 per cent for males).

Variations in post-retirement work intentions classified by age of employee suggest that, as would be expected, the percentage who say that they would never work again increases with age, running from 10 per cent for those aged less than 25 years to 36 per cent for those aged 56 years or more. In focusing on the prime early retirement category, it can be seen that 46 per cent said that they would consider part-time employment, 25 per cent said that they would consider self-employment, while the remaining 29 per cent said that they would never work again.

6.5 EARLY RETIREMENT IN THE IRISH PUBLIC SECTOR

This section changes the focus to consider the experience of early retirement schemes in the public sector. Throughout the section the emphasis will be on a contrast between the experience in the two sectors. In Section 6.5.1, management's perception of early retirement is considered. Issues examined include the incidence of early retirement schemes, as well as their perceived advantages and disadvantages.

6.5.1 Incidence and Perceived Advantages/Disadvantages of Early Retirement Schemes

It was shown in Section 6.3.1 that when the sample of firms was adjusted using an enterprise-based weight, 6 per cent of private sector companies offered early retirement to their employees. The comparable public sector figure is 22 per cent. This suggests that this option is much more prevalent in the public sector. When weighted in proportion to their number of employees, however, it was found that 37.8 per cent of relevant public sector employees worked in organisations which provided this option. The comparable private sector figure is 38.1 per cent. This suggests that, in general, there is little difference in the percentage of each sector's workforce covered by such schemes.

Those organisations which did not offer such schemes to their staff were asked whether their introductions would offer the potential for employing additional staff who would not otherwise be employed. A total of 80 per cent of relevant organisations said that they felt that the introduction of such schemes would offer the possibility of employing more staff. This was in stark contrast to the view held by private sector management for whom the comparable figure was only 31 per cent.

Table 6.10 summarises information on the perceived advantages (if any) of early retirement schemes among public- and private sector companies. It can be seen that two main contrasts are apparent between the sectors. First, management in public sector organisations have a much higher tendency to perceive such schemes as being more advantageous to their organisation than do their private sector counterparts. It is apparent that the percentage of private sector companies which feel that there are no advantages to early retirement schemes is almost three times as great as that for the public sector (35 per cent compared to 12 per cent respectively). Secondly, there is a significant contrast between public and private sectors in the extent to which public sector management mentioned that such schemes facilitated employees. The table shows that just over 20 per cent of organisations mentioned this as an advantage in the public sector, whereas it was not cited by management in private sector enterprises.[6]

Table 6.10: Percentage of Public and Private Sector Organisations/Enterprises Mentioning Various Advantages (if any) of an Early or Phased Retirement Scheme in Their Organisation

	Private Sector	Public Sector
None	34.9	12.0
N.A./staff too young	3.8	0.0
Assists manpower planning/natural wastage	42.4	45.0
Allows new ideas/young blood	31.0	38.8
Facilitates employees	0.0	20.4
Other	9.8	15.3
Total	121.9	131.5

Note: See footnote to Table 6.3. Table based on sample reweighted in proportion to number of employees.

---

[6]   The reader will note from Table 6.3 that when the private sector management survey was weighted by enterprise only (i.e., not accounting for its contribution to total sectoral employment) a small percentage of firms in certain size-sector categories did mention that these schemes would 'facilitate employees'. When weighted in proportion to employment, however, the aggregate estimate goes to zero.

Table 6.11 presents details on the perceived disadvantages (if any) of early retirement schemes among public and private sector organisations/enterprises. The data suggest that managements in 45 per cent of private sector firms said that there were no disadvantages to these schemes. The comparable figure for the public sector was only 28 per cent. This trend counterbalances the substantially lower percentage of relevant public sector organisations (relative to their private sector counterparts) which said that there were no advantages to early retirement schemes (as discussed above in relation to Table 6.10). In general, a larger percentage of organisations in the public sector than in the private sector mentioned the expense of funding such schemes and also problems associated with the loss of experienced staff and consequent retraining costs. A total of 35 per cent and 41 per cent respectively of public sector organisations mentioned these two issues. Comparable figures for the private sector are 21 per cent and 32 per cent.

Table 6.11: Percentage of Public and Private Sector Organisations / Enterprises Mentioning Various Disadvantages (if any) of an Early or Phased Retirement Scheme in Their Organisation

	Private Sector	Public Sector
None	44.8	28.0
N.A./staff too young	5.0	0.0
Too expensive to fund	21.1	35.3
Lose experienced staff/retraining costs	31.7	41.5
Other	2.2	1.2
Total	104.8	106.0

Note: See footnote to Table 6.3.
　　　Table based on sample reweighted in proportion to number of employees.

6.5.2   Employees' Perception of Early Retirement

In the course of the public sector employee questionnaire respondents were asked the direct question: 'Would you yourself be seriously interested in taking early retirement at some stage?' A total of 71 per cent said that they would. The comparable figure for the private sector was 68 per cent. Given the nature of the topic under discussion, it is important to consider how this response varies across age cohort. Table 6.12 provides a comparison of public and private sector responses classified by age of respondent. This shows that there is virtually no difference between private and public sector in the response pattern of the lowest three cohorts. A substantial differential is apparent in the top two categories — being 16 percentage points in the 46–55-year cohort and 10 points in the top age category. The significance of this differential in these two categories (and especially in the 46–55-year cohort) is that this is the prime age group where early retirement schemes could be expected to have potentially greatest impact on employment creation.

At least two points should be noted in respect of the figures in the table. First, as noted in the discussion of Table 6.7 above, the fall in the percentage of respondents in the top age cohort who say that they would be interested in early retirement at some stage may simply reflect the fact that for many of those in this age group, retirement in the future would no longer be perceived as being 'early'. Secondly, it is slightly dangerous to infer actual future behaviour from hypothetical scenarios such as asking respondents whether or not they would realistically be interested in taking early retirement at some stage in the future. For respondents in the younger age cohorts, the financial and other reality of what early retirement could involve may not have been considered in full.

Table 6.12: Percentage of Employees in Public and Private Sector Organisations/Enterprises Who Stated that They Might be Seriously Interested in Taking Early Retirement at Some Stage

Age Cohort	Private Sector	Public Sector
	(Per Cent Saying They Would Be Interested)	
0–25 years	45.9	46.4
26–35 years	72.6	67.6
36–45 years	77.3	78.6
46–55 years	69.5	85.2
56+ years	39.5	49.5
Total All Ages	67.6	71.2

The final aspect of early retirement which was examined is the future work intentions of those who said that they would be seriously interested, at some stage, in availing of an early retirement scheme. The comparative information for both public and private sectors is presented in Table 6.13. Given the nature of the topic under discussion, age-differentiated figures on post-retirement employment intentions are presented, in addition to the aggregate total for each sector. Overall, it can be seen that generally comparable trends are evident in both the public and private sectors.

Table 6.13: Employees in Public and Private Sector Organisations Who Stated that They Would be Seriously Interested in Early Retirement, Classified by Work Intentions on Taking up Retirement.

	Private Sector						Public Sector					
	0–25 yrs	26–35 yrs	36–45 yrs	46–55 yrs	56+ yrs	Total	0–25 yrs	26–35 yrs	36–45 yrs	46–55 yrs	56+ yrs	Total
	(Per Cent of Employees)											
Full-time employment	0.4	0.4	0.7	0.0	0.0	0.4	0.0	0.0	1.7	2.3	0.0	1.1
Part-time employment	49.1	54.8	55.6	46.1	55.6	53.6	92.0	40.9	60.4	40.4	63.0	53.1
Self-employment	40.8	34.8	29.1	24.6	8.3	31.7	0.0	36.1	13.6	12.5	4.9	18.5
Never work again	9.6	10.0	14.6	29.3	36.1	14.2	8.0	22.9	24.4	44.7	32.2	27.3
Total	100	100	100	100	100	100	100	100	100	100	100	100

Only a tiny percentage of workers in each cohort said that they would like to take up full-time employment after availing of an early retirement scheme, whereas 53 per cent would like to take up part-time work. Although there are some differences (in the order of 4–6 percentage points), the percentages in the three oldest cohorts who would like to take up part-time employment are roughly comparable. The percentage of public sector employees who would consider self-employment is considerably less than that of their counterparts in the private sector. From the age-differentiated figures it is clear that the propensity in the public sector to consider self-employment as an option after early retirement is only about half that in the private sector among employees in the top three age cohorts. Finally, the percentage of public sector workers who said that they would 'never work again' after early retirement is substantially higher in the public sector — 27 per cent compared with 14 per cent in the private sector.

6.6 SUMMARY

This chapter considered a range of topics related to early retirement schemes in both the private and public sectors. These included the current availability of such schemes; managements' perceptions of their advantages and disadvantages; potential incentives which private sector companies felt that the government should introduce to encourage them to offer early or phased retirement schemes; an estimate of the additional take-up rate of such schemes; as well as the related post-retirement work intentions of those who said that they would seriously consider early retirement at a future date.

In terms of availability of such schemes, it was found that approximately equal percentages (35 per cent) of both the private and relevant public sector workforce worked in enterprises which offered workers an early or phased retirement option. In general, within the private sector the availability of an early retirement facility was related to firm size, being much more generally available in large firms.

Approximately two-thirds of private sector firms said that they saw no advantages to early retirement schemes, while just over 60 per cent said that they saw no disadvantages. The degree of indifference to such schemes among private sector companies can be gauged, by the fact that 42 per cent said that they saw neither any advantages nor any disadvantages, at least in part, to such schemes.

The percentage of relevant public sector organisations which said that there were no advantages to early retirement schemes for staff was only one-third that of the comparable private sector figure (12 per cent compared with 35 per cent respectively). Having said this, however, managements in a substantially lower percentage of relevant public sector organisations also said that they thought that there were no disadvantages (28 per cent compared with 45 per cent in the private sector). The main disadvantages of these schemes as seen by both the public and private sectors seem to be related to the loss of experienced staff and/or related retraining costs, as well as the cost of funding the schemes themselves. Although both issues were of major concern to both public and private organisations, they were of substantially greater concern to the former than the latter.

In suggesting possible inducements that the government could offer to encourage private sector firms to introduce early retirement schemes, the managements of private companies seemed to rely heavily on various forms of financial and compensatory incentives. These included, for example, the subsidisation of pension schemes; financial grants to employers to offer early or phased retirement schemes to their workers; tax relief on employee schemes; and a reduction in the eligibility age for State pensions.[7] All such suggestions would have implications for tax receipts and social welfare budgets.

In terms of possible take-up rates by employees, it was found that a total of 68 per cent of private sector employees across all age cohorts said that they might seriously consider availing of such an option at some time in the future. A total of 70 per cent of the prime age cohort for which early retirement would be applicable (46–55 years) said that they would seriously consider availing of such an option at a later date. The percentage of relevant public sector employees who stated an interest in early retirement in the future was roughly comparable with that in the private sector (71 per cent compared with 68 per cent). A substantial 15-point difference was apparent, however, in the prime age cohort of 46–55 years (85 per cent in the public sector and 70 per cent in the private sector).

Finally, perhaps the most significant aspect of employees' views and intentions regarding early retirement options is the post-retirement intentions of those who stated that they would be interested in taking up the option at some date in the future. Only 14 per cent of private sector and 27 per cent of relevant public sector workers said that they would wish never to work again after early retirement. Approximately 53 per cent of both relevant public and private sector employees said that they would like to take up part-time employment, while 32 per cent of private and 18 per cent of relevant public sector employees said that they would consider the option of self-employment after early retirement. The net effect on employment opportunities of any employment policy option would clearly depend, inter alia, on replacement ratios. Given the apparent attraction of early retirement for downsizing the workforce, an assumption of a high replacement ratio may well be optimistic. If replacement ratios

---

[7] As noted in footnote 2, the fact that some of the suggested tax incentives are already in place may suggest that many of the firms did not provide pension schemes for their employees and so were not familiar with the related tax arrangements.

were only moderate to low and most early retirees did, in fact, take up some form of part-time work, the net effect could be a shift of a section of the labour-force from one form of employment status to another. This would clearly have an adverse impact on net gains in terms of increased employment opportunities arising from the original early retirement policy.

CHAPTER 7

SABBATICALS AND EXTENDED LEAVE

7.1 THE ISSUES

The literature on extended leave, career breaks and sabbaticals is somewhat limited and does not give a clear picture of the impact of these measures on employment levels. Evans and Massey (1986) divide schemes which provide for substantial periods of leave into three broad categories:

- Sabbaticals as a reward for good service

- Unpaid leave: career re-entry, extended career breaks and leave for educational or other purposes

- 'Banking' leave arrangements.

The international experience of each of these categories in turn is discussed in the next section.

7.2 THE INTERNATIONAL EXPERIENCE

7.2.1 Sabbaticals as a Reward for Good Service

A number of companies have introduced policies of extended paid leave for their employees. Extended periods of leave may be granted, on full pay, to employees who have been in employment for specific lengths of time. They are usually free to spend this leave as they choose. Companies which offer these sabbaticals see them as providing staff with the opportunity to rejuvenate or refresh themselves. An example of such a scheme is The John Lewis Partnership in Britain. About 100 of the company's employees become eligible every year, and in 1984 the scheme cost £300,000 (May, 1985). The scheme was first introduced in 1979 and all partners and employees, including part-time ones, are eligible. They must have completed 25 years of service, and be 50 years of age, to avail of 26 weeks paid leave:

> The opportunity to withdraw for a while from everyday employment without financial disadvantage and with the assurance of return to the same job is something that only the employer can give (Evans and Massey, 1986: 167).

McDonald's also rewards long-serving staff with paid sabbaticals of eight weeks leave after 10 years of service. Another scheme is operated by the BBC for staff with, on average, 15 years service. There are generally no conditions laid down and the leave can be taken for any purpose. Full pay is provided and some additional help towards expenses. Humphreys (1986), in his study of work sharing in the Irish public service, held the view that paid leave of absence is too erratic and irregular to be of relevance to job creation in terms of temporary employment. Certainly in the cases mentioned above, job creation was not a motivator. Personnel practices were of primary concern and other types of issues were to the forefront in managing paid leave, such as releasing senior people for protracted periods of absence and managing the re-entry process.

7.2.2 Unpaid Leave

Other forms of extended leave are more generally unpaid, and therefore may provide some measure of potential for job creation, especially those for prolonged periods in the form of sabbaticals and career breaks.

Britain

In Britain, the banks have been to the forefront in promoting career breaks, mainly oriented towards the care of young children. The National Westminster Bank, in 1981, guaranteed re-entry at the same grade to those members of staff who left under the re-entry scheme, and also provided training on return. A further scheme did not guarantee the job back, but put individuals on a reserve list until an equivalent post became vacant. Both schemes were initially available for a five-year period, which could be extended. Applicants usually had five years service and were expected to work a further 20 years on return.

The Midland Bank introduced a similar scheme in 1985. Its main purpose was to encourage women to return to work. The company also wanted to attract career women into the bank and to utilise its investment in staff training. The scheme was open to both men and women, and up to five years leave could be taken. Contact was encouraged during the absence through attendance for a minimum number of days per annum.

Roche (1991) found that sabbaticals in Britain were much more common in the 'creative' sectors and in administration, journalism, executive management and academia. Their main purpose was to form part of a strategy to refresh and retain the core workforce.

Denmark

In Denmark, an 'Act on Leave for Employees' was passed in 1993. Section 10 of this Act makes provision for parental leave to look after children from birth to 8 years when certain conditions have been fulfilled, namely:

- The employee has worked for one or more employees for at least 120 hours in the last 13 weeks before the start of the leave.

- The employee is entitled to at least 13 and at most 26 weeks.

- Both parents are entitled to the leave; thus, a total length of 52 weeks leave is permitted.

- The employee is not entitled to remuneration from the employer.

- Instead, an allowance of 80 per cent of the maximum allowance for unemployment relief.

Sweden

In Sweden, the opportunities for individual choice and flexibility have been greatly extended through state legislation on extended leave (Weigelt, 1991). The Parental Leave Act is the most widely utilised. Both parents are entitled to leave up until the child is 18 months old and are also allowed to work 75 per cent of their normal working hours until the child is 8 years old. Statistics on take-up rate indicate that the majority of leave is taken by women. Only 27 per cent of married fathers took parental leave and, of those, two-thirds took less than two months. The Education Leave Act allows employees to take leave for extended periods to pursue education. There is no earnings compensation, as there is with the Parental

Leave Act. Labour force surveys in Sweden show that about 1 per cent of employees are on leave because of educational pursuits.

Ireland

The career break scheme for the Irish Civil Service was first introduced in 1984 with two primary objectives:

- To facilitate those who wish to combine a career with domestic and other responsibilities and interests

- To create new employment opportunities by filling vacancies created by those taking a break.

In this programme there was a clearly stated desire to use career breaks to create jobs. Figures for 1986 show that two-thirds of participants were women aged under 30 (Evans and Massey, 1986). It is not clear from the figures what the breakdown of the replacements actually was. In terms of meeting the first objective, the scheme was not entirely successful. About a quarter of those analysed in 1986 gave care of children or other domestic reasons as their reason for applying. The majority travelled abroad and took other jobs.

Thus far, little in the literature indicates the level, if any, to which such extended leave schemes have contributed to employment retention or creation. The potential exists to replace people who are on leave, but the evidence regarding replacement is sparse.

7.2.3 'Banking' Leave Arrangements

'Banking' leave is a procedure where periods of extended leave can be earned by a variety of methods. Peugeot-Citroën in France provide an example of a highly developed form of such a scheme. Points can be accumulated on the basis of attendance, shift work, night work, weekend and bank holiday working or working under special conditions (Tavernier, 1978). Using this system employees can convert points gained into hours that can be banked. In addition, they are encouraged to take the leave as extended leave or early retirement, rather than as longer holiday leave. Rather than contributing to employment, the scheme has resulted in reduced absenteeism and improved production planning. Other similar schemes are in operation in Britain in the BBC, Massey Ferguson, Lucas, Heinz, and the Prudential.

More recently, in Germany, proposals have been made to give employees extended holidays in order to save jobs and cut costs. Herr Rexrodt, the German Economics Minister recently stated:

> There are many other possibilities than just the four-day week. We must also go for the amount of time people work in a year or in their entire life. If we exhaust all the possibilities of more flexible working time, hundreds of thousands of jobs can be saved (Gow, 1993: 4).

In Belgium, the idea of career breaks is not new. Legislation enacted in 1985 allowed workers to take breaks from six months to five years, during which they received state allowances of about £200 per month. In 1993, this legislation was updated to enable easier access by creating an automatic entitlement for selected workers and avoiding the need for collective agreements. Hence workers obtained greater freedom of choice. Furthermore, they are given a degree of protection against dismissal and they must be replaced by an unemployed job seeker if the break exceeds six months in duration.

7.2.4 Conclusion

There appears to be little evidence of job creation taking place as a result of sabbatical or extended leave periods. That does not rule out its role, however, as part of a package of measures designed to retain or extend employment. Nevertheless, the employment effect is quite limited, as Curson and Palmer (1986: 192) have concluded:

> We enquired about extended leave arrangements as a possible means of creating jobs because it had been suggested that they might assist in achieving that result. However very few organisations offer extended leave, and where they do, it is often restricted to certain groups or grades that no conclusions about either costs or job creation can be drawn.

7.3 SABBATICALS AND EXTENDED LEAVE IN THE IRISH PRIVATE SECTOR — MANAGEMENT'S VIEW

This section considers managements' views and perceptions of sabbaticals and extended leave in the private sector main areas. First, the extent to which career breaks are in fact offered to private sector employees is looked at, and an estimate provided of the number of such employees who took a sabbatical or career break over the previous five years. Secondly, there is a discussion of the replacement policy of private sector firms which had staff on sabbatical or career break at some time in the five years preceding the survey. Thirdly, managements' views on the advantages and disadvantages of career breaks are considered, as well as their perception of the reasons for career breaks in their firm over the five years preceding the survey. There is, first of all, a presentation of some information on managements' attitudes to the possibility of offering extended parental leave to their staff.

7.3.1 Current Situation Regarding Career Breaks

Table 7.1 presents details on the extent to which career breaks or sabbaticals are offered to staff by private sector companies. It shows that these are available in just under 10 per cent of firms. The highest percentages of firms offering this option were in the larger manufacturing/building (31 per cent) and larger non-distributive services (36 per cent). When the respondents were weighted in proportion to their total employment it appeared that just over 35 per cent of the private sector workforce was covered by a career break option.[1] At the time of the survey only 2 per cent of firms had any staff members on a career break.

Table 7.1: Whether Firm Offers Sabbaticals or Career Breaks and Whether any Employees are now on Such Breaks

Does Firm Offer Unpaid Career Breaks?	Manuf. / Bld		Distributive Services		Non-Distributive Services		Total, All Enterprises	Total, Weighted by Employment
	< 100 Emps.	100+ Emps.	< 20 Emps.	20+ Emps.	< 20 Emps.	20+ Emps.		
	(Per Cent of Enterprises)							(Per Cent of Employees)
Yes	5.1	31.5	10.8	15.9	6.6	36.4	9.5	35.3
No	94.9	68.5	89.2	84.1	93.4	63.6	90.5	64.7
Weighted (Unweighted N)	7,000 (75)	500 (64)	17,500 (52)	900 (44)	12,400 (69)	1,000 (44)	39,300 (348)	554,600 (348)

---

[1] The disparity between the percentage of firms, on the one hand, and employees, on the other, is a direct reflection of the higher than average propensity among larger firms to offer these arrangements to their workforce.

The relatively small subset of firms (approximately 6 per cent) which had had some staff members on career break at any point in the five years preceding the survey were asked to give a break-down of their grade and gender. From this an estimate can be de-rived of the total number of private sector employees who took an extended break over the period in question. Table 7.2 shows that a total of just over 8,700 persons took a career break in this period. Approximately two-thirds of these were taken by females.

Table 7.2: Estimated Numbers of Employees Who Took Sabbaticals or Career Breaks in the Past Five Years, Classified by Gender and Occupational Grade

	Male	*Female*	*Total*
Total number of breaks	3,075	5,650	8,725
(Per Cent)	(35)	(65)	(100)
	Per Cent		
Professional/managerial	14	12	26
Clerical	5	22	27
Skilled manual	9	2	11
Unskilled manual	8	28	36
Total	35	65	100

Note: Table based only on enterprise weight. In this context it would be technically inappropriate to use a weight based on enterprises in proportion to their number of employees.

It can also be seen that a total of 26 per cent of career breaks were taken by employees in the professional/managerial grades; 27 per cent by clerical workers; 11 per cent by skilled manual workers and the remaining 36 per cent by unskilled manual workers. It is clear from the table that most breaks were accounted for by fe-males in the unskilled manual grade (28 per cent), followed by the clerical grades (22 per cent).

Information on the reasons given by employers for employees wanting to take a career break is presented in Table 7.3, which shows that the main reasons given are related to travel (36 per cent) and family reasons (25 per cent). Only about 7 per cent of breaks were taken to try out self-employment, while a further 7 per cent were taken to try another job. The reader is reminded that the information in Table 7.3 relates to the reasons as per-ceived by the management, rather than by the employee.

Table 7.3: Reasons Given by Management for Career Breaks in the Five Years Preceding the Survey

Reasons Given by Management for Career Breaks	Total	
	Number	*Per Cent*
Education	775	8.9
Travel	3,150	36.0
Self-employment	575	6.6
Other employment	625	7.2
Family reasons	2,225	25.5
Other reasons	1,375	15.8
Total	8,725	100.0

In the course of the management survey, the firms which had staff on sabbatical in the preceding five years were asked how they had dealt with the situation in terms of temporary staff replacements. A total of 70 per cent of the firms in question (which of themselves represented just over 6 per cent of all firms) said that they had replaced none of the employees during their break; a further 7 per cent said that they had replaced some but not all of the employees; and a further 22 per cent had replaced all of the employees who had taken a break. When the firms survey was adjusted in line with the employee/enterprise weight, it is estimated that just under 54 per cent of the employees who took a sabbatical or career break were replaced in their absence.

Finally, firms were asked whether, over the preceding five years, they had to turn down any applications from employees to take an extended, unpaid career break or sabbatical. Among those who offered such breaks, about 9 per cent said that they had turned down at least one application. Among those who did not offer this option to their workforce, only 2 per cent reported having turned down an application. The main reasons given by employers for having turned down applications concerned the fact that a particular employee was essential to the operation of the business or enterprise in question.

7.3.2 Employers' Perceptions of the Advantages and Disadvantages of Career Breaks

Section A of Table 7.4 provides details on managements' perceptions of the *advantages* of career breaks. From this it can be seen that 85 per cent of all firms (accounting for 55 per cent of total private sector employment) felt that career breaks offered no advantages to employers. A higher percentage of smaller than larger firms said that there were no advantages to offering career breaks to employees. For example, it can be seen that in each of the three broad sectoral groups outlined in the table, there is at least a 20 percentage point differential between smaller and larger firms

Table 7.4: Advantages of Career Breaks as Perceived by Employers

	Manuf./Bld		Distributive Services		Non-Distributive Services			
	< 100 Emps.	100+ Emps.	< 20 Emps.	20+ Emps.	< 20 Emps.	20+ Emps.	Total, All Enterprises	Total, Weighted by Employment
	(Per Cent of Enterprises)							(Per Cent of Employees)
A. Advantages of Career Breaks								
None	82.8	63.4	93.5	70.5	78.5	54.5	85.0	54.8
Allows employees to gain experience	10.6	21.1	3.8	15.9	17.7	22.7	10.3	26.5
Removes surplus staff	0.5	3.1	—	4.5	1.3	6.8	0.8	1.6
Improves staff morale	5.1	15.0	2.8	11.4	3.8	13.6	4.1	10.9
Reduces payroll and related costs	1.5	3.1	1.3	—	—	4.5	1.0	9.8
B. Disadvantages of Career Breaks								
None	43.8	11.7	26.9	20.5	26.3	9.3	28.9	20.4
Costs and problems of training temporaries	31.7	51.2	43.8	40.9	25.0	48.8	36.0	38.2
Costs and problems of retraining after break	2.7	12.2	1.3	11.4	11.6	14.0	5.4	19.7
Breaks continuity of employee/client relationship	9.0	17.3	7.8	20.5	25.4	23.3	14.3	14.8
Generally disruptive for firm	15.0	18.2	26.6	15.9	17.2	11.6	18.7	13.4
Imposes additional work on remaining staff	—	—	2.8	2.3	—	2.3	1.4	0.5
Weighted (Unweighted N)	7,000 (75)	500 (64)	17,500 (52)	900 (44)	12,400 (69)	1,000 (44)	39,300 (348)	554,600 (348)

holding the view that career breaks confer no advantages to employers. Foremost among the advantages cited was the belief that career breaks allowed employees to gain experience elsewhere (mentioned by 10 per cent of the enterprises which accounted for 26 per cent of employees); and that career breaks could improve staff morale (cited by 4 per cent of firms, accounting for 11 per cent of employees).

Section B of Table 7.4 presents information on managements' perceptions of the *disadvantages* of the career break option. From this it is apparent that 29 per cent of enterprises (accounting for 20 per cent of the workforce) can see no disadvantages to offering this facility to staff. A higher percentage of smaller than large firms said that there were no disadvantages to the introduction of career breaks. This is especially true of the manufacturing/ building and non-distributive services sectors. Among the main disadvantages cited were: the costs and problems associated with training replacements (mentioned by 36 per cent of firms account- ing for 38 per cent of employees); general disruption to the opera- tion of the firm (mentioned by 19 per cent of enterprises covering 13 per cent of employees); and breaks in the continuity of em- ployee/client relationships (14 per cent of firms, accounting for 15 per cent of the relevant private sector labour force).

7.3.3 Employers' Views on Extended Parental Leave

One aspect of unpaid leave about which information was specifi- cally collected was the extension of maternity leave on the birth of a child. The following question was put to managements to assess their views on the possibility of offering up to two years unpaid maternity leave:

> In some countries employees are allowed to take an extended period of unpaid maternity leave (say, two years) to look after young children. After the unpaid leave the employee is enti- tled to return to the job she left. Would you be in favour of such a scheme being introduced in Ireland?

Managements' responses are outlined in Table 7.5, which shows that over half of the firms (54 per cent) said that they would be in favour of the introduction of such a scheme. The proposal met with more or less equal popularity among larger and smaller firms alike. Consequently, there is little difference in the percent- age of firms answering in the affirmative (54 per cent) when weighted by an enterprise-based weight, and the percentage agreeing when weighted by a firm-based weight which varied in direct proportion to numbers of employees (55 per cent). There is clearly some evidence that the suggestion was rather less well received by the manufacturing/building sector, especially among larger firms, than by the other two sectors.

Table 7.5: Answers to the Question 'Would you Favour an Extension of Unpaid Maternity Leave?'

Would You Favour an Extension of Unpaid Maternity Leave?	Manuf. / Bld		Distributive Services		Non-Distributive Services			
	< 100 Emps.	100+ Emps.	< 20 Emps.	20+ Emps.	< 20 Emps.	20+ Emps.	Total, All Enterprises	Total, Weighted by Employment
	(Per cent of Enterprises)							*(Per Cent of Employees)*
Yes	43.1	36.2	59.8	42.9	53.5	51.2	54.0	55.0
No	56.9	63.8	40.2	57.1	46.5	48.8	46.0	45.0
Total	100.0	100.0	100.0	100.0	100.0	100.0	100.0	100.0
Weighted	7,000	500	17,500	900	12,400	1,000	39,300	554,600
(Unweighted N)	(75)	(64)	(52)	(44)	(69)	(44)	(348)	(348)

7.4 EMPLOYEES' EXPERIENCES AND VIEWS OF CAREER BREAKS AND EXTENDED MATERNITY/PATERNITY LEAVE

The previous section considered the extent of coverage and incidence over the previous five years of unpaid sabbaticals as well as managements' perceptions of their advantages and disadvantages. In this section, the discussion turns to the views and experience of employees as regards career breaks or other forms of unpaid extended leave.

7.4.1 Incidence and Motivation Among Employees for Taking Career Breaks

The private sector employee survey indicated that just over 2 per cent of employees said that they had ever taken a career break. These were all relatively short breaks of between 1 and 9 months in duration. Females had a slightly higher probability of having taken such a break — 2.9 per cent as compared with 1.7 per cent for their male counterparts. The main reasons given for taking the breaks in question were largely classified by respondents as relating to children and family, and other personal reasons. Only one respondent emerged in the course of employee interviews who had ever applied for a career break and been turned down.

In view of this low level of experience of career breaks it is rather remarkable that as many as 27 per cent of employees said that they would like to take such a break, either currently or at some point in the future. The main reasons cited for wanting to take such a break are outlined in Table 7.6, which shows that 'travel' is the most frequently mentioned reason (41 per cent of respondents); followed by 'to try self-employment' (21 per cent); 'to try a new career' (20 per cent); and 'education/training' (16 per cent). Family reasons were mentioned by 10 per cent of employees in aggregate. There was clear evidence of strong differences in male/female responses in two areas, namely, 'to try self-employment' and 'for family reasons'. The former reason was cited by 31 per cent of males as compared with only 1.3 per cent of females, while the latter ('family reasons') was mentioned by only 3 per cent of males and 25 per cent of females.

Table 7.6: Reasons Cited by Employees Who Said That They Would be Interested in Taking an Unpaid Career Break or Sabbatical at the Moment or Some Time in the Foreseeable Future

	Males	Females	Total
	Per Cent		
To travel	39.0	46.5	41.4
For education/training	15.5	18.2	16.4
To try a new career	19.8	20.6	20.0
To relax/'recharge the batteries'	2.1	4.5	2.9
Family reasons	3.1	25.2	10.1
To try self-employment	30.8	1.3	21.4

7.4.2 Employees' Views on Extended Unpaid Parental Leave

In the course of the employee questionnaire, those respondents who had children were asked the following question about parental leave:

Some people say that it would be nice to take an extended period of unpaid maternity (or paternity) leave from work (say, two years) to look after children when they are very young. If you were able to do this, would you be interested in taking this sort of extended, unpaid leave to look after your children, provided you could be guaranteed of getting your job back at the end of this period?

A total of 45 per cent of respondents replied in the affirmative to this question. The percentage of females who said that they would like to take extended unpaid maternity leave (63 per cent) was substantially higher than that of males (39 per cent). Those who expressed an interest were then asked whether they would be able to afford, from a financial point of view, to take such an unpaid break. A total of 5.4 per cent of private sector employees said that they would like to take such a break *and* would be able to afford to do so. This corresponds to approximately 17,700 persons.[2] The aggregate figure of 5.4 per cent of private sector employees who had children and said that they would be in favour of extended unpaid parental leave and could afford to avail of this option marked substantial male/female differences in response outcomes. The percentage of relevant female employees who were in favour and could afford was 17.8 per cent, compared with only 1.5 per cent of their male counterparts.

7.5 EXTENDED LEAVE AND CAREER BREAKS IN THE IRISH PUBLIC SECTOR

This section briefly considers a number of aspects of extended leave as it applies to the relevant public sector organisations included in the survey. Issues examined include the extent and incidence of career breaks, as well as managements' perceptions of their advantages and disadvantages. In addition, the experience of career breaks among public sector employees is looked at, including the motivation for such breaks. Finally, there is a consideration of the potential take-up among public sector employees of an extended period of unpaid parental leave.

---

[2] A total of 59.1 per cent of the grossed sample of 554,600 employees said that they had children and so were asked the question on whether they would be in favour of extended unpaid parental leave. Of this figure, a total of 5.4 per cent said that they would be in favour of *and could afford* to take up such an option.

7.5.1 Incidence of Career Breaks

In section 7.3.1 above it was noted that 9.5 per cent of enterprises (accounting for some 35 per cent of relevant private sector employees) offered the career break option. Further, it was found that only 2 per cent of private sector firms actually had a staff member on such a break at the time of interview. The situation in the public sector contrasted strongly with this experience. A total of 82 per cent of public sector organisations said that this option was available to some of their employees. These 82 per cent of public sector organisations accounted for 89 per cent of relevant employees. Similarly, it was found that a total of that 63 per cent of relevant public sector organisations interviewed said that they had at least one employee on a career break at the time of interview. It is clear, therefore, from these figures that the opportunity to take a career break is much more prevalent among public sector organisations and public sector employees than among their private sector counterparts.

Table 7.7 compares the replacement policy adopted in the public and private sectors. It can be seen that in two-thirds of relevant public sector organisations all employees taking a career break were replaced. This compares with a figure of just over 22 per cent of private sector firms. At the other extreme, it can be seen that in only 5 per cent of public sector organisations were employees on career breaks replaced. The comparable figure for the private sector was 70 per cent.

Table 7.7: How Employers in the Private and Public Sectors Dealt with the Situation of Employees Taking Career Breaks

How Employers Dealt with Career Breaks	Public Sector	Private Sector
	(Percentage of Firms / Organisations)	
Replaced none of the employees	5.3	70.3
Replaced some but not all of employees	26.8	7.4
Replaced all of employees	68.0	22.3
Total	100.0	100.0

7.5.2 Perceived Advantages and Disadvantages of Career Breaks

Table 7.8 presents a comparison of the advantages and disadvantages of the career break option as perceived by public sector managements. This shows that public sector organisations were much more likely to cite advantages in career breaks than were their private sector counterparts (33 per cent of relevant public sector organisations saw no advantages, compared with 85 per cent of private sector firms). It is clear from section A in the table that four main advantages were mentioned on a more frequent basis among the relevant public sector organisations interviewed in the survey, namely: 'allows employees to gain experience' (36 per cent public sector, compared with 10 per cent for the private sector); 'improves staff morale' (19 per cent, compared with 4 per cent); 'allows organisation to retain valued staff' (8 per cent, compared with 0 per cent); and 'allows "new blood"' into the organisation' (10 per cent, compared with 0 per cent).

Table 7.8: Advantages of Career Breaks, as Perceived by Employers in the Public and Private Sectors

	Public Sector	Private Sector
	(Percentage of Firms/Organisations)	
A. Advantages of Career Breaks		
None	33.3	85.0
Allows employees to gain experience	35.8	10.3
Removes surplus staff	0.0	0.8
Improves staff morale	19.2	4.1
Reduces payroll and related costs	0.0	1.0
Allows organisations to retain valued staff	8.0	0.0
Allows 'new blood' into organisation	9.7	0.0
B. Disadvantages of Career Breaks		
None	17.4	28.9
Costs and problems of training temporaries	34.2	36.0
Costs and problems of retraining after break	16.0	5.4
Breaks continuity of employee/client relationship	11.8	14.3
Generally disruptive for firm	9.2	18.7
Imposes additional work on remaining staff	0.0	1.4
Temporary staff have to be let go subsequently	11.0	0.0

From Section B of the table it can be seen that, in terms of disadvantages, a lower percentage of public than private sector organisations feel that there is no disadvantage associated with offering career breaks to staff (17 per cent, compared with 29 per cent).

The main disadvantages cited included: 'costs and problems of training temporary staff' (34 per cent); 'costs and problems of re-training after break' (16 per cent); 'break in the continuity of employee/client relationships' (12 per cent); 'temporary staff have to be let go subsequently' (11 per cent); and 'generally disruptive to the firm/organisation' (9 per cent).

7.6 EMPLOYEES' EXPERIENCE OF CAREER BREAKS IN THE PUBLIC SECTOR

This section deals with the percentage of relevant public sector breaks; the motivation for such breaks; and future intentions and aspirations regarding these unpaid breaks. Finally, there is a discussion of the views of public sector employees on an extension of unpaid parental leave following the birth of a child.

7.6.1 Incidence, Motivation and Intentions Regarding Career Breaks

A total of 12 per cent of public sector employees interviewed said that they had at some stage taken an unpaid career break. This contrasts with the corresponding private sector figure of only 2 per cent. Approximately half of these breaks were reported to be of one year's duration, while a quarter were of less than a year's duration, and the remaining quarter were for more than a year. The main motivation behind the breaks was child care (about 50 per cent), followed by travel and personal reasons (each mentioned by about 15 per cent of respondents). Education, trying a new career and voluntary service were also mentioned by a small number of employees.

When asked about future intentions regarding a career break, a total of 26 per cent of respondents said that they would be interested in taking such a break at some time in the future. This compares with 27 per cent of respondents in the private sector. The main reasons given were: travel (32 per cent); education/training (18 per cent); to try a new career (11 per cent); to relax/'recharge the batteries' (19 per cent) and family reasons (19 per cent).

7.6.2 Extensions of Parental Leave

As with private sector respondents, employees in the public sector survey were asked whether they would be interested in taking some form of extended, unpaid leave for two years to look after children, provided that they could be guaranteed of getting their job back at the end of the period. A total of 56 per cent of the relevant respondents expressed a positive interest in this type of leave, while 27 per cent of those who said that they would be interested also said that it would be financially feasible for them to take such leave. This means that it would appear that such leave would present itself as a viable, realistic option to a sizeable proportion (of the order of 15 per cent) of public sector employees. The reader is reminded that, as discussed in Section 7.4.2 above, the comparable private sector figure was just over 5 per cent.

7.7 SUMMARY

This chapter has examined the incidence of career breaks; managements' perceptions of their advantages and disadvantages; and employees' experience of such breaks. A comparison between the relevant public and private sectors was given from both employers' and employees' perspectives.

It was seen that approximately 10 per cent of private sector companies offer the career break option to their staff, but that only 2 per cent of staff were actually on a break at the time of interview. This contrasts with the situation in the public sector, where approximately 82 per cent of relevant organisations offered the option of career breaks to its staff, and 63 per cent had at least one employee on a break at the time of interview. An estimated total of 8,700 persons had availed of a break in private sector companies during the five years preceding the study. Almost two-thirds of the breaks were taken by females. In terms of replacement ratios, private sector companies replaced 50 per cent of employees on breaks, whereas relevant public sector organisations replaced practically all employees taking such breaks. In general, managements in private sector organisations tended to see fewer advantages to the career break option than did their public sector counterparts. The main advantages cited by both the public and private sectors relate to the extent to which they allow employees to gain experience outside the company and the beneficial effects that they have on workers' morale. The main disadvantages mentioned relate to the costs associated with training of temporary staff and retraining of the permanent staff who take up the career break option. Other issues, such as the break in the continuity of employee/client relationship and the generally disruptive nature of such breaks, were raised on a relatively frequent basis by managements in both the public and private sectors.

The level of interest in such breaks at some time in the future was high among employees in both sectors (26–27 per cent). The main reasons given for this interest included travel; education/training; a chance to relax or 'recharge the batteries'; family reasons; and an opportunity to try a new career.

CHAPTER 8

CONCLUSIONS

8.1 INTRODUCTION

The aim of this chapter is to draw together the main conclusions reached in earlier chapters and to assess the implications of these results for policy. The policy objective of any of the initiatives reviewed is assumed to be to cause an increase in the numbers of currently unemployed persons who find jobs, whether on a full-time or part-time basis. A number of issues need to be addressed in carrying out such an assessment.

In the first place, it must be recalled that a number of the questions asked in the surveys were *hypothetical* in nature. At several points, respondents, both employers and employees, were asked for their preferences or for their predictions about how they would behave in different circumstances. It must always be borne in mind that the answers to such questions may not always reflect what will happen in fact. This can arise not from any inclination on the part of respondents to mislead, but simply from the fact that it is impossible to specify in an interview all the circumstances and changes in conditions that may surround any future situation. Thus, predictions based on responses given in the survey must be made very cautiously.

A second general issue relates to the matching of positions vacated with unemployed persons. The population of unemployed persons has certain defined characteristics in terms of age, sex, skill level and experience. If the jobs created by new initiatives, such as job-splitting or work sharing, do not match the unemployed in terms of skill and experience requirements, then the reduction in unemployment will be less substantial. Therefore, in examining each of the policy areas, an attempt is made to assess the nature of the jobs likely to be created and to comment on the correspondence between these jobs and the characteristics of the unemployed population.

Thirdly, there is the question of who bears the cost of any change in policy. This could be employers (for example, increased administrative burdens arising from work sharing); those currently employed (for example, if desired overtime hours are reduced); or the Exchequer (for example, if a new arrangement results in a substantially lowered tax take). As the different policies are reviewed throughout this chapter, the likely nature and magnitude of the costs involved are commented on.

Fourthly, it is vital to consider the *unintended consequences* which could flow from some of the policies. Prominent among these is the effect on labour supply of an increase in the availability of jobs. It could easily happen that, as the number of jobs on offer increases, new entrants, hitherto classified as 'inactive', might be attracted into the labour market, so that the effect of the policy on the level of unemployment is reduced or nullified. Among the inactive groups from which such new entrants could come are persons in education, retirement or home duties.

The issue of unintended consequences is dealt with in Section 8.4 below, which presents the results of a national survey designed to assess the broad magnitude of these so-called 'displacement' effects. Before turning to this, however, there is a sketch of the overall demographic and labour force context in which future policy is likely to be operating. This is covered in sections 8.2 and 8.3. There follow five sections which review each of the five types of work sharing in turn, from a policy perspective. The final section draws together the recommendations into a set of overall conclusions.

8.2 WORKING TIME AND THE COMPOSITION OF THE WORKFORCE

By focusing on the long-run demographics of the Irish workforce, this section seeks to provide a backdrop against which current and likely future employer and employee attitudes to working time flexibility and work sharing can be understood. By sketching such a backdrop, we may be in a better position to project the medium to long-term prospects for the uptake of the various types of work sharing options considered in earlier chapters. The degree to which a higher level of uptake of flexible working time options leads to increased employment or reduced unemployment, of course, is a separate issue and one that will be taken up in later sections of this chapter.

Significant differences between broad occupational groups emerged in the study in such areas as interest in further time off work, levels of overtime working, job sharing, career breaks and early retirement. Broadly, both the actual uptake of these flexible working time options and positive attitudes towards their uptake are highest among managerial and professional employees, next highest among clerical workers, and lowest among manual workers. This pattern probably reflects different employment priorities rooted primarily in differences in pay, levels of education and different experiences of employment. The pattern is not, however, consistently borne out by the survey findings. For example, while higher occupational groups appear more willing to take a pay cut to gain more time off work, the proportion of managerial and professional employees agreeing that they would like to avail of more time off from their current jobs in lieu of a pay rise is the lowest of all occupational groups.

Assuming that the dominant pattern of attitudes identified in the employee survey continues into the future, the climate towards flexible working time in the workforce is likely to become more positive over the long run, as the proportion of the workforce employed in occupational categories with more positive views continues to rise. Taking a long-term perspective on change in the occupational structure of the workforce reveals in Ireland, as in other industrial societies, a gradual growth in the proportion of the workforce occupied in 'higher' occupational categories — a phenomenon known by sociologists as 'structural mobility'. Thus, in the 1951 census only 5 per cent of working male employees were classified as professionals, managers and salaried employees, compared with just under 17 per cent in the mid-1980s. Other non-manual employees made up about 14 per cent of the male employee workforce in 1951, rising to 22 per cent in 1985. This growth in non-manual occupations, was balanced by an overall decline in manual categories from 34.6 per cent of the male employee workforce in 1951 to 21.8 per cent in 1985. (The latter trend masks a rise in the share of skilled manual workers in the manual occupational category (data derived from Breen et al., 1990: 55).) This trend is set to continue as Ireland moves through a trajectory of structural change familiar to industrial societies. Given this trend — and assuming no major exogenous change in the 'occupational differential' apparent in postures towards flexible working time — the overall incidence of positive attitudes towards availing of flexible working time options seems set to rise.

Public policy to support wider choice in working time options will therefore be working 'with the grain' of socio-economic change in the occupational or skill composition of the workforce.

In the specific instance of overtime working, a pattern is found, whereby non-manual workers are more likely to work overtime on a non-remunerated basis, apparently as a normal feature of administrative, managerial and professional careers in organisations. Clerical workers seem different, however, showing low levels of non-remunerated overtime and significant levels of remunerated overtime. As the proportion of the workforce occupying managerial and supervisory positions continues to rise, it appears likely that for growing numbers of employees, working beyond 'normal hours', without extra pay, will become more common. For these categories of employees, management faces no cost constraints on overtime, and no endogenous constraints are apparent. Indeed, quite the contrary, as organisations lay increasing emphasis on 'commitment', and as managerial careers become more professionalised, the pressures on managers to disregard any distinction between normal and required working time seem set to increase. Ireland may be a long way from the Japanese or North American patterns of executive working time, which involve managers working particularly long hours — comprising high weekly working hours, a near-complete blurring of the distinction between normal and expected working hours and a tendency to pass up holidays — as a normal feature of managerial careers, but the trajectory of change is in this direction. The effects on the health and well-being of manual workers regularly working long hours is often emphasised in support of measures to limit overtime. The same argument applies to non-manual, and particularly to managerial workers, though in this specific context it is less frequently encountered. While the European Union Directive will, however, squeeze the absolute permissible level of overtime working, a derogation is permitted for member states in the case of 'managing executives' or 'other persons with autonomous decision-making powers'.

Among manual and clerical categories, where paid overtime is the norm, recent innovations in standard working time regimes internationally, as considered in the review of experience with overtime working, may presage a significant managerial squeeze on paid overtime working. These themes will be reviewed in more detail in the section below, dealing with the survey results on overtime working.

Changes in the occupational composition of the workforce are related in part to the changing *sectoral composition* of the workforce. Long-run change in this dimension of workforce composition involves the familiar trend towards the growing importance of service industries in the economy (see Breen et al., 1990: 155–8). Judging by current working time preferences, long-run change in the sectoral composition of employment within the private sector will have little decisive impact, either way, on the popularity of flexible working time options. Interest in job sharing, sabbaticals, early retirement, and attitudes to overtime working do not appear to be related in any major way to industrial sector. Significant differences are, however, apparent between the public services and other sectors. The public services emerge as an area in which flexible working time options have considerable appeal and in which, indeed, a number of initiatives were pioneered on a significant scale. A decline in the relative scale of public service employment may thus work against the popularity of flexible working time.

A further dimension of workforce demographics with a more clear-cut bearing on flexible working time is the pattern of long-run change in the gender composition of the workforce. A cohort-analysis of female participation rates by Blackwell (1989: 10–11) shows that for younger cohorts of women there is now a greater tendency to remain in the workforce when peak child-rearing years arrive. Between 1971 and 1991, the percentage of married women participating in the workforce rose from 8.0 per cent to 23.2 per cent; the participation rate for single or widowed women declined from 47 per cent to 41 per cent. Over the same period, the male participation rate also fell. Both these dimensions of change are a reflection primarily of longer spells in education and a growing incidence of earlier retirement. The really important trend, as regards flexible working time, concerns the growing number of married women remaining in the workforce or returning to work after having children. This trend is the outcome of public policy changes which interact with secular changes: the removal of the 'marriage bar' in the public service; the increased earnings potential of women resulting from higher education and equal pay and opportunities legislation; the decline in average family size. In Ireland, these factors in combination are leading to convergence in the labour market behaviour of men and women, although the level of female participation in the workforce still lags well behind the EU average (see Blackwell, 1989: 16).

Given the pronounced gender bias in the popularity of flexible working time options, growth in the numbers of married women opting to remain in the workforce will provide a direct stimulus to the growing popularity of flexible working time options. A separate question is whether the rising labour market participation of married women might also act as a catalyst for change in male working time preferences. The sociologist, Michael Rose (1988), has suggested that this indeed can be expected to occur. As more married women opt to remain in work, working time regimes built up around 'male career norms' come under pressure, and the job and career principles they reflect may be called into question. More opportunities arise for men to avail of flexible working time options, and men may become more inclined to do so, especially men in dual-career families or partnerships (Rose, 1988: 148–51). Judging by the data in the Irish employer and employee surveys, however, women's changing career profiles have yet to have any significant impact on men.

A further relevant dimension of workforce demographics is the pattern of long-run change in the age structure of the working population. Given that either popularity or feasibility of flexible working time options varies by age category, changes in the age structure of the population will alter the relative popularity of different options. Job sharers in the survey, for example were concentrated in the prime age categories of the female workforce, and interest in job sharing was also strongest among employees in this category. Interest in career breaks, on the other hand, is more heavily skewed towards younger age categories, and career break schemes in the Irish civil service have been availed of primarily by employees under 30. Interest in parental leave, on the other hand, is quite evenly spread over employees from working age up to 55 years, so the popularity of this flexible working time option is unlikely to be affected by workforce demographics.

The clear trend in Ireland is towards an ageing workforce. This is likely to depress the popularity of career breaks over time as the proportion of the working population in the younger age categories declines. As the numbers in the prime age categories rise, growing numbers of employees, especially female employees, are likely to want to avail of job sharing. The number of persons in the workforce aged 45–64 years will have grown by 33,000, or 10 per cent, over the period 1981–96, and relative growth in this segment of the workforce is set to continue (NESC, 1993: 70). This trend will lead to a gradual increase in the proportion of the workforce for whom early retirement options may prove both attractive and feasible, especially if the higher popularity of early retirement among younger workers, revealed in the employee survey, reflects a *cohort effect*. There may, of course, be good public policy reasons for not promoting early retirement, but the numbers in a position to countenance retiring early are set to rise as the Irish workforce ages.

8.3 EMPLOYERS AND THE CONFIGURATION OF THE WORKFORCE

To complete this discussion of the future labour market context, this section considers whether broad lines of change evident in employer and management approaches to configuring the workforces of organisations have any bearing on the availability of flexible working time options. As was apparent in the examination of the international evidence on working time in earlier chapters, one of the main concerns animating business strategy over the past decade has been the search for flexibility in its various dimensions. This has involved a growing emphasis on such things as numerical or 'headcount' flexibility, including flexibility in managing working time to match the available supply of labour to variations in product or service demand; a growing emphasis on wage flexibility; and a growing emphasis on the flexible deployment of labour as between jobs and activities, through the removal of demarcations and other restrictions on work organisation. The new management agenda has been linked to such things as the vogue in so-called 'human resource management' and the rising incidence of 'non-standard' work and workers (part-timers, fixed-term contract workers, etc.) Though several of the main theories seeking to identify how these concerns might change the configuration of the workforce in organisations have been heavily criticised, the concerns themselves are well documented in a series of research studies and are likely to remain of major importance.

It has already been outlined how major employers in a number of countries have sought to reduce or eliminate paid overtime, without increasing employment, by making standard working time arrangements more flexible, through flexible rostering arrangements. It has also been indicated how flexible rostering arrangements have been used to absorb recent rounds of reductions in normal working hours in some countries, especially Germany and Britain. Whether the new managerial concern with flexibility will have a benign impact on employer attitudes to flexible working time options is more doubtful. While managers may be seeking to promote higher levels of flexibility in labour utilisation, and may be willing to countenance such things as early retirement, job sharing, career breaks and extended maternity leave, if they provide convenient means of cutting headcount or expanding part-time employment, this appears unlikely to translate into general support for employment-focused, or indeed employee-focused, flexible working time options, such as those considered in the present study. What the surveys indeed reveal is little enthusiasm among employers for job sharing, career breaks, or early retirement. There is a general belief that these schemes carry few commercial benefits and make sense only as ways of responding to employee preferences. In short, the general advocacy of employment-focused and employee-focused flexible working time options cannot be said to be 'going with the grain' of the new management flexibility agenda.

8.4 EFFECTS OF INCREASED JOB OFFERS ON LABOUR SUPPLY

This section considers in more detail the issue of 'unintended consequences' of work sharing initiatives. As explained above, these arise primarily from effects on labour supply of increases in the numbers of jobs available.

8.4.1 The Household Survey

All of the work sharing initiatives which have been reviewed have as their objective the provision of more job offers. The creation of these new opportunities will only lead to an equivalent reduction in unemployment if no new entrants are attracted into the labour force from outside the labour force — that is, from categories of persons who had been classified as 'inactive'. If large numbers of new entrants are attracted into the labour force by any of the policies suggested, this will substantially reduce the effectiveness of the policies. For this reason, the study included an additional piece of data collection to investigate labour supply effects.

Each month, the ESRI and TEAGASC conduct a household survey on behalf of DG II of the European Commission relating to consumer attitudes. The target sample in this survey is a national random sample of 1,000 households. This survey has frequently been used by the ESRI to mount ad hoc surveys of the population on various topics. In the present instance, it was decided to use two rounds of the Consumer Survey (carried out in April and May 1994) to ask some questions about people's desire to take jobs, especially part-time ones, if such jobs became more easily available.

The questionnaire used is shown in the Appendix. It begins by defining the target population for the survey as persons aged between 16 and 60 who are retired or on home duties. The other main category of person outside the labour force is that of 'student'. It was decided to exclude these because of the difficulty of distinguishing between jobs they would get after qualification, jobs held during term, and vacation jobs. Thus, our estimates of labour-supply effects based on the survey data exclude the possibility that some persons might leave education to take up newly available jobs.

The questionnaire went on to obtain some background information on the eligible respondents — their age and sex, whether and when they had a job, their job search activities and their interest in taking up a part-time job. Respondents were then asked how many hours they would like to work and how much they expected to earn if employed. The questionnaire concluded with some questions on social welfare entitlements.

8.4.2 Results of the Survey on Labour Supply

In the two rounds of the Consumer Survey, a total of 1,024 households were contacted, containing an estimated 2,560 persons aged 16 or over. Some 701 of these (27 per cent) were in the target group for this study's survey of economically inactive persons (i.e. aged between 16 and 60 and currently either in retirement or home duties). Extrapolating these figures on a national basis gives a total of just under 700,000 persons who could potentially be attracted back into the labour force by an increase in job availability. The rest of the survey was concerned with estimating how interested these individuals were in a return to work.

Almost all of the persons identified were female (692 out of 701). About 11 per cent said that they had actively tried to find work within the previous three months. This percentage is strongly related to age, with about a quarter of the those under 30 saying that they had sought work, compared with only 6 per cent of those over 50. (See Table 8.1.) Respondents were then asked the following question:

Suppose the government set up some scheme which would make it easier for someone like you to find a part-time job, to do some work on a so-called job sharing or part-time basis. Do you think that you would be *realistically* interested in taking up a part-time job outside the home?

A total of 60 per cent said that they would. Table 8.2 shows that the proportions expressing interest were again higher in the younger age groups, but the relation with age is not quite so marked, as can be seen from Table 8.1. The effect of a number of other variables on respondents' job-seeking behaviour and interest in a part-time job was also examined. It was found that those who had left the labour force within the previous five years were somewhat more likely to be have sought a job or to express interest in part-time employment. Respondents who had left the labour force as a result of redundancy were much more likely to be interested in a job than were those who had left for other reasons (mainly to care for their family).

Table 8.1: Did Respondent Actively Seek Work in the Past Three Months?, Classified by Age

Seek Work in Past Three Months?	Under 30	30–39 years	40–49 years	50 or over	Total
	Percentage of Respondents				
Yes	25.5	16.7	10.1	6.3	88.7
No	74.5	83.3	89.9	93.7	11.3
Total	100.0	100.0	100.0	100.0	100.0

Table 8.2: Did Respondent Express Interest in Part-Time Work?, Classified by Age

Interested in Part-Time Work?	Under 30	30–39 years	40–49 years	50 or over	Total
	Percentage of Respondents				
Yes	68.1	71.8	63.0	47.4	59.8
No	31.9	28.2	37.0	52.6	88.7
Total	100.0	100.0	100.0	100.0	100.0

What types of job are these respondents interested in and do they have a realistic appreciation of the likely wage rates? Table 8.3 shows that over 60 per cent of respondents expressing interest in a job would like what amounts to half-time employment — that is, about 20–24 hours per week. Only about 9 per cent said that they would like a full-time job. The mean expected wage rate seems quite realistic at about £4 per hour.

Table 8.3: Desired Hours and Mean Expected Hourly Rate of Pay, Classified by Age

Desired Hours	Age Group				Total
	Under 30	30–39 years	40–49 years	50 or over	
	Percentage of Respondents				
Under 15 hrs	6.3	6.0	4.7	4.2	5.0
15–19 hrs	18.8	11.1	12.7	14.2	13.1
20–24 hrs	50.0	58.1	59.3	65.8	60.1
25–29 hrs	18.8	12.0	16.0	8.3	12.9
30+ hrs	6.3	12.8	7.3	7.5	8.8
Mean Expected Hourly Pay	£ Per Hour				
Average Pay	4.17	4.31	3.91	3.68	3.97

In summary, then, it can be said that there is a substantial pool of persons, who are predominantly female and not at present classified as unemployed, who express a strong interest in just the sort of jobs that work sharing would make available. To the extent that work sharing measures are successful in creating new opportunities, such persons will undoubtedly be attracted back into the labour force. While it could be argued that this development is desirable in itself, it will certainly reduce the effect of work sharing on measured unemployment.

8.5 THE CONTROL OF OVERTIME

The nub of the issue of whether controls on overtime can lead to job creation without damaging competitiveness or increasing labour costs relates first to the level of overtime working in Ireland and second to the degree to which overtime working is 'endemic' or 'systematic': that is, worked in large measure as a matter of custom and practice, or to meet employee expectations, or largely for reasons of inertia that relate to management not having the will to change or being unwilling to risk changes to existing working arrangements.

The data presented in this study indicate that levels of overtime working in Ireland are indeed high by any standards. A large majority of private sector workers (81 per cent) are employed in companies in which some form of remunerated overtime is under-taken. Some 62 per cent of employees work in companies in which overtime is worked on a regular weekly or daily basis; and 82 per cent of the employees interviewed said that they had worked some form of overtime during the 12 months preceding the survey. Similarly, about 97 per cent of relevant public sector workers are employed in organisations where some remunerated overtime is undertaken. So any public policy changes that seek to change the manner in which overtime is regulated could potentially impact on large numbers of companies and employees.

However, the pattern emerging from a series of questions seeking to establish the rationale and character of overtime working appears to point decisively *against* the view that much overtime working lacks a clear-cut economic or business rationale. In all, 84 per cent of the private sector workforce and 89 per cent of public sector employees are employed in companies which feel that remunerated overtime is necessary if they are to continue in business at current levels of output. Questions probing the reasons why overtime is worked elicited replies which emphasised demand-related factors, like fluctuations in demand and the removal of bottlenecks. Judging from the pattern of management replies, 'inertial' or 'systematic' forces sustaining overtime appear to be of relatively little importance: 'custom and practice', 'providing pay increases for employees' and 'trade union agreements' do not emerge as strong avowed influences on management behaviour for using remunerated overtime. Somewhat ambiguous in this respect, perhaps, are replies indicating that remunerated overtime is worked to 'meet normal demand': over 55 per cent of employees work in companies which thought this either a very important or important factor. When companies are asked to give the single most important reason for remunerated overtime, however, this factor drops sharply in importance, accounting for replies in companies employing an estimated 4.2 per cent of the private sector workforce. The demand-related factors, on the other hand, hold their place as major influences on management behaviour in utilising paid overtime.

Only in the case of the larger organisations among the 13 per cent of private sector companies considering remunerated overtime as not being essential for their continued operation at current levels of output (all such organisations, large and small, account for an estimated 17 per cent of the workforce) is evidence encountered of strong influences exerted by custom and practice or the weight of employee expectations. Though the evidence suggests that this state of affairs may be most pronounced in larger distributive service companies, the relatively small potential public policy impact of measures to combat systematic overtime (at most 17 per cent of the private sector workforce) and the difficulty of targeting the areas concerned pose difficulties for public policy intervention.

The emphasis by employers in both the public and private sectors on the demand related reasons for overtime working points to the economic and business obstacles that are likely to be encountered in most instances by policy measures seeking to tighten the regulation of paid overtime. These obstacles are likely to be more pronounced still because of the ease with which employers appear to be able to find employees 'very willing' or 'willing' to work overtime — even if such a disposition might conceivably be tempered by an apparent willingness on the part of many employees to give up overtime if it helped the unemployed. What is more, overtime working is viewed by a clear majority of manual workers — the group with the highest prevalence of paid overtime working — as important in maintaining their standard of living. The strong perceived taxation disincentive attaching to overtime work clearly does little to reduce the propensity of people to work overtime, nor their reliance on overtime to maintain their standard of living. Furthermore, the international evidence, reviewed in the chapter on the control of overtime, suggests that high overtime premia, set down in legislation, have proven to be of limited effectiveness in controlling employers' willingness to resort to overtime.

If policy measures were to be introduced to curb overtime working with a view to encouraging job creation, the import of the findings on the prospects and likely features of any employment created would bear consideration. If the major rationale for overtime working in companies is to meet fluctuations and bottlenecks in patterns of demand, any jobs created by curbs on overtime are likely to be geared to expanding recruitment during periods of anticipated peaks and bottlenecks. As such, the jobs that might result are likely to be part-time and possibly temporary or seasonal full-time jobs; they are clearly unlikely to be full-time and permanent jobs, as the creation of such jobs would be tantamount to costly labour hoarding in normal production periods or production troughs.

Also, given the limited effectiveness of legislating punitive overtime premia, and the substantial non-paid overtime currently

worked by administrative and professional managers, the imposition of a legal upper limit on working hours would appear to be
the most effective measure for controlling overtime. (Again, it
should be borne in mind that the European Union Working Time
Directive permits member states to derogate from legal limits to
working time in the case of managerial and related workers.) A
legislative approach, based on the promulgation of legal norms in
respect of maximum permissible working time, might follow some
of the European models, considered earlier, by combining the retention of paid overtime up to a given hours ceiling and making
provision for time-off-in-lieu of overtime above that ceiling. The
latter principle has won a measure of acceptance in Irish industrial relations, through SIPTU's involvement in the Shannon
Aerospace annual hours agreement. From the employee survey
results, however, it appears that time-off-in-lieu, whether on its
own or in combination with cash, is not extensively used in the
Irish private sector as a means of compensating employees for
overtime. About 51 per cent of those working overtime in the private sector are compensated by cash payments alone and 31 per
cent (almost all managerial or professional workers) claim to receive no compensation at all. Comparable figures for the public
sector are 35 and 38 per cent respectively.

The dominance of cutting PRSI as a government response
likely to encourage employers to substitute employment for overtime emerges decisively from the survey of employer opinion on
the desirability of possible public policy responses.

Notwithstanding this response, the reduction or elimination of
overtime through the creation of additional employment must
also now be regarded as but one line of response open to companies. Curbs on overtime introduced in order to create jobs could
act as a catalyst for an employer response of a very different kind.
Gaining momentum in recent years internationally is an approach to working time scheduling which seeks to eliminate overtime without creating additional employment by introducing
flexible normal working time regimes. In this line of response the
normal working week or year is defined in terms of the average
hours employees are expected to work at normal rates of pay over
a period of, say, a week, a month or even a year. In any given
period of time, the actual hours people work are allowed to vary
within defined upper and lower limits in order to allow working
hours to respond flexibly in response to fluctuations in demand.
Arrangements of this kind have figured in many collective agree-

ments, reducing normal working hours in the past decade in Britain, Germany and other countries. Examples of such arrangements can be found in Ireland — for example, the 'annual working hours' agreement between Shannon Aerospace and SIPTU — and have figured prominently in recent major disputes, such as that at TEAM Aer Lingus. It seems likely that the inspection effect that arises from managerial experience with such measures, combined with competitive pressures, will dictate that management-initiated, and even public policy-initiated, curbs on overtime will strengthen this line of response to the control of overtime at the expense of an employment-focused response.

8.6 JOB SHARING

Only about 5 per cent of private sector companies offer job sharing arrangements, but these account for a not inconsiderable 31 per cent of the private sector workforce. Over a quarter of companies operating job sharing claim that they intend extending existing schemes; of these, nearly 80 per cent claim that they will employ additional staff as a result. The percentage of organisations in the public sector which offer job sharing is much higher, at 79 per cent.

In the public sector, an estimated 8,000 people job share, while about 5,300 people currently job share in the private sector. The latter accounts for 3 per cent of all those employed in companies that claim to permit job sharing, and about 1 per cent of the private sector workforce. Even allowing that many of those employed in companies offering job sharing may work in jobs for which job sharing is not operationally suitable or available, and that, besides, many employees may be completely disinclined to avail of job sharing arrangements even where available, there nevertheless appears to be significant scope for the further uptake of existing opportunities, if the incentives available — whether to employees, employers or both — were to be increased.

The scope for the further extension of job sharing also emerges from the employee survey, where just under a fifth of all employees expressed an interest in job sharing; and, of these, more than a third also said that they could afford to job share.

What incentives might increase the popularity of job sharing for employers or employees? What must first be noted is that 73 per cent of private sector employers were unable or disinclined to identify any government measures that might induce firms to introduce job sharing. Of the remainder, the only factor mentioned by significant numbers, other than cutting employers' PRSI, was financial support for training. For employees, the tax benefits and net take-home pay benefits accruing from job sharing are already considerable, and it may bear note that only 1 per cent of private sector employees in the survey pointed to the pay advantages associated with job sharing. This might of course mean that they were unaware of such benefits, but it seems better interpreted as indicating that the net pay effects are not of primary importance in attracting employees generally to job share.

The broadly positive attitudes and propensities towards job sharing need to be balanced by other indications from the surveys pointing to constraints of various kinds. First, three-quarters of firms, employing more than half the private sector workforce, saw no advantages to the firm in operating job sharing. On the other hand, over 70 per cent of firms, representing 77 per cent of employees in the private sector, were willing to identify disadvantages. Second, firms not operating job sharing were categoric that they did not intend doing so. Such a negative perception of job sharing is interesting in the light of international research findings which point at least to the potential for substantial benefits for the employer, as well as some disadvantages, of course. Assuming that these benefits can be attained in practice in Irish business circumstances, and given the small proportion of firms which operate job sharing and are in a position to endorse the advantages accruing from job share arrangements, a major exercise in information, communication and education in the potential advantages of job sharing seems necessary if the concept is to be looked on more favourably by employers in general. Employees seem to have no difficulty pointing to advantages associated with job sharing: only 24 per cent believed that there were none. Job creation as an advantage, however, received little mention.

The importance of highlighting the known potential advantages of job sharing to employers is all the more apparent when findings on the origins of job sharing schemes in the Irish private sector are examined. In spite of the fact that the majority of employees were willing to identify advantages attaching to job sharing (76 per cent) and that over 20 per cent were interested in job sharing, management responses indicate that the impetus for the introduction of job sharing in Ireland has come overwhelmingly from local or head-office management, rather than from employees themselves, or from their unions.

One way of making progress in this area would be for the social partners to arrange and publicise widely case studies of successful job sharing schemes, highlighting their benefits to the employers and employees involved and their impact on job creation. Simple accounts of the tax and social welfare consequences of job sharing could also be developed in this way. Guidelines on best practice in introducing and managing job sharing arrangements could also be jointly agreed.

A further public policy constraint that arises in the further extension of job sharing concerns the effect that job sharing may have on the situation and opportunities of women workers. All 28 of the job sharers interviewed in the employee surveys undertaken in both public and private organisations were women. Data from the company survey suggest that at least three-quarters of all job sharers are women. Of those interested in undertaking job sharing and claiming to be able to afford to job share, 81 per cent are women. The job sharers and potential job sharers identified in the survey tend, perhaps predictably, to be in the phase of the life cycle when childbearing and child-rearing responsibilities are greatest.

Given current preferences, incentives to encourage the further uptake of job sharing will very disproportionately tempt women to trade full-time jobs for part-time jobs, either temporarily or permanently. On the other hand, the availability of job sharing might also prevent women from leaving the workforce entirely. Job sharing is also more advantageous than conventional part-time work in that the evidence clearly suggests that the pay, conditions and promotional prospects enjoyed by job sharers are similar to the conditions enjoyed by full-time workers, except that they are split over two people. Hence the conclusion presented in Chapter 6 that job sharers in general cannot be viewed as a 'marginal workforce', enjoying pay and conditions that do not bear comparison with those of full-time workers.

In terms of the promotion of equal opportunities between men and women at work, job sharing can be seen to have complex effects. As stated above, the great majority of job sharers and potential job sharers are women, but some women who trade full-time careers for part-time careers might otherwise have traded full-time careers for parenting and opted to leave the workforce altogether. So the wider availability of job sharing will keep more women in the workforce and to this degree lead to a greater degree of equality of opportunity, but may also relegate women to a 'slower track', in terms of career progression and promotion, as compared with men.

8.7 CHANGES TO STANDARD WORKING HOURS

Significant differences still exist in the reported standard working hours of different categories of workers. The standard weekly working hours of managerial and professional/administrative staff appear to be higher and more variable than those of other workers. These categories also tend to work higher levels of non-remunerated overtime, as seen in Chapter 5. What these findings point to is that the distinction between 'standard' and total working hours is less well-defined in the case of these workers than other categories of private sector employee. It would seem from the data collected in the management survey that clerical workers still enjoy an hours 'differential' over manual workers (see Table 4.1). However, this differential — which historically has been wide — has closed to within about one hour per week. The cut in the standard working hours of all workers working 40 or more hours per week, provided for in the Programme for National Recovery (PNR) (1987–90) affected a substantial number of firms. The great bulk of all reductions in working time recorded over the past five years have come about under the PNR.

In general, the standard hours worked in the public sector appear to be below comparable grades in the private sector. The largest gap (of approximately 7 hours) is for the higher administrative grades and the lowest (of 1 hour) for the routine grades. In general, during the past five years, standard hours in the public sector, though somewhat lower, do not appear to have fallen by as much as in the private sector. As in the private sector, any reductions which did take place were achieved under the PNR.

The impact of the recent round of reductions in normal working hours, as reported by employers, indicated that it had little direct effect on employment or productivity and stronger direct effects on overtime working and labour costs. About 20 per cent of firms, employing about a third of the private sector workforce, claim that overtime increased in direct response to the hours round. Almost half of all companies, employing over 60 per cent of the workforce, reported increased labour costs. Only 8 per cent of all companies, employing 7 per cent of the workforce, reported an increase in full-time employment, and 3 per cent, accounting for 21 per cent of employees, reported an increase in part-time employment. In general, trends in the public sector were similar, although the employment impact is reported to have been higher, with 26 per cent of organisations stating that full-time employment rose.

The modest impact which the hours round appears to have had on employment is consistent with data on recent experience with hours reductions in other European countries. Given the modest scale of the cut in normal hours in Ireland — one hour in the week for workers working 40 or more hours — it is not surprising that employers were generally able to absorb the reduction without additional recruitment.

More surprising, perhaps, in the light of this finding, is the number of employers stating that a further reduction in standard hours — the magnitude of the hypothetical cut was not specified in the question put to respondents — would lead to an increase in employment. Approximately a third of both public and private bodies thought that additional full-time employment would be necessary in the event of a further cut in hours, and roughly the same proportion thought that additional part-time employment would be necessary. Given their recent experience of the negligible effect that the cut of one hour had on employment, and the likelihood that in answering the question they were thinking of further reductions of the same modest scale, this finding gives some cause for surprise. It could be that employers are of the view that little further scope exists for absorbing hours cuts through increased cost or higher productivity, and that employment rises would now be inevitable in the wake of further cuts. These views are consistent with opinions expressed on the same issue that further hours cuts would impact negatively on productivity. Employers also thought that overtime would be likely to rise, but surprisingly, in the light of experience in the UK and Europe, very few believed that further cuts in hours would facilitate negotiations on flexible working time. The best inference that can be drawn from the overall pattern of the findings on the issue of further cuts in working time is that employers believe that little slack remains to be taken up in adjusting to further cuts in hours, with the result that additional employment would become necessary with a consequent decline in productivity. Judged in the light of the employment record of the recent 39-hours round, it seems prudent to conclude that even if a further round had a bigger impact on employment, the net impact would remain modest. A more sizeable cut in normal working time would, of course, be difficult for employers to absorb without resorting to additional employment. However, such a reduction in hours is likely to meet with very intense employer resistance since it would carry high risk in respect of cost and competitiveness. It is only in the context of further European movement on normal working hours that further progress of any kind seems likely in Ireland.

How likely are employees to demand and campaign for further cuts? The proportion of private sector employees agreeing with the statement that they would like to get more time off even if this meant a reduction in pay is only 22 per cent. The comparable public sector figure was 21 per cent. Similarly, only 19 per cent of private sector and 26 per cent of relevant public sector employees agreed with the statement that if they were due a pay rise they would prefer to take all or some of it in the form of time-off-in-lieu. Although there is clear evidence to suggest that female employees are more positively disposed than their male counterparts to time-off in preference to financial payment, these expressions of viewpoint by employees on pay/leisure trade-offs hardly point to strong demand for further cuts in working time, which might find expression, in the short to medium term, in pressure on trade unions to make further headway with the long-established union objective of the 35-hour week. However, the role that unions have played historically in intensifying employee leisure preferences through concerted working time campaigns must also be borne in mind.

8.8 CAREER BREAKS AND EXTENDED LEAVE

Just under 10 per cent of private companies claim to offer employees career breaks or extended leave arrangements, but only 2 per cent of companies said that any of their staff were on career breaks at the time of the study. The situation in the public sector appears to be quite different. About 82 per cent of public sector organisations said that the option of career breaks was open to at least some of their employees, and 63 per cent had at least one employee on a career break at the time of the study. In all, an estimated 8,700 people had availed of career breaks in the private sector during the five years preceding the study. The vast majority of these were women. Private employers replaced just over 50 per cent of the employees on career breaks, whereas practically all public sector employees taking such breaks were replaced. As with job sharing, few private firms identified advantages to the employer in operating career break schemes, and many more were willing to identify disadvantages. In contrast, only a third of public sector organisations were unable to identify advantages. The proportion of employees interested in availing of a career break is about 27 per cent — a higher general level of interest than registered in the case of job sharing. To the degree that international research has identified at least significant potential advantages to employers, a major effort is again required to communicate these to the business community, and to locate and disseminate successful Irish case studies, if employers are to look more favourably on career breaks.

Of particular note is the level of shared employer and employee interest in extending optional maternity leave. Just under half of all companies, employing more than half of the private sector workforce, would favour an extended period of unpaid maternity leave of up to two years. Forty-five per cent of employees with children would wish to avail of extended parental leave — 63 per cent of women and 39 per cent of men. Only 5 per cent of both would wish to avail of extended parental leave and said that they could afford to do so. This still amounts to nearly 18,000 employees. Given a reasonable replacement ratio for staff availing of such leave — replies to the question on career breaks suggest a replacement ratio in the region of 50 per cent — the employment effects of facilitating extended parental leave would be far from negligible. Under current legislation on maternity leave, female employees have the statutory right to avail of additional leave of four weeks on expiry of paid maternity leave; men have no right to either paid or unpaid paternity leave. One option in responding to employee preferences on maternity/paternity leave would be to amend current legislation to allow women to avail of a longer period of unpaid maternity leave and to give men a statutory right to unpaid paternity leave. No direct expenditure liability on the exchequer would arise, though such a scheme would affect tax revenue, however marginally. However, the principle of introducing new statutory rights to extended leave in the case of women, and unpaid paternity leave in the case of men, is likely to meet with objections from the sizeable number of employers who do not favour this option. The majority of employers who favour extended maternity leave may not embrace the concept of paternity leave, and, besides, may react negatively to the promulgation of 'rights' to leave or extended leave.

In practice, extended parental leave will lead considerably more women than men to trade jobs for time off for prolonged periods. The same issues arise as in the case of job sharing in determining the impact of parental leave policy changes on equal opportunities as between men and women. More women than men will be tempted to diverge from conventional linear or unbroken careers by trading jobs for time-off for long periods of time. At the same time, the availability of the option of extended maternity leave is likely to encourage some women who would otherwise have quit the workforce to withdraw instead on a temporary basis and to resume their careers after a break from the workforce.

8.9 EARLY RETIREMENT

Only 6 per cent of private companies offer special arrangements for early or phased retirement, and these cover about 38 per cent of the workforce. Larger firms are considerably more likely to operate such arrangements than are small firms. Of firms not currently offering early or phased retirement schemes, 17 per cent, covering over 30 per cent of the workforce, believe that such schemes hold the potential for employing new staff. The incidence of such schemes in the public sector is of the same order of magnitude, covering just under 38 per cent of employees.

Two-thirds of all private sector firms can see no advantages to the employer in early- or phased-retirement schemes. The remaining third, which do see advantages, account, however, for two-thirds of the workforce. A much lower percentage of relevant public sector organisations (covering 12 per cent of employees) said that there were no advantages to a system of early or phased retirement. One possibly ominous advantage that dominates the list given by firms was that early retirement 'assisted manpower planning'. This could mean that early retirement allows firms an opportunity to rebalance the age structure of their workforce by replacing older staff with younger staff. It is at least as likely to mean that early retirement provides a convenient means of cutting headcount. Disadvantages are identified by two-thirds of all private firms, accounting for 45 per cent of the workforce. The proportions of firms identifying advantages and disadvantages, and their levels of workforce coverage, are more closely balanced in the case of early and phased retirement than in the case of other work sharing options where perceived disadvantages greatly exceeded perceived advantages. A minority of all companies were willing to identify ways in which government policy might provide incentives for early retirement arrangements, but these accounted for 55 per cent of the workforce. Moreover, in this area the replies of employers were quite specific and focused, laying emphasis on such things as cutting tax on retirement pensions and lump sums and subsidising pension schemes or providing grants to employers.

Should the State act in this area, it is likely to follow public schemes in other countries by premising any public subsidisation of early retirement on mandatory replacement from the live register. Otherwise, public subsidies would simply increase the incentive to employers to cut the headcount.

One finding of note in the area of early retirement was that a large majority of employees interested in retiring early (86 per cent in the private sector and 73 per cent in the public sector) would like to take up part-time employment or self-employment following retirement. The level of interest in part-time employment was highest at 54 per cent. Thus, even assuming that those leaving through early retirement schemes of various kinds were replaced in significant proportion in the companies from which they retired, large numbers are likely to remain in the workforce and the majority of these would intend to find part-time employment. Short of introducing subsidised early retirement schemes based on mandatory replacement, the assumption of a high average replacement ratio in early retirement seems optimistic given the known attractions of early retirement to larger companies seeking to 'downsize' their numbers. If replacement ratios are low and most early retirees wish to seek part-time work, then general public policy support for early retirement could amount primarily to an exercise in encouraging a section of the workforce to move from one kind of employment status to another. There might be little overall gain in employment opportunities and little effect on the level of unemployment.

The principle of inducing early retirees to leave the workforce raises serious ethical concerns regarding the right of people to seek work and would also clash with government policy on age discrimination and the treatment of the aged.

One further finding of the employee survey is noteworthy. Leaving aside respondents in the 25-years-or-less age category, the proportions of respondents who said that they were seriously interested in taking early retirement broadly *decline* as the age of respondents rise. In the private sector, for example, 57 per cent of

those aged 56 years or more express serious interest in early retirement, compared with 76 per cent of those in the age category
36–45 years. It is not possible to determine from the cross-
sectional survey data whether this reflects a life-cycle effect. If it
does, then the actual level of interest is of the magnitude reflected
by the replies of older workers, and is likely to remain so. Alternatively, higher levels of avowed interest in early retirement
among younger age groups could reflect a *cohort effect*, such that
levels of support for this option among those in the target age
category for early retirement will continue to rise as younger
workers with different values and priorities enter the pre-
retirement phase of their working lives.

8.10 SOCIAL CHOICE, EMPLOYMENT AND PUBLIC POLICY OBJECTIVES

The data presented in this study show that significant numbers of
employees favour more flexible working time arrangements than
those currently prevailing in most companies in Ireland. The
wider availability of job sharing, career breaks, extended and parental leave and early retirement would thus respond to diverse
employee preferences with respect to the balance between working time and life outside employment. The wider provision of
working time options which allow employees to tailor their working lives better to their general lifestyles would represent, in itself, a social and cultural advance. Many employers currently operate flexible working time regimes, and more seem willing to
make traditional regimes more flexible. It has to be recognised,
however, that the data indicate clearly and unambiguously that
employers see little advantage for themselves in flexible working
time and are much more disposed to identify disadvantages. Such
a posture represents a serious brake on the pace of change in
working time regimes.

The impact of greater working time flexibility on employment
and unemployment in Ireland, while it may not be inconsiderable,
is unlikely to be profound. Existing job sharing arrangements are
being availed of by a small number of people in the private sector,
although 10 per cent of employees claim both that they are interested and that they could afford to job share. Fewer than 9,000
people in the private sector have availed of career breaks over the
past five years and it would appear that about half of this number
were replaced. Few employees show a strong preference for further

cuts in normal hours, although significant numbers of employers claim that any further cuts would require additional recruitment. The great majority of those expressing a serious interest in early retirement would wish to go on working, half of them in part-time jobs.

The impact on other social and public policy objectives, in the Irish case, of greater working time flexibility and of the control of overtime can also be considered in the light of the survey data. Tighter curbs on overtime would impact most strongly on the living standards of manual workers: for large numbers of manual workers overtime earnings have come be viewed as a major buttress to desired standards of living. Employer responses also imply that tighter restrictions on overtime could impair business performance and reduce competitiveness.

Job sharing, career breaks and extended parental leave encourage more women than men to trade full-time continuous jobs and careers for extra time off. While the alternative for many women might be to leave the workforce entirely, it should still be recognised that the gender imbalance in the choice of flexible working time options involves underscoring for women career paths and employment histories that diverge significantly from those of the great majority of men. What is sometimes called the 'male career model' — involving continuous full-time work and a willingness to put in long hours on a paid or unpaid basis — still, by and large, determines which employees are marked out for promotion to top jobs, high incomes, prestige, responsibility and authority. As such, the work histories or career paths associated with career breaks, extended maternity leave and job sharing carry significant costs for women.

REFERENCES

Alston, J.P. (1986): *The American Samurai: Blending American and Japanese Management Practices*, Berlin: W. de Gruyter.

Anon. (1989): "Does Job Sharing have Potential in Your Business?", *Profit-Building Strategies for Business Owners*, 19(7): 9–10.

Anon. (1990): "Giving Employees Time, Flexibility", *Employee Benefit Plan Review*, 44(11): 16–18.

Arkin, W. and Dubrofsky, L.R. (1978): "Job Sharing", in R. Rapoport. and R. Rapoport. (eds.), *Working Couples*, London: Routledge and Kegan Paul.

Bahls, J.E. (1989): "Two for One: A Working Idea", *Nation's Business*, 77(6): 28–30.

BIE (Bureau of Industry Economics) (1984): "Reducing Standard Hours of Work: Analysis of Australia's Recent Experience", *Research Report No. 15*, Canberra: Australian Government Publishing Service.

Bienefeld, M. (1972): *Working Hours in British Industry: An Economic History*, London: Weidenfeld and Nicolson.

Blackwell, J. (1989): *Women in the Labour Force*, Dublin: Employment Equality Agency.

Blanpain, R. and Engels, C. (1995) "Belgium", in R. Blanpain, J. Rojot and E. Kohler (eds.): *Legal and Contractual Limitations to Working Time in European Member States*, Louvain: Peters

Blase, K. (1992): "Take Care of Yourself: Part-time Leadership in Education a Healthy Concept for the 1990s", *Women in Management Review*, 7(7): 17–23.

Blyton, P. (1985): *Changes in Working Time: An International Review*, New York: St Martin's Press.

Blyton, P. (1987): "The Working Time Debate in Europe", *Industrial Relations*, 26(2): 201–207.

Blyton, P. (1989a): "Time and Labour Relations", in P. Blyton, J. Hassard, S. Hill and K. Starkey (eds.): *Time, Work and Organisation*, London: Routledge.

Blyton, P. (1989b): "Hours of Work", in Bean, R (ed.): *International Labour Statistics: A Handbook, Guide and Recent Trends,* London: Routledge.

Blyton, P. (1992): "Learning from Each Other: The Shorter Working Week Campaigns in the German and British Engineering Industries", *Economic and Industrial Democracy,* 13(3): 417–30.

Boisard, P. (1982): "La réduction des heures travaillées", *Cahier du Centre d'Etudes de l'Emploi,* Paris: PUF.

Bosch, G. (1986): "The Dispute over the Reduction in the Working Week in Germany", *Cambridge Journal of Economics,* 10(3): 271–90.

Breen, R. and Halpin, B. (1989): *Subsidising Jobs: An Evaluation of the Employment Incentive Scheme,* Economic and Social Research Institute, General Research Series Paper No. 144, Dublin: ESRI.

Calmfors, L. (1985): "Work Sharing, Employment and Wages", *European Economic Review,* 27(3): 293–309.

Calmfors, L. (1988): "Work Sharing and Overtime", *Scandinavian Journal of Economics,* 90(1): 45–62.

Carby, K. and Edwards-Stuart, F. (1981): *The Overtime Dilemma,* Information Report 31, London: IPM.

Carr, D.E. (1986): "Overtime Work: An Expanded View", *Monthly Labor Review,* 109(11): 36–9.

Casey, B. (1991): *Redundancy and Early Retirement: The Interaction of Public and Private Policy in Britain, Germany and the USA,* London: Policy Studies Institute.

Champy, J. (1995) *Reengineering Management: The Mandate for New Leadership,* New York: Harper Collins.

Christopherson, S. (1991): "Trading Time for Consumption: The Failure of Working-Hours Reduction in the United States", in K. Hinrichs, W.K. Roche, and C. Sirianni (eds.): *Working Time in Transition — The Political Economy of Working Hours in Industrial Nations,* Philadelphia: Temple University Press.

Cole, R.E. (1972): "Permanent Employment in Japan: Facts and Fantasies", *Industrial Relations Review,* No. 26.

Cole, R.E. (1992): "Work and Leisure in Japan", *California Management Review,* 34(3): 52–63.

Commission of the European Communities (1978): *Work Sharing — Objectives and Effects,* Commission staff paper, Annex to SEC (78) 740, Brussels: CEC.

Commission of the European Communities (1980): *Community Guidelines on Flexible Retirement,* COM (80): 393 final, Brussels: CEC

Confederation of British Industry (1980): *Jobs — Facing the Future,* London: CBI.

Curson, C. and Palmer, S. (1986): "Conclusions and Considerations", in C. Curson (ed.): *Flexible Patterns of Work,* London: IPM.

Cuvillier, R. (1984): *The Reduction of Working Time: Scope and Implications in Industrialised Markets,* Geneva: International Labour Organisation.

De Neuborg, C. (1991): "Where Have All the Hours Gone? Working-Time Reduction Policies in the Netherlands", in K. Hinrichs, W.K. Roche, and C. Sirianni (eds.): *Working Time in Transition — The Political Economy of Working Hours in Industrial Nations,* Philadelphia: Temple University Press.

De Rongé, A. and Molitor, M. (1991): "The Reduction of Working Hours in Belgium: Stakes and Confrontations", in K. Hinrichs, W.K. Roche, and C. Sirianni (eds.): *Working Time in Transition — The Political Economy of Working Hours in Industrial Nations,* Philadelphia: Temple University Press.

Department of Employment (1978): "Measures to Alleviate Unemployment in the Medium Term: Work Sharing", *Department of Employment Gazette,* 86(4): 400–402.

Deutschmann, C. (1991): "The Worker-Bee Syndrome in Japan: An Analysis of Working-Time Practices", in Hinrichs, K., Roche, W.K. and Sirianni, C. (eds.): *Working Time in Transition — The Political Economy of Working Hours in Industrial Nations,* Philadelphia: Temple University Press.

Dixon, P.B. (1987): "The Effects on the Australian Economy of Shorter Standard Working Hours in Construction and Related Industries", *Institute of Applied Economic and Social Research,* Working Paper No. 2: 29–32.

Drew, E. (1990): *Who Needs Flexibility: Part-time working — The Irish Experience,* Dublin: EEA.

Drèze, J.H. (1985): *Work Sharing: Why?, How?, How Not?,* Economics Paper No. 42, Louvain: Université Catholique de Louvain.

Edwards, P.K. and Whitson, C. (1991): "Workers are Working Harder: Effort and Shop-floor Relations in the 1980s", *British Journal of Industrial Relations,* 29(1): 593–601.

Ehrenberg, R.G. and Schumann, P.L. (1982): *The Average Workweek as an Economic Indicator,* New York: National Bureau of Economic Research Occasional Paper 69.

Ehrenberg, R.G. and Schumann, P.L. (1982): *Longer Hours or More Jobs?,* New York: Cornell.

Elsendoorn, G. and van Ginneken, C. (1986): *"ATV in kline bedrijven",* Zoetermeer: EIM.

Employment International (1993a): "Social Affairs Council Adopts Working Time Directive", December: 7–9.

Employment International (1993b): "European Social Policy Green Paper", December: 26–33.

Equal Opportunities Commission (1981): *Women and Under Achievement at Work,* Research Bulletin, No. 5, Spring.

Equal Opportunities Commission (1981): *Job Sharing,* Manchester: EOC.

ETUI (European Trade Union Institute): (1985): *Flexibility and Jobs: Myths and Realities,* Brussels: ETUI

European Economy (1980): *Adaptation of Working Time: Impact of a Reduction in the Annual Duration of Work,* Luxembourg: Directorate General for Economic and Financial Affairs, CEC.

European Foundation for the Improvement of Living and Working Conditions (1986): *Shift Work Review: Research of the European Foundation, 1981–84,* Dublin: EFILWC.

European Industrial Relations Review (1993a): "Working Time Directive — Common Position", No. 235: 15–18.

European Industrial Relations Review (1993b): *The Reduction and Restructuring of Working Hours,* No. 231: 25–28.

European Industrial Relations Review (1993c): *Agreements on Early Retirement and Career Breaks,* No. 237: 24–26.

Evans, A.A. (1975): *Hours of Work in Industrialised Countries,* Geneva: International Labour Organisation.

Evans, A.A. and Curson, C. (1986): "Overtime and its Alternatives", in Curson, C. (ed.): *Flexible Patterns of Work,* London: IPM.

Evans, A.A. and Massey, P. (1986): "Sabbaticals, Extended Leave and Career Breaks", in Curson, C. (ed.): *Flexible Patterns of Work,* London: IPM.

Evans, A.A. and Attew, A. (1986): "Alternatives to Full Time Permanent Staff", in Curson, C. (ed.): *Flexible Patterns of Work,* London: IPM.

Fields, G. (1992): "Towards Great Consumer Society — Japanese Vision", *Tokyo Business Today,* 60(8): 20.

Flint, J. (1988): "It's a New World", *Forbes,* 142(11): 172.

Fredriksson, I. (1988): "Job Sharing in Sweden: Some Examples", *Economic & Industrial Democracy,* 9(3): 397–400.

Galand, O., Gaudin, J. and Vrain, P. (1984): "Contrats de Solidarité de préretraite et stratégies d'entreprises", *Travail et Emploi,* 22, December.

Geoghegan, M. (1985): *An Analysis of Working Time in Ireland during the Twentieth Century,* unpublished MBS dissertation, University College Dublin, Department of Industrial Relations.

Goldhar, J.D. and Jelinek, M. (1985): "Computer Integrated Manufacturing: Organisational, Economic, and Strategic Implications", *Interfaces,* 15(3): 94–105.

Gow, D. (1993): "More Time Off Could Save German Jobs", *The Guardian,* 4 November.

Greis, T. (1984): *The Decline of Annual Hours Worked in the United States since 1947,* Philadelphia: Industrial Research Unit, The Wharton School, University of Pennsylvania.

Gröhn, K. (1979): *Views on Shortening Daily Working Hours,* Research Department, No. 15, Ministry of Social Affairs and Health, Helsinki: Julkaisuja Publications.

Handy, C. (1994) *The Empty Raincoat: Making Sense of the Future,* London: Hutchinson.

Harrison, B. and Kelley, M.R. (1993): "Outsourcing and the Search for Flexibility", *Work, Employment & Society,* 7(2): 213–35.

Hart, R.A. (1984a): *The Economics of Non-Wage Labour Costs,* London: Allen and Unwin.

Hart, R.A. (1984b): *Shorter Working Time: A Dilemma for Collective Bargaining,* Paris: OECD.

Hill, S. and Blyton, P. (1987): "Flexibility and Patterns of Work", paper presented to a conference entitled "The Japanization of British Industry", at the University of Wales Institute of Science and Technology, September.

Hinrichs, K., Roche, W.K. and Wiesenthal, H. (1985): "Working Time Policy as Class-Oriented Strategy: Unions and Shorter Hours in Great Britain and West Germany", *European Sociological Review,* 1(3): 211–29.

Hinrichs, K. (1991): "Working-Time Development in West Germany: Departure to a New Stage", in K. Hinrichs, W.K. Roche, and C. Sirianni (eds.): *Working Time in Transition — The Political Economy of Working Hours in Industrial Nations,* Philadelphia: Temple University Press.

Hoel, M. and Vale, B. (1986): "Effects of Unemployment of Reduced Working Time in an Economy where Firms Set Wages", *European Economic Review,* 30 (5): 1,097–1,104.

Hourihan, F. (1993): "Search for Cures", *Community Report,* 3(4): 5–9.

Hughes, J.A. (1978): "A Shorter Working Week: How the Department of Employment Got it Wrong", *Workers Control Bulletin,* No. 6, Nottingham Institute for Workers' Control.

Humphreys, P.C. (1986): *Work Sharing and the Public Sector,* Dublin: Institute of Public Institution.

IDS (Income Data Services) and IPM (Institute of Personnel Management) (1992): *Pay and Benefits — European Management Guides Series,* P. Burgess (ed.), London: IPM.

ILO (International Labour Organisation) (1984): *Working Time: Reduction of Hours of Work, Weekly Rest and Holidays with Pay,* Geneva: ILO.

ILO (International Labour Organisation) (1990): "The Hours We Work: New Work Schedules in Policy and Practice", *Conditions of Work Digest,* 9(2), Geneva: ILO.

Industrial Relations Europe (1993a): "As VW Cuts Hours, Some Plead For Longer Working Week", 21(252): 5.

Industrial Relations Europe (1993b): "Work Time Cuts Measure Now Looks a Damp Squib", 21(252): 3.

Industrial Relations Europe (1993c): "Labour Ranks are Split over Possible Hours Claim", 21(251): 4.

Industrial Relations Europe (1993d): "Red Tape Around Working Time is All Set for Abolition", 21(252): 6.

Industrial Relations Europe (1993e): "Unions Urge Overtime Curbs to Tackle Unemployment", 21(249): 6.

Ingram, P.N. (1991): "Changes in Working Practices in British Manufacturing Industry in the 1980s: A Study of Employee Concessions Made During Wage Negotiations", *British Journal of Industrial Relations,* 29(1): 1–13.

Irish Times (1987): "62% Favour Job Sharing", 2 September.

Jacobi, O. and Muller-Jenstch, W. (1990): "West Germany: Continuity and Structural Change", in G. Baglioni and C. Crouch (eds.): *European Industrial Relations: The Challenge of Flexibility,* London: Sage.

Jacobsen, P. (1995): "Denmark", in R. Blanpain, J. Rojot and E. Kohler (eds.): *Legal and Contractual Limitations to Working Time in European Member States,* Louvain: Peters.

Jallade, J.P. (1991): "Working-Time Policies in France", in K. Hinrichs, W.K.Roche, and C Sirianni. (eds.): *Working Time in Transition — The Political Economy of Working Hours in Industrial Nations,* Philadelphia: Temple University Press.

Japan Institute for Social and Economic Affairs (1996), 'Japan 1996: An International Comparision', Tokyo: Japan Institute for Social and Economic Affairs.

Jones, E.B. (1974): "An Investigation of the Stability of Hours of Work per Week in Manufacturing, 1947–70", College of Business Administration, University of Georgia, Research Monograph No. 7.

Katz, R. and Goldberg, A.I. (1982): "Working Extra Hours: Worker Involvement in the Modern Era", *Personnel Review*, 11(1): 31–34.

Kennedy, K.A. (1993): "Long Term Trends in the Irish Economy", *Irish Banking Review*, Summer,: 16–25.

Kish, L. (1965), *Survey Sampling*, New York: Wiley.

Klein, J.A. (1989): "The Human Costs of Manufacturing Reform", *Harvard Business Review*, 2: 60–66.

Kniesner, T.J. (1976): "The Full-Time Workweek in the United States, 1900–1970", *Industrial and Labor Relations Review*, 4(2): 95–113.

Kochan, T.A. (1985): "Contemporary Employment Stabilization Practices" in T.A. Kochan. and P. Barocci (eds.): *Human Resource Management and Industrial Relations*, Boston: Little Brown.

Kraft, K. (1989): "Expectations and Adjustment of Hours and Employment", *Applied Economics*, 21(4): 487–95.

Losey, M.R. (1992): "Workplace Policies Should be Family-Friendly", *Modern Office Technology*, 37(5): 84–5.

Mangan, J. and Steinke, J. (1987): "Working Time Reductions in Australia: The Economic Effects", *Human Resource Management Journal*, 2(July): 4–11.

Mangan, J. and Steinke, J. (1988): "Working-time Reductions: A Survey of the Australian Experience", *Industrial Relations Journal*, 19(4): 322–7.

Marchand, O. (1984): "L'emploi en 1982-83: simple répit dans la divergence entre demande et offre", *Economie et Statistique*, 166: 25–38.

Marinelli, M. and Bermann, K. (1991): "Divide and Conquer — Everything!", *Supervision,* 52(4): 3–5.

May, S. (1985): "Sabbaticals: The John Lewis Experience", in D. Clutterbuck (ed.): *New Patterns of Work,* Aldershot: Gower.

McCarthy, M.E. and Rosenberg, G.S (1981): *Work Sharing: Case Studies,* Kalamazoo, Michigan: Institute for Employment Research.

McKendrick, J.E. (1989): "Stretching Time in '89", *Management World*, 18(4): 10–11.

McKinlay, A. and McNulty, D. (1992): "At the Cutting Edge of New Realism: the Engineers' 35 hour Week Campaign", *Industrial Relations Journal*, 23(3): 205–13.

McLaverty, P. and Drummond, H. (1993): "Work, Effort and Performance", *Employee Relations*, 15(3): 37–44.

McNabb, R. (1989): "Compensating Wage Differentials: Some Evidence for Britain", *Oxford Economic Papers*, 41(2): 327–38.

Mele, D. (1989): "Organisation of Work in the Company and Family Rights of Employees", *Journal of Business Ethics,* 8(8): 647–55.

Mertens, D. (1979): "L'aménagement du temps de travail in Emploi et nouveaux modes de vie", at a conference of the Institut d'Éducation, Fondation Européene de la Culture, Paris, November.

Metcalf, D. (1982) *Alternatives to Unemployment, Report No. 610,* London: Policy Studies Institute.

Metz, N.M., Reid, F. and Swartz, G.S. (1981): *Sharing the Work: An Analysis of the Issues in Work sharing and Job-Sharing,* Toronto: University of Toronto Press.

Moser K. and Kalton, G. (1971): *Survey Methods in Social Investigation,* London: Heinemann

Moss Kanter, R. (1986): "The New Workforce Meets the Changing Workplace: Strains, Dilemmas and Contradictions in Attempts to Implement Participative and Entrepreneurial Management", *Human Resource Management,* 25(4): 505–37.

NBPI (National Board for Prices and Incomes) (1970): *Hours of Work, Overtime and Shift Working,* Report No. 161, Cmnd. 4554, London: HMSO.

Neifer-Dichmann, E. (1991): "Working Time Reductions in the Former Federal Republic of Germany: A Dead End for Employment Policy", *International Labour Review,* 130(4): 511–22.

NESC (National Economic and Social Council) (1993): *A Strategy for Competitiveness, Growth and Employment,* Dublin: National Economic and Social Council, Report No. 96.

O'Riordan, W. (1984): "The Effect of Variations in Hours Worked Per Week in Irish Industry, 1956–71", *Irish Journal of Business and Administrative Research,* 6(1): 39–47.

Owen, J. (1976): "Workweeks and Leisure: An Analysis of Trends, 1948–75", *Monthly Labor Review,* August: 3–8.

Owen, J. (1979): *Working Hours: An Economic Analysis,* Lexington: D.C. Heath.

Parr, J. (1988): "Direct Marketing: Industry Scrambles to Fight Mail's Higher Tab", *Advertising Age,* 59(44): 15–16.

Rehn, G. (1977): "Towards a Society of Free Choice", in J. Wiatr and R. Rose (eds.): *Comparing Public Policies* (Wroclaw et al.: Zaklad Narodowy imienia Ossolinskich/Wydawnictwo Polskiej Akademii Nauk).

Roche, W.K. (1987): "Leisure, Insecurity and Union Policy in Britain: A Critical Extension of Bienefeld's Theory of Hours Rounds", *British Journal of Industrial Relations,* 25(1): 1–17.

Roche, W.K. (1988): "Worksharing and Unemployment Reduction", in Kerins, A.T. (ed.): *Unemployment — The Need for Change,* Dublin: Boole Press.

Roche, W.K. (1991): "The Chimera of Changing Employee Time Preferences: Working Hours in British Industrial Relations since World War II", in K. Hinrichs, W.K. Roche, and C. Sirianni (eds.), *Working Time in Transition — The Political Economy of Working Hours in Industrial Nations,* Philadelphia: Temple University Press.

Rose, M. (1988): "Attachment to Work and Social Values", in Gallie, D. (ed.), *Employment in Britain,* Oxford: Blackwell, Chapter 5

Ross, M. (1986): *Employment in the Public Domain in Recent Decades,* Economic and Social Research Institute, General Research Series, No. 127, Dublin: ESRI.

Sakai, K. (1990): "The Feudal World of Japanese Manufacturing", *Harvard Business Review,* 6: 38–49.

Scheur, S. (1992): "Denmark: Return to Centralisation", in A. Ferner and R. Hyman (eds.), *Industrial Relations in the New Europe,* Oxford: Blackwell.

Schönemann-Paul, H., Körmendji, E. and Gelting, T. (1992): *"Den faste arbejdstijd erfortid",* Copenhagen: Spectrum.

Schor, J.B. (1991): *The Overworked American: The Unexpected Decline of Leisure,* New York: Basic Books.

Seal, K. (1991): "Job Sharing Finds Share of Interested Users", *Hotel & Motel Management,* 206(16): 66.

Sinclair, P.M. (1987): *Unemployment: Economic Theory and Evidence,* Oxford: Blackwell.

Sirianni, C. (1991): "The Self-Management of Time in Postindustrial Society" ,in K. Hinrichs, W.K. Roche, and C. Sirianni (eds.), *Working Time in Transition — The Political Economy of Working Hours in Industrial Nations,* Philadelphia: Temple University Press.

Smith, C. (1988): "Working on a Change: Japan Steps Gingerly Towards a five-day Week", *Far Eastern Economic Review,* 140(15): 62–3.

Smyth, D.J. and Karlson, S.H. (1991): "The Effect of Fringe Benefits on Employment Fluctuations in US Automobile Manufacturing", *Review of Economics & Statistics,* 73(1): 40–49.

Syrett, M. (1983): *Employing Job Sharers, Part-Time and Temporary Staff,* London: Institute of Personnel Management.

Tavernier, G. (1978): "Car Workers Shift to Flexible Leisure Time", *International Management,* October: 39–40.

Thomas, E.G. (1987): "Workers who Set their Own Time Clocks", *Business & Society Review,* 61(Spring): 49–51.

Trade Union Research Unit (1981): *Working Time in Britain,* London: Anglo-German Foundation.

Trejo, S. (1991): "The Effects of Overtime Pay Regulation on Worker Compensation", *American Economic Review,* 81(4): 719–40.

Tsujimura, K. (1980): "The Effect of Reductions on Working Hours on Productivity" in N. Shunsaku (ed.): *The Labor Market in Japan: Selected Readings,* Tokyo: University of Tokyo Press.

Turnridge, G. (1981): "The Economic Impact of a Uniform Move to a 35 hour Week", *Economic Affairs Research Services,* Research Discussion Paper, No. 8, October.

UCG (University College Galway) (1980): *A Study of Overtime Working in Ireland,* Study No. 790118, Department of Industrial Engineering, UCG.

UCG (University College Galway) (1982): *Case Studies in Overtime and Work Sharing,* Department of Industrial Engineering, UCG.

Van der Linden, J.T. (1987): "Labour Time Reduction as an Instrument for Full Employment: A Revival from the Discussion of the 1930s", *International Journal of Manpower,* 8(1): 3–9.

Verespej, M.A. (1989): "The New Workweek", *Industry Week,* 238(21): 11–21.

Volg, A.J. (1992) "Do Americans Work Too Hard", *Across the Board,* 29,(7): 15–20.

Walsh, B.M. (1979): *Work Sharing and the Unemployment Problem in Ireland,* Report to the Federated Union of Employers, Dublin: Economic and Social Research Institute.

Walton, P. (1985): "Job Sharing" in D. Clutterbuck (ed.): *New Patterns of Work,* Aldershot: Gower.

Watson, G. (1992): "Hours of Work in Great Britain and Europe: Evidence from the UK and European Labour Force Surveys", *Employment Gazette,* November.

Weigelt, U. (1991): "On the Road to a Society of Free Choice: The Politics of Working Time in Sweden", in K. Hinrichs, W.K.Roche, and C. Sirianni (eds.): *Working Time in Transition — The Political Economy of Working Hours in Industrial Nations,* Philadelphia: Temple University Press.

Westbrook, R. and Williamson, P. (1993): "Mass Customisation: Japan's New Frontier", *European Management Journal,* 11(1): 38–45.

Wheelwright, S. and Hayes, R. (1981): "Japan — Where Operations Really are Strategic", *Harvard Business Review,* July/August: 67–74.

White, M. and Ghobadian, A. (1984): *Shorter Working Hours in Practice,* London: Policy Studies Institute.

White, M. (1980): *Shorter Working Time*, Report No. 589, London: Policy Studies Institute.

Whybrew, E.G. (1968): *Overtime Working in Britain,* Research Paper 9, Royal Commission on Trade Unions and Employers' Associations, London: HMSO.

Wickham, J. (1993): *New Forms of Work in Ireland,* A report presented to the European Foundation for Living and Working Conditions on behalf of Infratest Sozialforchung, Munich.

Womack, J.P., Jones, D.T. and Roos, D. (1990): *The Machine that Changed the World,* New York: Macmillan.